# Commitment-Led Marketing

# REVIEWS
for
*Commitment-Led Marketing*

"After years of using customer satisfaction measures I was extremely frustrated at the lack of correlation between satisfaction and subsequent customer defection rates. The measurement of commitment, via the Conversion Model™ provided the vital link I had been looking for."

*Alan Gilmour, Brand and Marketing Director, Lloyds TSB*

"The Conversion Model™ enabled us to establish real insight into loyalty and we effectively fused it with a segmentation process. This has allowed us to really grapple with the core market dynamics and establish key marketing objectives in an increasingly competitive and diverse marketplace . . ."

*Mark Horton, Group Head of Marketing, Northcliffe Newspaper Group*

"Since I first came across the Conversion Model™ back in 1990, I have always found it was the perfect tool for measuring the health of brands I've worked on . . ."

*David V. Spangler, Director, The Council for Marketing and Opinion Research (CMORE) and former Research Director of Levi Strauss & Co.*

"The Conversion Model is a compelling strategic marketing tool that offers a true understanding of institutional investor behaviour. It is a predictive indicator of potential market share gains and losses with a phenomenal degree of precision."

*Patricia Toney, Manager, Marketing Research, Chicago Board of Trade*

"To grow a business, convert customers to your offering and then keep them committed. . . . a very powerful answer is in this book."

*John Deighton, Professor of Business Administration, Harvard Business School*

". . . using the Conversion Model™ has given us significant insights into brand choice across a range of countries and cultures. . . . The added dimension of commitment has allowed us to understand more comprehensively what is in the mind of our consumers – a real plus in terms of giving us the competitive edge."

*Janett Edelberg, Joseph E. Seagram & Sons*

# Commitment-Led Marketing

*The Key to Brand Profits is in the Customer's Mind*

Jan Hofmeyr and Butch Rice

JOHN WILEY & SONS, LTD

Chichester • New York • Weinheim • Brisbane • Singapore • Toronto

Copyright © 2000 by John Wiley & Sons Ltd,
Baffins Lane, Chichester,
West Sussex PO19 1UD, England

National        01243 779777
International  (+44) 1243 779777
e-mail (for orders and customer service enquiries): cs-books@wiley.co.uk
Visit our Home Page on http://www.wiley.co.uk
or http://www.wiley.com

*Other Wiley Editorial Offices*

John Wiley & Sons, Inc., 605 Third Avenue,
New York, NY 10158-0012, USA

WILEY-VCH Verlag GmbH, Pappelallee 3,
D-69469 Weinheim, Germany

Jacaranda Wiley Ltd, 33 Park Road, Milton,
Queensland 4064, Australia

John Wiley & Sons (Asia) Pte Ltd, 2 Clementi Loop #02-01,
Jin Xing Distripark, Singapore 129809

John Wiley & Sons (Canada) Ltd, 22 Worcester Road,
Rexdale, Ontario M9W 1L1, Canada

**British Library Cataloguing in Publication Data**

A catalogue record for this book is available from the British Library

ISBN 0-471-49574-3

Typeset in 11/15pt Goudy by Mayhew Typesetting, Rhayader, Powys
Printed and bound in Great Britain by Biddles Ltd, Guildford and King's Lynn
This book is printed on acid-free paper responsibly manufactured from sustainable forestry, in which at
least two trees are planted for each one used for paper production.

# Contents

# Preface

Our work has its origins in what some may think was a bizarre beginning. It started in the field of religious studies when Jannie was teaching and researching at the University of Cape Town. A particular field of interest for him was the process of religious conversion. One of the things that distinguishes this process is that it is sometimes sudden and sometimes gradual. Psychologists had failed to find either a mechanism or a conceptual framework to account for what causes this difference. It was the chance discovery by Jannie of catastrophe theory that allowed for the development of such a framework.

From religion Jannie's work moved into politics. At that time South Africa was in the grip of a revolution. Many white South Africans had realized that change was inevitable, but they continued to be stuck in dysfunctional patterns of political activity. The theory of commitment and conversion was applied in an attempt to understand what might make whites willing to accept non-racial democracy.

It was at that point that our paths crossed. While Jannie had been involved in developing a general theory of commitment and conversion and applying it to South African politics, I had been building Research Surveys (Pty) Ltd, by then South Africa's most successful marketing research company. Research Surveys carried out the fieldwork for that early political research. The businessman recognized the commercial potential of what the academic was doing and the rest, as they say, is history.

We called our approach *The Conversion Model*™ and launched it in South Africa in 1989 without any idea of its full commercial potential. In 1990 we launched in the United States and subsequently around the world. You can now do Conversion Model™ work in any country in the world. Our network has a sales presence in some 70 countries and over 120 cities. More than 2800 projects have been commissioned by clients in nearly 200 product categories for more than 80 of the world's leading multinationals. From small beginnings in the political cauldron that was South Africa in the mid-1980s, the commitment-based approach to marketing, which is at the heart of this book, has become a global phenomenon.

We have written our book in an attempt to make the foundations of our approach explicit to the marketing world. When we started, most marketers were talking about brand loyalty. Then, in the early 1990s, many marketers started talking about customer satisfaction. It is only now, some ten years later, that marketers are beginning to talk widely about commitment. In our view, commitment is fundamental. It's one of those things that just isn't going to go away. Developing commitment is something that human beings do. It is something that we see in thousands of years of human activity. And it's a part of our natural language.

This book is our contribution to moving 'commitment' to the centre of the stage in the world of marketing. We have based the book on many examples from the projects that we and our partners have completed in the past ten years. In order to preserve client confidentiality, we have sometimes had to disguise our examples, but we have never done so in ways that distort reality.

Although our approach to the conceptualization and measurement of commitment may be just one of many, we hope, with the publication of this book, to place the concept of commitment and its value to marketers under the spotlight. Above all, we hope that you, the reader, find our ideas and practical examples stimulating and useful.

*Butch Rice*

# Acknowledgements

This book is the culmination of more than ten years of hard work by a great many people around the world. When so many have been involved, deciding who should be acknowledged by name is a difficult task.

Few marketers were talking the language of commitment when we started out in 1990. The fact that the concept of commitment is now common currency is at least partly due to the support of some visionary marketing researchers. In the United States, Verne Churchill, then the President of Market Facts, Inc., deserves special mention. Without his enthusiasm and support, we would never have secured our first projects on 'foreign' soil so quickly. Others who played a crucial role in that first year abroad were Iona Marty, Jeanine Douglas, Kate Emerson, Carl Edstrom, Susan Ford and Nan Martin – young executives of Market Facts, Inc. who were willing to recommend a little-known approach to their key accounts. On the client side, a special word of thanks to Dave Spangler, then of Levi Strauss, who was the first client in the United States to take us seriously.

In the ensuing years, we were supported by a formidable team around the world. They number hundreds and work for many of the world's finest marketing research companies. We remain convinced that, taken as a group, they are the single most powerful network of marketing researchers in the world. People like Elaine Howard of Market Facts Inc., Julie Bevan of RSGB, and Michael Voss of TNS (Emnid) – we are sorry we cannot name you all, but you know who you are. Thank you, to you all. It has been an honour and a pleasure to work with you.

On the technical side, some people deserve special mention. To Bob Ceurvorst of Market Facts, Inc. and Trevor Richards of RSGB in the UK, a special word of thanks for your contributions over the years. Others who have delighted us at conferences with their innovations include Debra Hall of Research Solutions in New Zealand, Rick Bennett of Market Facts of Canada, and Dave Hannay of TNS Financial Services in the UK.

We come now to clients – without whom we would have nothing to talk about. We wish to thank a range of clients for permission to mention some of their work in this book. They include Nissan (Ireland), Lloyds TSB in the UK, Langeberg (the marketers of All Gold tomato sauce in South Africa), e.tv and the ANC, the party of Nelson Mandela and currently the government of South Africa. To Market Facts, Inc. and Taylor Nelson Sofres, a special word of thanks for the non-proprietary research used in this book. Finally, to Research Surveys, owners of the Conversion Model™, thank you for permission to use graphic illustrations of the theory behind the Conversion Model in Chapter 3.

Special thanks go to Alan Gilmour of Lloyds TSB, who was one of the first major clients who was willing to share his experiences with the rest of the world. We acknowledge, with appreciation, the contribution he has made in extending our knowledge of how best to apply the philosophy of commitment to marketing.

Our enterprise is centred in Cape Town, South Africa, one of the most beautiful cities in the world. At its heart sits a small core of talented and dedicated people. Thank you to the members of the Conversion Model team past and present, who have been willing to work long hours against tight deadlines to get the job done. Your unwavering commitment to looking after our partners has been exemplary. A special word of thanks to Lesley van der Walt, the leader of the team and our companion for nine of the past ten years. Without your commitment, it would not have been possible to achieve what we have.

To Beverley, Butch's secretary of 18 years, a big thank you for the many hours of typing and support. And to Nicoli, Jannie's secretary of five years, as everyone knows, life would be chaotic without you. And then to Sam and Sienne who helped 'construct' this book by chasing down references and coordinating what finally went to the publishers, a big thank you.

We were fortunate in having an impressive publishing professional at our side. Claire, you have been a fantastic guide through this process – critical and supportive in the nicest possible way. And thanks also to all the other professionals at Wiley. At every stage of the process we've known that we've been in safe hands.

Last but not least, our families. For years now, we have been involved in a punishing schedule of international travel. We cannot say enough about the support we've had from our families through this period. To Marjory and Sheila, the appreciation that we have for the sacrifices you have made knows no bounds. We have always known, no matter where we were, that there was a 'safe place' to which we could return. We hope, as you look back at the past ten years, that you will feel that it's been worth it.

*We would like to thank:*

Andrew Ehrenberg for permission to use the schematic outline of the strong and weak theories of advertising used in Chapter 6.

Don Schultz for allowing us to reprint the diagram that appears in Chapter 7 that contrasts new versus old marketing.

Telmar for their permission to reprint the figure in Chapter 6 that shows ad liking and average ad awareness.

# 1

## The Key to Brand Profits

### *What you can expect to find in this book*

Our behaviour as human beings is often puzzling. For example, why do people stay in unhappy marriages? And why do some marriages look perfect from the outside, but suddenly collapse into divorce? Why do many people stay in jobs they dislike, going to work day after day, dreading walking through the doors of the company that employs them, but never resign?

Our seemingly high tolerance for dissatisfaction is reflected in many situations in the world of marketing. Why do people keep on driving cars that they hate? And keep on using banks that they detest? On the other hand, why is it that some consumers say they are perfectly happy with the brands they are using, yet switch at the next purchasing occasion?

 *Is our quest for satisfied customers correct? If satisfaction is a poor predictor of human behaviour, should we be putting the emphasis on customer satisfaction that we do?*

If we do not understand the apparent paradoxes of consumer behaviour, we run the risk of wasting massive amounts of marketing funds. We advertise unnecessarily. We conduct customer satisfaction studies, investing millions of dollars to improve our satisfaction scores, only to be puzzled by the fact that defection rates do not change. We are timid about price increases, and are surprised when competitors are sometimes able to increase their prices without the negative impact on their brand share that we expected.

> **"Why is it that some consumers say they are perfectly happy with the brands they are using, yet switch at the next purchasing occasion?"**

The key to successful marketing is knowing what's in the consumer's mind and managing the relationship appropriately. This is what we have called *commitment-led marketing*. It is about understanding that customer satisfaction is a poor predictor of behaviour, but that commitment is an excellent predictor. It is about knowing what consumers are going to do before they know it themselves. It is about not wasting money. It is about boosting your bottom line.

In this book we provide solutions to some of marketing's most vexing questions. For example:

- How should brand loyalty *really* be defined?
- What is the difference between loyalty and commitment?
- How can commitment be used to build strong brands?
- What are the implications of commitment for our understanding of brand equity, and what role does commitment play in building brand equity?

Key to improving profitability is the reduction of wastage in marketing expenditure. With this in mind, we explain why some ad campaigns are much more effective than others, giving guidelines on how to identify these in advance.

 *Regarding relationship marketing, one of the key questions is: what about consumers who do not want a relationship with the brand? How do we identify them, and how should the relationship be managed, if at all?*

> **"The key to successful marketing is knowing what's in the consumer's mind and managing the relationship appropriately."**

Commitment-led marketing permeates all facets of the marketing effort: advertising, relationship marketing, new product development, the choice of appropriate channels of distribution, pricing strategies and the ability to predict the future with accuracy.

Commitment-led marketing enables you to formulate global strategies that are practical and profitable, with the key emphasis always being on building the relationship between the brand and consumers to optimal levels.

# A new look at marketing challenges

Commitment-led marketing is about understanding your consumers in terms of the commitment they have to your brand, and then using that information to decide how best to manage the relationship. Commitment is a state of mind. It is the happiness of the marriage between the consumer and the brand. Some marketers get confused between the concepts of loyalty and commitment. Loyalty is about what consumers *do*. Commitment is about what consumers *feel*.

| **"Commitment is a state of mind."** |
| --- |

Here is an example to help explain the point. Over the last couple of years, a friend of ours has regularly flown on United Airlines when travelling from the USA to Australia as part of his around-the-world routing. An inspection of the United Airlines database would identify him as one of their most loyal customers. Every time he landed in the USA on South African Airways, he left for Australia on United Airlines. Behaviourally, he was loyal. However, his behaviour did not reveal what was in his mind. The only reason that he flew United Airlines was because they were the partners for South African Airways on their around-the-world package. To be honest, United is one of his least favourite airlines. His behaviour does not reveal what is in his mind, which is extreme convertibility and a high availability to most other airlines.

Commitment-led marketing is about managing the relationship with customers according to what is in the mind. United Airlines should have been treating our friend with kid gloves, attempting to find out the causes of his imminent defection, rather than sending letters of congratulations on reaching the next tier of their frequent flyer programme, because of his behaviour. What he *did* was not in line with what he *felt*. He was *loyal*, but not *committed*.

| **"Commitment-led marketing is about managing the relationship with customers according to what is in the mind."** |
| --- |

Committed customers are the backbone of the value of a brand. Your committed customers are those least likely to defect and, hence, those most likely still to be using your brand in the years to come.

> **"Committed customers are the backbone of the value of a brand."**

# The value of committed customers

The concept of commitment is not simply intellectually intriguing. There are many reasons why any marketer would like as many committed customers as they can get. Our experience during the past decade has taught us many lessons about why marketers should care about nurturing and growing their committed customer base. This section presents some of our learning points. In later chapters, we will provide additional evidence to support the conclusions outlined in the following subsections.

## Committed customers are willing to pay more

The more committed a consumer is to a brand, the less important price becomes in the purchase decision. This applies across all product categories.

Spotting committed consumers making a purchase decision is easy. As they sweep past the supermarket shelves, they select the brand to which they are committed, and put it into the trolley without a second glance. In contrast, when they buy brands to which they are not committed, they are more likely to be seen examining other brands, making price comparisons, or reading the ingredient details on the pack before making a final choice.

One of the outcomes of adopting a philosophy of commitment-led marketing is more appropriate pricing, particularly in brand portfolio situations. The larger the number of committed consumers using a brand, the more justified the brand will be in demanding a price premium. Conversely, if a brand has few committed consumers, it will be price sensitive, dictating a very different pricing strategy.

Think about things to which you are committed. They could range from the car that you drive, to your favourite beer, an antiperspirant or a regular holiday destination. Whatever it is, the more committed you are, the less important price is in the final selection process.

## Committed customers stay with the brand longer

We have conducted numerous validation studies around the globe, covering many product categories, in order to investigate the relationship between commitment and the length of time the consumer stays with the brand. The findings of all these studies have been consistent: the higher the commitment, the less likely it is that the consumer will defect from the brand. Putting it another way, the higher the commitment, the longer the consumer stays with the brand.

The impact of commitment on lifetime value is significant. It is not unusual to find that the time that a committed consumer spends with the brand is ten or twenty times that of an uncommitted consumer. Committed consumers see little reason to change and will stay with the brand to which they are committed year in and year out.

## Committed consumers give you more of their business

In most markets, consumers use more than one brand. They use a repertoire of brands, with the size of the repertoire varying by consumer and by category. However, the more committed the consumer, the greater the share of the repertoire given to the brand to which they are committed.

Figure 1.1 shows an example from a beer study in Asia, illustrating the dramatic way in which commitment impacts on the share of requirements that the brand satisfies.

A committed consumer gives more of their business to the brand, is willing to pay more, and will stay with the brand a lot longer than an uncommitted consumer, because of their lower probability of defection. Hence, the lifetime value of a committed consumer is a multiple of that of an uncommitted consumer, who flirts with your brand but does little else.

## Committed consumers soak up your advertising

When flighting advertising campaigns, your committed consumers are those most likely to see and like your advertising. Our powers of selective perception are strong. There is a circularity in advertising which is not always recognized. Although somebody who sees your advertising is more likely to buy your brand, it is also true that those who use your brand are more likely to see your advertising. And those who use your brand and are *committed* to it are usually those most likely to be soaking up your advertising.

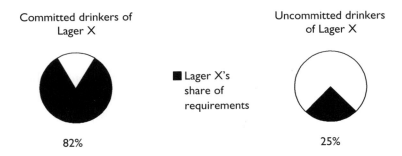

**Figure 1.1** *Share of requirements that Lager X satisfies*

The role of advertising is continually debated. One issue on which the research industry is reaching consensus is that advertising, in most cases, is not 'persuasive'. Advertising works best at *maintaining* relationships, rather than attracting new users. With committed consumers of the brand being those most likely to see and like the advertising, the more committed consumers your brand has, the more effective your advertising will be.

Table 1.1 shows the differences in recall of a brand's advertising between consumers committed to a brand, and those using other brands who are strongly unavailable to the brand being advertised.

In the UK, committed Persil users are nearly twice as likely to be aware of Persil's advertising than are those consumers who are unavailable to the brand. This pattern is consistent across all countries, although the ratio of advertising effectiveness differs. This will obviously be a function of the execution of the advertising and advertising weight.

With 64% of committed consumers of detergent brands being aware of their brand's advertising, compared to 36% of those unavailable to the brand, the effect of advertising on committed consumers is approximately 80% more than on those who are unavailable to the brand.

## Committed consumers act as advocates

At the high end of commitment, committed consumers act as advocates for the brand, exhorting others to use it. In effect, they are an extension of your sales force. The more committed consumers you have, the more effective your marketing efforts will be.

**Table 1.1** *A comparison of the advertising recall of consumers who are committed to a brand to that of those who are strongly unavailable to it\**

| Country | Brand | Total (%) | Committed (%) | Unavailable (%) |
|---------|-------|-----------|---------------|-----------------|
| UK | Persil | 23 | 32 | 17 |
| France | Ariel | 43 | 59 | 29 |
| Germany | Sunil | 44 | 64 | 36 |
| Poland | Vizir | 79 | 87 | 57 |
| India | Surf Excel | 71 | 83 | 38 |
| Japan | Super Top | 76 | 75 | 48 |
| Canada | Tide | 46 | 59 | 32 |
| Argentina | Skip | 49 | 54 | 29 |
| **Average** | | **54** | **64** | **36** |

*Source*: Conversion Model Licensee Network non-proprietary study, 1999.

\* The table shows the percentage of consumers who claim to have seen advertising 'recently' for the brands in question.

The reverse is also true. When consumers switch from a brand to which they were committed, but which lets them down, they will often form an unusually strong commitment to the new brand to which they have switched. In tandem with this, they will actively attempt to dissuade others from using the brand from which they have switched. They become marketing terrorists, waging ongoing guerrilla warfare against the brand which let them down, akin to jilted lovers. This phenomenon is particularly prevalent in the service industries.

## What makes a consumer committed?

One of the most important requirements in obtaining commitment from a consumer is that brand choice has to matter. If brand choice does not matter to a consumer, it is almost impossible to achieve commitment from that consumer. It is these consumers (we call them *uninvolved*) who switch brands despite being satisfied with the brand they were using, leaving marketers bemused. Although the brand satisfied their needs, they are quite capable of brand switching at every purchase occasion because brand choice in the product category is relatively unimportant.

In addition to brand choice being important to consumers, they must also be convinced that the brand to which they are committed is superior to other brands in the marketplace. Hence, commitment is very much a function of competitive offerings.

Committed consumers are not ambivalent about their favourite brands. They are confident that the brand to which they are committed is the right brand for them, and act accordingly, both in their purchasing behaviour and in the way in which they decode all information about the brand. They soak up information that confirms the wisdom of their decision, in whatever form this communication takes, whether it be advertising, editorial or discussion with friends about the product category.

## How do we use all of this?

This book describes the ways in which commitment-led marketing can become an integral philosophy of an organization. Commitment-led marketing permeates every facet of marketing, both strategically and tactically. This section looks at some of the areas where we have implemented this philosophy with positive effect.

### Advertising

The area of advertising provides one of the richest sources of 'quick hits' in terms of cost savings, for it is here that we commonly encounter some of the biggest opportunities for increasing profit, by reducing wastage. We define wastage as the expenditure of marketing funds on consumers who are unlikely to switch to the brand in the near term.

The first question any marketer should be asking is whether they should be advertising at all. By using the philosophy of commitment-led marketing, it is fairly easy to answer this question unequivocally.

If the majority of consumers in a market are committed to brands other than yours, it becomes extremely difficult to justify using advertising as a means of boosting sales, other than to attempt to create awareness for your brand. Even then, there are usually more cost-effective ways of achieving this.

By understanding the commitment of consumers to all brands in your market, you are able to assess whether or not advertising is appropriate for your brand. The suitability of all channels of communication can be better assessed when the commitment of consumers to the brands they use is understood. As an example, it has been our experience in most markets that many brands that advertise on national television should not be doing so. Typically, only the top two or three brands in a category can justify national television campaigns. This is because the wastage for smaller brands is unacceptably high. When your brand has a relatively small share in a market, it has, by definition, relatively few users. You will also have fewer committed users than the brand leader, in all probability. As the number of users of a brand correlates strongly with the overall effectiveness of your advertising, your advertising will be relatively ineffective. As your brand has only a relatively small share, the majority of consumers in the product category will be using other brands. If they are *committed* to these brands, the implications for your advertising campaigns are even more serious, as your advertising is unlikely to raise awareness levels of your brand significantly.

> **"We define wastage as the expenditure of marketing funds on consumers who are unlikely to switch to the brand in the near term."**

By using the concept of commitment, marketers are now able to quantify, with accuracy, the wastage in their advertising campaign. No longer do we have to accept that half of advertising works and half doesn't, but that we don't know which half, as Lord Leverhulme once said. We can now be as accurate as saying, for example, that more than 90% of consumers are unavailable to a specific brand, because they are committed to other brands. Advertising, on its own, is unlikely to have any effect on their behaviour – hence, more than 90% of adspend will be wasted.

By using this approach, we are able to set objectives for what we hope our advertising can realistically achieve, what the tone of the advertising should be, and what an appropriate investment in advertising should be, as well as specifying the target audience far more tightly.

> **"Many brands that advertise on national television should not be doing so."**

We have successfully integrated measures of commitment into single-source databases, allowing media planners to plan media schedules on the basis of those consumers open to the message, rather than on demographics alone. By understanding the commitment of consumers, the effectiveness of your media spend can be dramatically enhanced.

## Relationship marketing

Relationship marketing is one of the latest catchphrases in the marketing industry, with many marketers switching their budgets from above-the-line communication to direct marketing programmes, using their customer databases as the platform for the programme. But in the same way as there is wastage in an advertising campaign, there is wastage in direct marketing programmes. Just as a consumer skips over a double-page spread in a magazine, he or she will often discard direct marketing material without even examining it.

> **"In the same way as there is wastage in an advertising campaign, there is wastage in direct marketing programmes."**

Using commitment-led marketing, we are able to attach measures of commitment to each customer in a database, accurately identifying those likely to respond positively to direct marketing efforts and those likely to ignore our efforts. Obviously, this has a significant impact on the cost of such programmes, as wastage is significantly reduced.

## New product development

Would you have guessed that tomato sauce is one of the categories in which we have encountered the highest commitment to a brand? Certainly in South Africa, the allegiance to the leading brand of tomato sauce, All Gold, is such that people are more likely to divorce their spouse than change their brand of tomato sauce.

The importance of measuring the commitment of consumers to the brands they are using before embarking on new product launches was dramatically underscored in South Africa, when Nestlé launched a new brand of tomato sauce in 1994. Trading on its dominance in the mayonnaise category, Nestlé's logic was simple. Its Crosse & Blackwell mayonnaise enjoyed a very strong image, and, up to then, consumers had to be content with only one major brand of tomato sauce – All Gold. All

Gold had an approximately 60% share of the market, with no other competitive brand enjoying any significant strength.

It would appear that the time was right for a bit of brand stretching for Crosse & Blackwell. The dominant position in the mayonnaise category could be extended to an expanded positioning of being a leader in the overall sauce category, rather than just mayonnaise. Accordingly, with the usual professionalism of Nestlé, an attractive pack was designed, a quality product was developed and tested in blind taste tests, convincingly beating All Gold, and it was subsequently launched with an aggressive launch campaign.

However, what Nestlé did not measure was the commitment of consumers to All Gold. More than 90% of consumers using All Gold are committed to it, making it one of the strongest brands in the world. When Crosse & Blackwell tomato sauce was launched, our advice to the marketers of All Gold was to sit tight and not overreact.

> **"The main reason for the majority of new products failing is that the commitment of consumers to the products they are already using is not taken into account."**

Nestlé fell far short of its original marketing target, and has only managed to achieve a share which remains stubbornly in single digits, despite subsequent price promotions. The brand least affected by Nestlé's launch was All Gold. Crosse & Blackwell gained its share at the expense of smaller brands, whose users had a lower commitment to them than did All Gold's consumers.

We believe that the main reason for the majority of new products failing is that the commitment of consumers to the products they are already using is not taken into account. No matter how favourably the product performs in product tests, it is more likely to fail if consumers are already strongly committed to their favourite brands. In recognition of this, some marketers use measures of commitment to identify the market which will be easiest to enter, both geographically and by product category.

The commitment of consumers to brands in the same category can vary enormously by geography. Figure 1.2 gives an example, showing the commitment of consumers to the bank they use most often, across a range of geographies.

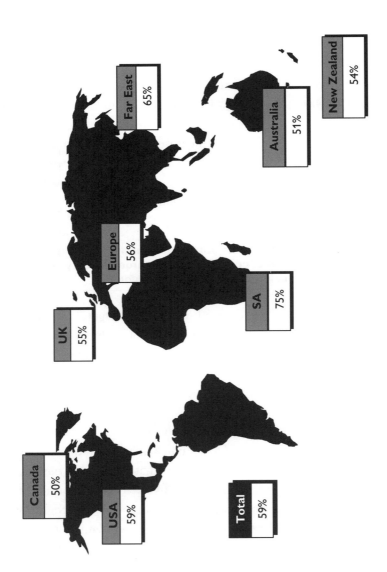

**Figure 1.2** *Global commitment norms for most frequently used brand: banking*

It can be seen that South Africa would be the most difficult market to enter with a new bank, due to the unusually high commitment to banks in South Africa. Given this high commitment, it is unlikely that price inducements would work, and even the most persuasive advertising is unlikely to have a significant impact on banking usage patterns.

> **"Typically, marketers have too many variants of their brands on shop shelves."**

Many marketers launch brand variants when brand share is under threat, hoping to attract new users. Our experience has shown us that those most likely to buy variants of the mother brand are those consumers who are already committed to the brand. New variants seldom significantly enhance the brand franchise. Rather, they run the risk of diluting brand equity, by reducing the visibility of individual variants in a range.

Fairly recently, Unilever[1] announced it would be culling the number of its brands globally from 1600 to 400. We were not surprised to hear this. Typically, marketers have too many variants of their brands on shop shelves.

## Channels of distribution

Some of the biggest shifts in marketing that will happen in the next decade will be because of changes in channels of distribution. For example, the implications of an increase in popularity of Internet shopping are obvious. In contrast, in the general retail trade, some retailers are offering shoppers the option of home deliveries. In banking, the option of Internet banking is now available as well as telephone banking. The impact of these trends is potentially significant and poses new questions for the marketer.

[?] *One of the questions that needs answering is: is my consumer committed to my brand, but not that committed to my channel of distribution? For example, if a competitor makes a service or product which is marketed on the Internet, will my consumers be seduced into what they perceive to be a more convenient channel of distribution, switching brands in the process?*

It is a relatively easy procedure to measure the commitment of consumers, not only to the brands they use, but also to the channels of distribution.

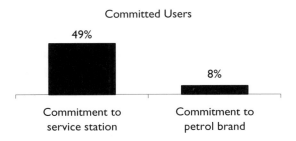

**Figure 1.3** *Commitment to petrol brand and service station*

*Source*: Bairfelt, S. and Richards, T. (1995) From customer satisfaction to customer segmentation, ESOMAR/JMA/ARF Triad Conference, New York.

A nice example of this was provided by Shell in the United Kingdom,[2] which measured the commitment of consumers to the brand of petrol they used most often, as well as to their service station. The results are shown in Figure 1.3. It can be seen that, perhaps predictably, consumers were far more committed to their favourite service station than they were to their favourite brand of petrol. Hence, if the brand of petrol sold at their service station were to change, it would be unlikely to have much impact on their purchasing behaviour.

## Pricing strategies

By understanding the commitment of consumers to all competitive brands in the market, the marketer is able to assess how price sensitive the overall market is, as well as the price sensitivity of their brand compared to other brands. We seldom find markets in which all brands have the same degree of price sensitivity. The larger the segment of consumers committed to the brand, the less price sensitive the brand will be in comparison.

Commitment-led marketing is also invaluable for assisting in understanding the reason for consumers buying private label brands. Marketers are sometimes unsure as to whether the primary reason for purchasing a private label or own brand is affordability or price sensitivity.

**[?]** *Putting it another way, is it because consumers cannot afford anything else, or is it because they see all brands as being pretty much the same, and buy the cheapest?*

If we find that the majority of 'own brand' purchasers are uncommitted, it is safe to deduce that they are buying because they cannot afford anything else. Although they buy the brand, they do not have a strong relationship with it and would prefer to be buying another brand in the category. Hence, the 'own brand' is not really a brand, in the classical sense, but simply a commodity representing the cheapest member of the category. On the other hand, if we find that the own brand enjoys a significant number of consumers who are committed to it, we can deduce that it is a brand in its own right, competing with other brands on the same basis.

## Predicting the future

Consumer commitment correlates with future behaviour. By contrasting the number of committed consumers your brand has with those of competitors, you are able to predict the likely direction of share change for all brands in the marketplace. The more committed consumers your brand has, the less vulnerable it will be to competitive attack.

When we started investigating the concept of commitment, back in the late 1980s, the very first study in which we utilized the concept investigated the impact of a banking merger on the commitment of the customers of the two financial institutions. Six months after the merger, we returned to our original respondents, to see what their defection levels were. Figure 1.4 shows the results.

This strong correlation between the original segmentation and subsequent defection patterns was to be the first of many validation studies showing that commitment is the crystal ball of marketers. Commitment correlates with future behaviour, enabling the marketer to identify those consumers most likely to defect, and those most likely to be retained. Among non-users of the brand, the marketer is able to identify those most likely to be acquired, and those consumers on whom marketing efforts will be wasted, as they are unlikely to switch brands in the foreseeable future.

By assessing the commitment of consumers to your brand, as well as the availability of those who are not using your brand, you are able to formulate the appropriate marketing strategy. At the most basic level of strategy formulation, marketers need to decide whether they should formulate an attacking strategy or a defensive one.

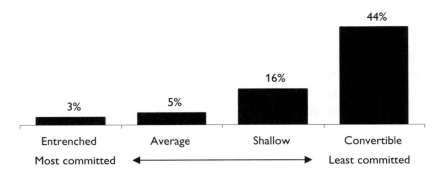

i.e. 3% of the respondents who were entrenched users of their bank had defected to another bank six months later, and so on.

**Figure 1.4** *Defection rates after six months*

**?** *What you need to know is not only whether your brand can increase its share, but where that increase will come from. Which of your competitors are most vulnerable, and how could those consumers be wooed away from your competitors?*

Commitment-led marketing enables you to simulate future competitive attack. With many global players, marketers see competitive regional launches sweeping around the globe in advance. It is a fairly simple task to import the brand that is soon to be launched in your territory and simulate the effect of the launch before it occurs. This enables the marketer to assess what impact, if any, the competitive launch will have on their brand. In addition, not only is the amount of potential damage to the commitment of the brand's users quantified, but the reasons for the new brand inflicting damage are fully understood, enabling the marketer to formulate adequate defensive strategies well before the attack takes place.

## Category threats – a real problem

Typically, category threats are far more serious for a brand's health than are competitive brand threats. An illustration of this was provided by the financial services industry some years ago, when unit trusts were first launched. While some life assurance companies were still focusing on each other's marketing efforts, the threat provided by the new category of investment was significantly larger.

Again, it is fairly straightforward to measure the commitment of consumers, not only to the brands they use, but to the product categories themselves. Dealing with a competitive brand threat is fairly easy. Dealing with a new category threat can be very challenging.

Further examples of category declines are provided by Levi Strauss, with the shrinkage of the jeans market in the USA. Obviously, the IT industry provides examples on an ongoing basis of new categories of services and software, as well as hardware, changing the underlying structure of the market. When new dimensions are introduced to a market, consumers reassess what the alternatives are to the brand they are currently using. In the process of this reassessment, traditional brand dominance can be overturned, as the established brands may lack strength on the new dimensions that have been introduced.

A striking example of this was provided by Arm and Hammer baking soda toothpaste, which was launched in the USA some years ago. By introducing the dimension of baking soda, an ingredient not included in a traditional toothpaste, Arm and Hammer was able to secure a significant share of the market, in which it had not been a traditional competitor.

## Global strategy formulation

An examination of commitment norms in most categories shows the short sightedness of attempting to have an invariant global marketing strategy. We often find that South Africa and Australia are included in the same region for global marketing purposes, but these two countries are diametrically opposed in terms of commitment. For most product categories, South Africa is one of the highest commitment markets in the world, while Australia is one of the lowest.

Both countries have the same sort of climate, providing the platform for sizeable beer drinking markets. Figure 1.5 shows commitment to the brand of beer drunk most often across a range of geographies. It can be seen that in Australia commitment to the brand of beer drunk most often is significantly lower than in South Africa, Europe and the Far East. Hence, price sensitivity in the beer market will be higher in Australia. For marketers thinking of entering the beer market, Australia would be a far easier market to enter, as the Australian beer consumer is more likely to be prepared to try a new brand. In South Africa and the Far East, even if a new beer were

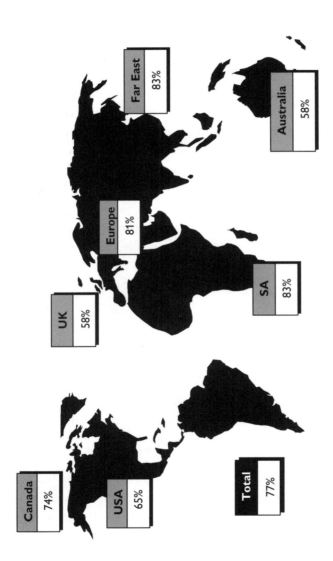

**Figure 1.5**  *Global commitment norms for most frequently used brand: beer*

launched at a competitive discount, it would be ignored by the majority of beer consumers. In recent years, attempts have been made to launch new brands of beer in South Africa, with disastrous effects, confirming the impact that commitment has on the potential for new entrants.

> **"An examination of commitment norms in most categories shows the short sightedness of attempting to have an invariant global marketing strategy."**

**[?]** *Why is it that different geographical markets differ so much in terms of commitment for the same product categories?*

One of the most important reasons is the structure of society. The more affluent and better educated the consumer, the less likely they are to be committed to the brands they use. Hence, it is predictable that Australia has a far lower degree of brand commitment than South Africa, as the Australian consumer is more likely to be well educated and relatively affluent. This has the immediate implication of an apparent marketing paradox. The more affluent the consumer, the less likely they are to be committed, and, hence, the more price sensitive they will be. This finding has been validated by many researchers, although at first it appears counterintuitive. Among poor consumers, commitment to the brands they use is often unusually strong. They cannot afford to take the risk of trying a competitive brand which might not satisfy their needs. Accordingly, they will be relatively price insensitive in terms of their regular brand repertoires.

There are other demographic characteristics which impact on commitment. Age is one of them. The younger the consumer, the less committed they are likely to be, hence the instability of youth markets.

There are also cultural overlays to commitment. In Canada, we find that French-speaking Canadians are more likely to be committed than English-speaking Canadians, while in South Africa, Afrikaans-speaking South Africans are more likely to be committed than English-speaking South Africans.

In addition to the structure of society, the number of competitive brands in the market also impacts on commitment. The more brands there are in the market, the lower commitment is likely to be.

Before embarking on a global strategy, it is critically important to understand the commitment to brands in every market in which the marketer operates, in order to ensure that the strategy takes all local idiosyncrasies, in terms of commitment, into account.

## The relationship is king

In summary, commitment-led marketing is about understanding what is in your consumer's mind and managing the relationship with the consumer appropriately. It is about:

- charging the right price, and formulating the appropriate communication strategy;
- advertising when you should be, and not advertising when you shouldn't;
- spending the right amount on a customer, no more and no less;
- making your business more sound strategically;
- increasing the value of your brand and helping you understand the market in a way you have not been able to before;
- boosting profitability, cutting costs and having seamless relationships with your customers.

By segmenting your customers according to their commitment to your brand and segmenting the non-users of your brand according to their availability to your brand, you are choosing one of the most actionable segmentations available, which will correlate strongly with future profitability. The key to brand profits is in your customer's mind.

## References

1.  *Esomar News Brief*, no. 10, November 1999, p. 17.
2.  Bairfelt, S. and Richards, T. (1995) From customer satisfaction to customer segmentation. Esomar/JMA/ARF Triad Conference, New York, June.

# 2

## Getting Started

*A basic introduction to how commitment works*

In this chapter we introduce a basic definition of commitment. We also look at different commitment and availability profiles that brands can have and what the implications of these are for marketing strategy.

## What is commitment?

Undoubtedly, there are different ways of measuring commitment. But the different definitions all agree on one thing – commitment is psychological rather than behavioural. Commitment is about what is in the mind rather than about what we do. And, as we have said, what consumers *do* and what consumers *feel* can be very different. We cannot deduce what consumers feel by observing their behaviour. Somebody who appears loyal could, in fact, be completely uncommitted, and switch brands at the next purchasing occasion. But what consumers feel dictates the way in which the relationship between the consumer and the brand should be managed.

We have measured commitment for the past ten years by using the Conversion Model[TM],[1] a proprietary model of commitment which was developed in the late 1980s in South Africa, before being launched in the USA in 1990. However, the Conversion Model is not the only way of measuring commitment. Although it was the first measure of commitment to be used in marketing, it has spawned numerous lookalikes which claim to measure the same sort of thing.

> **"We cannot deduce what consumers feel by observing their behaviour."**

Embedded in the work that we have undertaken has been a very explicit understanding of what it takes to make consumers change their choice of brands. This conceptualization is not restricted to the purchasing of brands, but encompasses all human behaviour. The theory that we have developed also explains why consumers sometimes do not switch brands, even when they are extremely dissatisfied.

> **"Satisfaction correlates poorly with future behaviour"**

The model uses four dimensions to measure commitment. These dimensions are described below. A more comprehensive explanation is provided in later chapters.

1.  Satisfaction with the brand. If you wanted to better understand the reasons for brand switching, the obvious starting point would be how satisfied the consumer is with the brand. The less satisfied the consumer, the less likely they are to be committed to the brand. Conversely, the more satisfied they are, the more likely they are to be committed. However, satisfaction correlates poorly with future behaviour, as evidenced by many researchers, including ourselves.[2,3] Understanding satisfaction does not help us to fully understand why consumers do what they do. Having said that, satisfaction is an essential component of understanding the relationship between consumer and brand.

2.  Perception of the alternatives. One of the reasons that consumers don't switch brands when they are dissatisfied is that they feel that the alternatives are just as bad as the brand they are using, or even worse. So, the reason for a consumer staying with a bank with which they are unhappy could be that they feel that all banks are equally bad. There would be no point in swapping one set of problems for another.

    One implication of this is that the monitoring of consumer perceptions of competitive alternatives is essential for the formulation of effective marketing strategies. The evaluation of a brand does not happen in isolation. It is a comparative measure against the competition. This also means that a high customer satisfaction score does not necessarily mean that the relationship with the customer is secure. If the consumer perceives a competitive brand in an even better light, they could be on the brink of defection.

> **"One of the reasons that consumers don't switch brands when they are dissatisfied is that they feel that the alternatives are just as bad as the brand they are using, or even worse."**

3.  The importance of brand choice. If brand choice doesn't matter, it is difficult to achieve commitment. The product category, as well as brand choice, has to be something relatively important in the consumer's life for commitment to be possible. We are continually surprised by the degree to which the importance of brand choice is higher than we expect it to be. For example, in a study conducted by RSGB (part of the Taylor Nelson Sofres Group) during 1999, it was found that 58% of UK consumers felt that brand choice in the laundry detergent category was extremely or very important. For the majority of UK consumers, brand choice in the laundry detergent category is a relatively important issue in their lives – something which might surprise some marketers (Figure 2.1).

    The more that brand choice matters, the more likely it is that the consumer will take time and trouble to make a final decision about which brand to choose. Having made the choice, the natural reaction to dissatisfaction is to attempt to fix the relationship, rather than switch. Think of typical high-involvement categories – banks, cars, jobs (and marriage!). When things go wrong, our first reaction is to try to sort things out rather than switch. The higher the commitment, the higher the level of dissatisfaction that will be tolerated before defection.

    When brand choice doesn't matter to consumers, we call them 'uninvolved'. The challenge of making brand choice matter is one of the most difficult that a marketer can face. How do you make something important in a consumer's life, when they couldn't care less? In most cases, when brand choice is unimportant to a consumer, it is best to accept the reality of the situation, and manage the relationship appropriately, by not wasting funds on strategies that are unlikely to change the status quo.

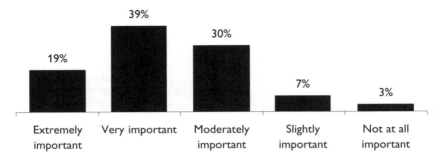

**Figure 2.1**   *How important is brand choice to UK consumers when buying laundry detergent?*

*Source*: RSGB/Taylor Nelson Sofres non-proprietary study, 1999.

> **"If brand choice doesn't matter, it is difficult to achieve commitment."**

4.  Degree of ambivalence. Ambivalence is a key dimension in the model of commitment that we use. The more ambivalent the consumer is about which brand to choose, the more likely it is that the final brand choice will be delayed until the last possible moment. For consumers such as these, point-of-purchase stimuli become critically important, as they will often only make their final choice at the shop shelf.

The brand which is most visible, or the cheapest, or the one stacked highest in a promotional display will often be the one that is bought. The tug of war between the brands about which the consumer is ambivalent is usually only decided just before the purchase is actually made.

> **"The more ambivalent the consumer is about which brand to choose, the more likely it is that the final brand choice will be delayed until the last possible moment."**

These four dimensions are the building blocks we use to determine whether a consumer is committed or not. As an example, for somebody to be classified as being strongly committed to a brand, brand choice has to matter a great deal. They would have to be convinced that the brand they were using was significantly better than any competitive brand. In addition, there would be no ambivalence about their perception. These consumers would be classified as belonging to the most highly committed consumer segment, as a result of their position on the four dimensions used to build the commitment model.

An allocation algorithm is used to classify people into the appropriate segment. At no time is the person asked directly what their commitment is. They simply respond to a battery of questions. Their responses are combined to produce a score, which then allocates them to a commitment segment. Using this approach effectively eliminates overclaim, which is a massive problem for marketing researchers in regions such as Africa, Asia and parts of South America.

The battery of questions needed to measure a person's position on the four dimensions usually takes less than five minutes to administer, and is typically administered via survey questionnaires. The data can be collected via face-to-face interviews, by telephone, by mail or over the Internet.

## Putting the segmentation into practice

When classifying consumers in terms of their level of commitment to a brand, the relationship that they have with *every* brand in the marketplace is identified. It is necessary to understand their relationships with all brands, in order to understand the relative attraction of other brands compared to those they are currently using. Broadly speaking, users and non-users of a brand are segmented as shown in Figure 2.2. Users of the brand are placed in one of four segments:

1.  Entrenched: users of the brand who are unlikely to switch brands in the foreseeable future.
2.  Average: users of the brand who are unlikely to change in the short term, but with some possibility of change in the medium term.
3.  Shallow: users of the brand who have a lower commitment than average, with some of these consumers already actively considering alternatives to the brand.
4.  Convertible: users of the brand who are most likely to defect.

Non-users are also classified into one of four segments:

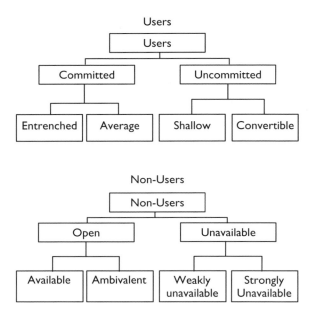

**Figure 2.2**   *The Conversion Model segments*

5. Available: non-users of the brand who prefer the brand to their current brands though they have not yet switched, and who have been identified as psychologically ready to switch.
6. Ambivalent: non-users who are as attracted to the brand as they are to their current brands. Hence, they are 'open' to the brand.
7. Weakly unavailable: non-users whose preference lies with their current brands, though not strongly.
8. Strongly unavailable: non-users whose preference lies strongly with their current brands. These people are least likely to switch to the brand in the near term.

As shown above, we often speak of *committed* or *uncommitted* people, with the understanding that the committed segment consists of those consumers who are 'entrenched' or 'average' in terms of their relationship with the brand, while uncommitted refers to those people who are 'shallow' or 'convertible' in their relationship. Among non-users, the 'available' and 'ambivalent' segments are referred to as *open*, when condensing the segments. Weakly and strongly unavailable segments are combined into the *unavailable* segment.

It takes some time to learn the language of commitment segmentation, but it is worth spending a little time trying to memorize the names of the segments. Remember, 'committed' and 'uncommitted' is just shorthand for reducing a four-segment classification to two segments. A lot of the time it is not necessary to look at the additional complexity of four segments – just knowing how many are committed or uncommitted is enough. Marketers sometimes get confused between the concepts of convertibility and availability. Convertible consumers are using *your* brand, and are most likely to *defect*, while *available* consumers are using *another* brand, and are most likely to be *acquired* by your brand in the near term.

Take a little time to try to memorize the labels. It will make for easier assimilation of the information to follow.

## How the basic commitment segments should be interpreted

It is important to keep on reminding oneself that commitment identifies consumers who have the *potential* to defect from the brand, or to be acquired by the brand. The way in which the segments are interpreted is more qualitative than quantitative. We know that convertible consumers are most likely to defect from the brand, but we don't know just how likely, in the absence of any follow-up research. In the same way, we know that relatively few entrenched consumers defect from the brand in any given year, but, again, we cannot quantify exactly how many.

When we carry out validation studies we return to the respondents we originally interviewed, to ascertain the brands they are consuming, after a period of at least six months has elapsed. This enables us to quantify the defection rates and acquisition rates per commitment and availability segment for the product category in which the validation study has been conducted.

Figure 2.3 shows an example from a beer study in Canada. In this study, Market Facts of Canada returned to the original respondents after a 12-month period. The respondents were part of the household panel maintained by Market Facts of Canada. As they are members of

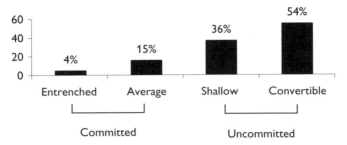

**Figure 2.3** *The relationship between commitment and subsequent defection rates for beers in Canada, showing the percentages in each category who had defected from the brand after 12 months*

*Source*: Market Facts of Canada non-proprietary study, 1994.

a panel, they are regularly interviewed, and it is easy to identify exactly which respondents took part in specific studies. All interviews were carried out by mail. The results of the recontact study are shown in Figure 2.3. It shows that 4% of the beer drinkers originally identified as being *entrenched* had defected from the brand during the 12-month period subsequent to their original classification. In contrast, 54% of those identified as being *convertible* had defected to another brand. Hence, commitment proved to be an excellent predictor of the number and profile of those beer drinkers most likely to defect, and those least likely.

Turning to beer drinkers who were not drinking Brand X at the time of the original interview, we find that their conversion to Brand X was as shown in Figure 2.4.

Half of beer drinkers *available* to the brand actually switched to it during the course of the 12-month period subsequent to the initial interview. Of those classified as being *strongly unavailable*, only 7% switched.

By identifying those most likely to leave the brand, as well as those most likely to be acquired by the brand, the marketer is able to quantify the size of the fluid centre of the market. It is from these consumers that brand share change is most likely to be derived in the near term. Not only is the size of the segment established, but

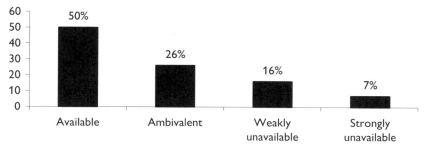

**Figure 2.4** *The relationship between availability and subsequent adoption rates for beers in Canada, showing the percentages in each category who had switched to the brand after 12 months*

*Source:* Market Facts of Canada non-proprietary study, 1994.

perceptions and motivations of these consumers are also measured, giving the marketer an insight into what needs to be done in order to control defection rates more effectively, while accelerating the acquisition of new consumers.

We thought that this validation study was a pretty tough test for the model, as the beer market in Canada is an extremely aggressive one, with Molson's and Labatt's at each other's throats on a continual basis. In addition, there are microbreweries and American beers. A plethora of different types of beers had also been launched in the period under review, including dry beers, iced beers, bottled draughts and so on. Given the turbulence of the marketing environment, the model performed extremely well at identifying those beer drinkers most likely to switch brands in the near term.

> **"By identifying those most likely to leave the brand, as well as those most likely to be acquired by the brand, the marketer is able to quantify the size of the fluid centre of the market."**

What the figure does *not* show is the size of the segments in the original study. Those available to the brand might have been as few as 5% of all consumers, or as many as 50% of the market. It is important not to confuse the *size* of the segment with the defection or conversion rate of each segment in specified time periods.

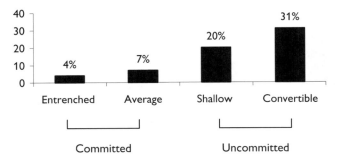

**Figure 2.5** *Defection rates for banks in Canada*

*Source:* Market Facts of Canada non-proprietary study, 1994.

Figure 2.5 presents another example, this time from banks, showing the results of a similar type of validation study. The charts show the defection rates of customers of banks in Canada after a 12-month period. Although there is a strong statistical relationship between the commitment segmentation and the subsequent behaviour of these consumers, the defection rates for banks are different from those for beer. It is more of a hassle to extricate yourself from a relationship with a bank than it is to switch your brand of beer at the next purchase opportunity.

## Some basic profiles

The commitment and availability profile of your brand, compared to other brands, dictates the marketing strategy that is appropriate for the most effective brand management. Some examples are presented in this section.

### Acquisition or retention?

Figure 2.6 shows a hypothetical brand profile of a brand that has more committed than uncommitted consumers – every marketer's dream. The brand is relatively secure, as the majority of its users are committed. We can see from the figure that 40% of all consumers are committed users of the brand, while 10% are uncommitted users of the brand. Putting it another way, 80% of the brand's users are committed – an outstanding achievement, in terms of brand strength.

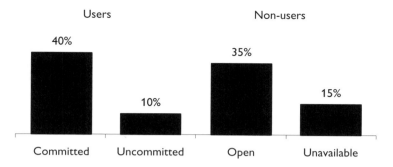

**Figure 2.6** *A brand with more available non-users than uncommitted users*

Unavailability is remarkably low, with only 15% of consumers (30% of non-users) unlikely to consider purchasing the brand in the near term; 35% of all consumers are not using the brand, but are open to using it. When those non-users *open* to the brand significantly outnumber those users who are *uncommitted*, an attacking strategy is appropriate. It should be noted that the chance of encountering an open segment as large as 35% of the market is very unlikely. If this were the case, it would most probably be due to one of two reasons – either because of an appalling out-of-stock situation, so that consumers could not find the brand on shelf, or because of an aspirational availability that was unrealistic. For example, most motorists would be available to the latest Lamborghini as a replacement for their current car. However, it is unlikely that they would be able to afford one.

One of the most important factors in deciding on the appropriate marketing stance is the difference between the size of the segment of consumers at risk of being lost to the brand and those who are open to being acquired. The greater this difference, in terms of open non-users outnumbering uncommitted users of the brand, the more justified the marketer will be in adopting an aggressive acquisition strategy, concentrating on acquiring new users, rather than focusing on the retention of current users, the majority of whom are secure in their relationship with the brand, and unlikely to defect in the near term.

> **"When those non-users *open* to the brand significantly outnumber those users who are *uncommitted*, an attacking strategy is appropriate."**

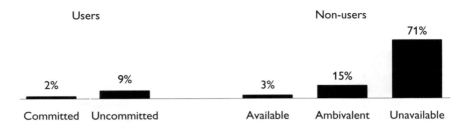

**Figure 2.7**  *Conversion Model segments  for Surf powder*

*Source:* RSGB/Taylor Nelson Sofres non-proprietary study, 1999.


## When consolidation is appropriate

The converse is also true. When the brand has more uncommitted consumers than committed consumers, a consolidation strategy is called for. The emphasis should be on retaining consumers, rather than trying to acquire new ones. Figure 2.7 shows a commitment and availability profile of a brand that should be defending rather than attacking. This time the profile is not hypothetical: it represents the profile of Surf washing powder in the UK. This time we show those non-users open to the brand in more detail, breaking them into their sub-segments of consumers who are immediately available to the brand, and those who are ambivalent. Those who are available to the brand prefer it to their current brand, and have a poor relationship with their current brand. It can be seen that Surf is in all sorts of trouble – 11% of consumers are using Surf, with 9% being uncommitted. Putting it another way, only 18% of Surf users are committed to the brand (2% of 11%), while 82% are uncommitted. With the majority of Surf users uncommitted and only 3% of the total market immediately available to the brand, it is clear that the emphasis should be on consolidation, with the focus being on improving the position of the brand before attempting to acquire new users. In a situation like this, where 71% of the market is unavailable to the brand, it is clear that the brand has its back to the wall, typically pointing to problems in product delivery, value for money perceptions or something else equally significant in terms of brand health.

> **"When the brand has more uncommitted consumers than committed consumers, a consolidation strategy is called for."**

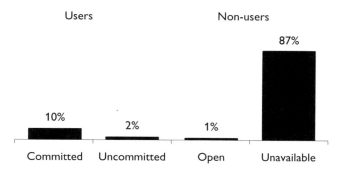

**Figure 2.8** *A Niche brand*

## Niche brands

Sometimes we encounter an interesting profile which looks something like Figure 2.8. This was the type of profile we encountered when investigating a breakfast cereal market some years ago. The product in question was a health cereal, which looked and tasted like cardboard. To consume the cereal voluntarily required an almost fanatical obsession with health. The marketer had been advertising the brand for some years in an effort to boost sales, but to no avail.

An examination of the commitment profile showed that the majority of consumers of the cereal were strongly committed. Their risk of defection was slight. On the other hand, the probability of growing the brand in the near future was even smaller, as few non-users were available. Exacerbating the situation was the fact that 87% of consumers were unavailable to the brand. These were consumers who were aware of the brand, and might even have tried it, but felt no attraction to it.

Our recommendation to the marketing team was to reduce the adspend significantly, and concentrate on satisfying the needs of current users of the brand. There was little potential for growing the brand, and advertising was unlikely to change the situation. Given the high commitment of the brand's users, the brand share was likely to remain stable for the foreseeable future.

Some years later, the marketing team told us that this was one of the best decisions they had ever taken. They had stopped trying to achieve the impossible, cut unnecessary advertising support, and increased the profitability of their brand by increasing the price, which they were able to do without adverse effects, due to the strong commitment of their user base. Brand share had remained rock steady. This type of profile is particularly prevalent in niche markets.

## Overall success of a brand

The success or otherwise of a brand can be attributed to two broad areas. Figure 2.9 is a diagrammatic illustration of this.

Many brands are not strong in terms of commitment from their consumers, but are held in place by high visibility, a strong presence at point of sale and excellent distribution. For consumers for whom brand choice is not that important (the *uninvolved*), these brands are the easiest choice to make. They come to mind first and occupy the lion's share of shelf facings in stores. They are brands that have strong *market equity*.

This does not only apply to packaged goods categories. For example, in telecommunications, a mobile phone supplier could be chosen because it is the one whose name comes to mind first, because of the visibility of the logo on buildings, billboards, sponsorships and through advertising exposure, as well as the convenience of retail locations, rather than because of a clear-cut brand image. Sheer visibility is a significant contributor to the market equity of many brands, and hence their success.

> **"Many brands are not strong in terms of commitment from their consumers, but are held in place by high visibility, a strong presence at point of sale and excellent distribution."**

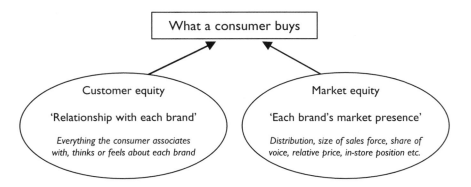

**Figure 2.9**   *Broad factors that determine the success or otherwise of a brand*

It sometimes happens that a brand enjoys high commitment among its users, but sales do not reflect this strong *customer equity*. In almost every case we have found that the problem lies in visibility and distribution. The brand is not achieving its true potential because it is difficult to find on shop shelves. Poor sales do not necessarily mean that brand health is weak. Customer equity can be strong, while market equity is weak.

> **"Poor sales do not necessarily mean that brand health is weak."**

# How do we manage the segments?

The appropriate management of the relationship varies from segment to segment. Here is a summary of some of the most important points to remember when deciding how best to manage the relationship between the brand and its consumers, according to the segment to which the consumer belongs. Those who use the brand are segmented into *committed* (entrenched or average) or *uncommitted* (shallow or convertible), while those who do not use the brand can be segmented into those who are *open* to the brand (available or ambivalent) or *unavailable* (weakly or strongly unavailable). Those consumers who are uncommitted can further be segmented into those who are involved and those who are uninvolved. Involvement simply refers to the importance of brand choice. If brand choice is important to consumers, we call them *involved*.

## Committed consumers

Conceptually, these are the easiest relationships to manage. These are consumers who like the brand, soak up the advertising and are not particularly price sensitive. But they do want reassurance about the wisdom of their choice.

If the commitment of consumers is not nurtured, their relationship with the brand can deteriorate with alarming rapidity. In a study conducted by Market Facts of Canada, it was found that in a 12-month period one in three committed banking customers became uncommitted.

Relationships with committed consumers need to be maintained. One of the mechanisms that does this really well is advertising. Obviously, it is not the only mechanism, but advertising is particularly appropriate for committed consumers. It serves to reassure consumers, as well as frame their consumption experience, enriching it in their minds.

The amount of effort that is required to maintain the relationship with committed consumers will differ from category to category. For some consumers, very little expenditure is needed to maintain a strong relationship with the brand. For others, however, regular reassurance is needed. It would be naive to assume that, in all markets, commitment will persist without maintenance.

> **"If the commitment of consumers is not nurtured, their relationship with the brand can deteriorate with alarming rapidity."**

We have applied measures of commitment in nearly 200 product categories. Norms for some of them are shown in Figure 2.10. The norms show the size of the segment of consumers who are committed to the brand that they use most often in the category. These norms have been constructed from studies across several major geographical markets, with more than one study having been conducted in each market.

Laundry detergents, beer and cigarettes enjoy high commitment from their consumers. These are brands which consumers are unlikely to switch frequently, in product categories in which price will play a weaker role in brand choice. Aggressive brand advertising is appropriate, in order to sustain the strong relationships that exist between consumers and the brands they use. In contrast, the commitment to retail chains and mobile network suppliers is relatively low. These are markets in which price will play a greater part in the final brand choice process, as well as convenience.

The figure reveals other insights. For example, it is interesting to note the low commitment of employees to the jobs they have. With only 42% of employees being committed, the majority of employees globally are not committed to their jobs. The lowest level of commitment that we have found among employees is in the UK, with the highest commitment being found among employees in South Africa.

Confectionery provides another interesting example of a high-commitment category. Although confectionery products are generally regarded as impulse items, the high commitment to confectionery brands means that consumers have favourite brands which they will buy time and

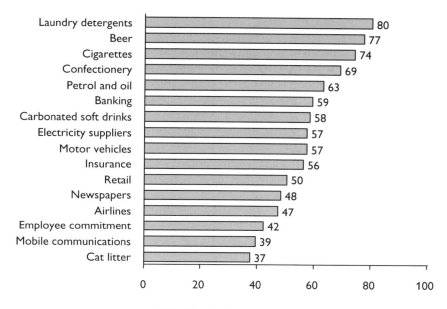

Percentage of users who are committed to brand used most often

i.e. 80% of laundry detergent users are committed to the brand of detergent they use most often, and so on

**Figure 2.10** *Global category norms*

again. Although the purchase of confectionery might often be on impulse, the brands which are chosen most often will tend to be fairly stable, in terms of purchasing patterns.

What is striking about the majority of these norms is how high they are. What they show is that consumers typically have a strong allegiance to the brands they use most often. When brand switching takes place, it tends to happen with brands on the periphery of a consumer's repertoire, rather than with their 'most often' brands.

Because of this high allegiance to brands, brand switching can be far more difficult to achieve than most marketers would hope, particularly when it comes to achieving the position of being the most favoured brand in the repertoire. Markets are typically more inert than marketers think they are, with significant changes only happening when new channels of distribution are introduced into the marketplace (such as egg, the first Internet-based bank in the UK) or when new meaningful dimensions are introduced to product categories (such as adding baking soda to toothpaste), causing consumers to reassess what the realistic alternatives are to the brands they are using.

> **"When brand switching takes place, it tends to happen with brands on the periphery of a consumer's repertoire, rather than with their 'most often' brands."**

## Uncommitted consumers

When we first started measuring the commitment of consumers, we thought that the commitment of all consumers could be improved if the correct strategy was in place. This is not the case. A lack of commitment to a brand can be due to many reasons – a lack of involvement in the category, dissatisfaction with the product or service, or, paradoxically, a very heavy involvement in the category, which leads to a dedication to brand experimentation and continuing trial of new brands.

When using research to understand uncommitted customers, it is essential that the reasons for commitment are fully understood as they will lead to very different strategies in terms of managing the relationship. The following subsections give a brief summary of how we do it.

### *The uncommitted consumer for whom brand choice is unimportant*

These are consumers for whom brand choice is so unimportant that they might be unaware of the actual brand they buy, remembering only the colour of the pack. They will make the brand choice that is the least hassle, and tend to be driven by convenience and price. These consumers often choose the brand leader, simply because it is the first brand that comes to mind when the shop assistant asks them what they are looking for.

Advertising is relatively ineffective at reaching these consumers, as they are among those least likely to 'see' and 'like' any advertising for the category. It will be screened out, as it is unnecessary information. If a brand has a large segment of consumers who are uncommitted because brand choice does not matter (the *uninvolved*), a key focal area of the marketing efforts should be point of sale and general visibility of the brand, rather than expensive advertising campaigns.

## Uncommitted but involved

If consumers are uncommitted, but brand choice does matter (the *involved*), the marketer faces a more complex challenge. If the brand belongs to a service category, it is likely that there have been problems experienced in service delivery, which need to be rectified. The exact nature of the problem needs to be identified, with appropriate action being taken.

However, we do encounter consumers who are uncommitted because they are 'committed to promiscuity'. Think of avid wine enthusiasts. Brand choice is extremely important to these consumers. But they are unlikely to ally themselves with any one brand of wine, as their thirst for knowledge drives them to continual experimentation. They show up in commitment segmentations as 'uncommitted but involved'. It would be foolhardy to try to improve the commitment of these consumers to any one brand. Rather, it needs to be recognized that they are unlikely to change in terms of their current brand relationships, but that they are likely to act as opinion leaders for those less well informed than they are. They are dedicated to experimentation, and soak up advertising in the category. Typically, they are aware of more advertising campaigns in the category than are other consumers. The more information we can give them about our brand, the better.

> **"We do encounter consumers who are uncommitted because they are 'committed to promiscuity'."**

## Available non-users

These are non-users who are not using your brand, but who are immediately available for acquisition. Identifying the size of this segment becomes particularly relevant when launching new categories, such as mobile phones. In one mobile phone study, we found that the size of the available non-user segment to *all* brands was so large, that any focus on inter-brand competition was irrelevant. Non-users were available to the *category*, with the result that the brand that was most easily available and first came to mind would be chosen. Obviously, this presupposed that the brand was competitively priced.

For most packaged goods categories, the size of the available segment is depressingly small. If the brand is not priced out of the consumer's reach, those who are interested in the brand should already be buying it.

> **"For most packaged goods categories, the size of the available segment is depressingly small."**

## Ambivalent consumers

Ambivalent consumers are not using your brand, but are ambivalent about it. The brand about which they are ambivalent is not any better or any worse than the brand which they are currently using. In order to woo these consumers, some sort of tie-breaker has to be offered to them. In some instances it might be price, while in others it might be a more convenient pack size or some other form of promotion. Typically, we would suggest that additional research be carried out among consumers who are ambivalent in order to better understand what might break the tie.

# What about the unavailables?

Typically, non-users who are available to or ambivalent about your brand are uncommitted users of competitor brands. Often, however, marketers focus more on the unavailable than on the available and ambivalent segments. This is because, for most brands, the unavailable segment is the largest of all segments. Hence, it entices the interest of marketers, purely because of its size. Typically, the segment of unavailable consumers is far larger than marketers think. Staying with our laundry detergent example from the UK, we see that the size of the consumer segment unavailable to individual brands is very large (Figure 2.11).

It can be seen that the majority of UK laundry detergent brands effectively operate in less than 50% of the market, which could come as a bit of a surprise to the marketers of some of these brands.

Let's understand the reasons why a consumer may be unavailable to your brand. It could be because:

- they know of the brand, may even have tried it, but see no reason to switch;
- they are committed to the brands they use;
- they are aware of the brand, but have a poor image of it;
- they don't know the brand exists.

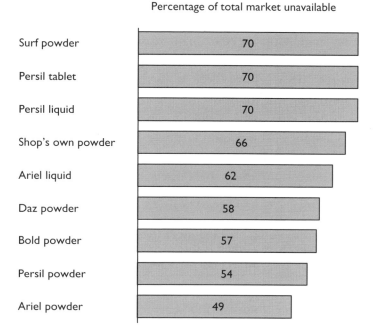

Figure 2.11   *Unavailable consumers to laundry detergent brands*

*Source*: RSGB/Taylor Nelson Sofres non-proprietary study, 1999.

Obviously, the latter reason for unavailability is the easiest one to remedy. If people are not buying the brand because they are unaware of its existence, it is comparatively easy to bring the brand to their attention, via advertising, for example. In this case, the main communication objective would simply be to say, 'here I am' in an intriguing enough way to induce trial.

Sometimes people are aware of the brand and have tried it, but are still not interested. We found an interesting example of this in the cider market, where a particular brand of cider had enjoyed a high degree of success among female drinkers. Consumers unavailable to the brand were mostly male drinkers who had tried the product, but found it too sweet, and thought it was mainly for women. In a situation like this, it was clear that a new product would have to be launched to satisfy the needs of these unavailable consumers, preferably a cider with a drier taste and more of a 'macho' image. There would be no point in continuing to try to entice unavailable male drinkers into using the current brand.

For mature brands, the most frequent reason for unavailability to the brand is that consumers are happy with what they are using. They see no reason to switch. It's not that there is anything wrong with the brand; consumers are happy just the way they are.

The size of the unavailable segment can be uncomfortably large. As discussed in Chapter 6, these consumers are least likely to be swayed by advertising. The most that advertising can hope to achieve is to bring the brand to their attention. Even then, their likelihood of 'receiving' the advertising in a positive way is low.

> **"For mature brands, the most frequent reason for unavailability to the brand is that consumers are happy with what they are using."**

Forced trial or sampling remains one of the best ways of getting unavailable consumers to consider the inclusion of the brand in their repertoire, particularly when the reason for their unavailability is a strong commitment to the brands they are currently using. Although expensive, sampling is still under-utilized in many industries. One which stands out is the airline industry. Many frequent flyers are strongly committed to the airlines they use, in addition to being locked in by loyalty programmes. The most seductive advertising is unlikely to induce a change. But a free flight to an overseas destination might well do so. Given the lifetime value of frequent flyers, it would be appropriate for airlines to consider adopting this strategy in order to woo them.

In summary, then, we can understand a lot more about why consumers are unavailable to our brand by simple segmentation. This will help us decide whether there is any realistic chance of wooing the unavailable segment to our brand in the foreseeable future. Typically, however, we do not expend that much intellectual energy on the unavailable segment, as we recognize that they are unlikely to be acquired in the near term. The attractiveness of sampling to them will depend very much on the cost of the sampling exercise and its possible return. This can easily be simulated via a survey, which will quantify the impact of sampling on availability to the brand, prior to embarking on a major exercise.

# Category in trouble

In addition to the eight commitment and availability segments, there is a ninth segment which we do not show often, simply including it in the 'strongly unavailable' segment. This is a segment of consumers that we have named *category in trouble*.

Consumers who belong to the category in trouble segment are there because we have identified them as having a low commitment to their brand, but also a very low availability to other brands in the marketplace. So, they are a sub-segment of the convertible segment (if they use a brand) or strongly unavailable (if they don't). They are definitely unavailable to our brand, as they have a low regard for it, but that's what they think about everything else in the market. They are called 'category in trouble' because they do not like any of the brands in the category. They are potential category defectors, as nothing in the category attracts them.

The segment of consumers who dislike everything in the category tends to be fairly small, rarely exceeding 5% of the total market. However, if the segment is comparatively large, it could point to new product development opportunities, as nothing in the market satisfies these consumers, despite their being active in the category. Fail to find a solution for them, and they will eventually leave the category.

The largest category in trouble segments we have ever encountered have been in the field of politics. In 1992, Market Facts conducted a study to measure the commitment of potential voters to the candidates for the presidency of the USA. They found that commitment levels were extremely low. The category in trouble segment was 15% of all voters, an unusually high percentage given that so many of the respondents thought the choice of someone for president to be a very important issue. Basically, voters were disillusioned by both of the conventional party choices – Clinton and Bush – at the time. This is one of the reasons why Ross Perot was able to do so well.

The record for the biggest category in trouble segment continued to be held by voters in the USA until the same research was repeated in the United Kingdom in 1996. This time RSGB, a leading marketing research company in the UK, looked at commitment to the three leaders of the main political parties that would contest elections in 1997. The three were John Major of the ruling Conservative Party, Tony Blair, the recently elected

leader of the main opposition Labour Party, and Paddy Ashdown, the leader
of the Liberal Democrats. In this case the category in trouble segment stood
at 25% – still a record. What the results told us was that conditions were
ripe for a major realignment in British politics. Subsequently, Tony Blair
managed to redefine Labour. The result was a landslide win for Blair's 'new'
labourites. In effect, he did what Ross Perot did in the USA but without
alienating his original constituency.

Another category in which we have found large category in trouble
segments, particularly in the USA, has been cigarettes. Here we encounter
category in trouble segments as high as 20–25% in certain demographic
segments, particularly among older smokers. Our interpretation of this is
that these are smokers who would dearly like to quit. Ex-smokers recall the
stage they went through prior to quitting, when they really disliked what
they were doing. But they kept on smoking in spite of themselves, because
they were addicted. If you had asked them what they thought of their
current brand of cigarettes, they would have given you a negative response.
They would have responded equally negatively about other brands of
cigarettes in the marketplace. They wanted to quit, but did not have the
strength to do so.

In more recent years, we have been paying more attention to the
category in trouble segment, but have not found many other interesting
examples like the ones from politics or the cigarette industry.

## Commitment is your crystal ball

One of the most important reasons why marketers should know how many
committed customers they have compared to their competitors is that
commitment has been shown to correlate with future behaviour. When
looking at the year ahead, commitment will give you a valuable insight into
which brands are likely to gain or lose market share, and from and to
whom.

A graphic example of this is provided by work we did in the early 1990s
in the cigarette market in the USA. We predicted that Marlboro was about
to decline, but our research claims were met with some disbelief on the part
of the client (who, incidentally, was not Marlboro). We were so pleased
when Marlboro Friday happened.

When we made our research presentation, the client liked everything we had to say, with the exception of the prediction about Marlboro. 'Do you guys realize you're talking about one of the strongest brands in American history?', we were asked. We were asked to recheck our figures, which we did. However, the prediction was clear. Marlboro was strategically vulnerable as a brand, and was about to slide. The number of uncommitted Marlboro smokers far outnumbered those non-Marlboro smokers who were available for acquisition. It is probable that the Marlboro defensive strategy would have been very different had they measured the commitment of their smokers.

## Blessed are the large . . .

Obviously, the commitment and availability segments are a measure of the strength of a brand. But how do we tell what kind of segment profile signals a really healthy brand?

One of the ways in which we decided this question in the early days was with a simple piece of arithmetic. To illustrate this calculation, let's look at two soft drink brands in the USA: Pepsi-Cola and Sprite. Their relative brand profiles in 1991 are shown in Table 2.1.[4] Sprite has more non-users who are available to it than does Pepsi, with the difference between available non-users and convertible users being 4% of the market. This number was arrived at by a simple subtraction. It seems a fair way to do it, given that we know the segments accurately enough to identify who is most or least likely to switch. The resulting numbers can then be used as a guide to potential market share loss or gain. In this particular case, one might be tempted to conclude that Sprite is more likely to grow in the near term than Pepsi.

However, our experience has taught us that this simplistic approach to interpreting the segments is wrong and points to an interesting application of 'double jeopardy'[5] found in the defection and acquisition rates of brands. What we have found is that:

- the bigger the brand, the fewer (proportionally) convertible users are lost;
- the bigger the brand, the more available consumers (proportionally) are gained.

**Table 2.1** *Brand profiles of Pepsi-Cola and Sprite, 1991*

|  | Pepsi-Cola (%) | Sprite (%) |
| --- | --- | --- |
| Users | 34 | 14 |
| Entrenched | 4 | 1 |
| Average | 19 | 6 |
| Shallow | 9 | 6 |
| Convertible | 2 | 2 |
| Near-term potential | +2 | +4 |
| Available | 4 | 6 |
| Ambivalent | 12 | 15 |
| Weakly unavailable | 13 | 20 |
| Strongly unavailable | 37 | 45 |
| Non-users | 66 | 86 |

*Source*: Market Facts, 1991 Soft Drink Study.

This means that although Pepsi and Sprite both have the same size convertible segment (2% of the market), Pepsi will be less likely to lose its convertible customers in the near term than Sprite will. In the same way, although Pepsi only has 4% of the market available to it, compared to 6% of the market available to Sprite, the acquisition rate of available consumers will be significantly higher for Pepsi than for Sprite.

At this stage, we do not have sufficient data to come up with a definitive model, but feel that this relationship will be roughly proportional to brand share, in terms of the acquisition of availables and the defection of convertibles. The larger the brand share, the more convertible consumers who will be retained by the brand and the more available non-users who will be acquired. We explore this in more detail in later chapters.

## Who gets what, and from whom?

Commitment-led marketing identifies not only the consumers of a brand who are convertible, but also to which brand or brands they are being attracted. In addition, we can identify from which brands our future growth is likely to come.

This type of analysis provides an overview of the tugs of war in the market, enabling us to quantify for each pair of brands the net share that can be lost or gained for each respective brand. This is a very handy way of identifying what the true threats are in the marketplace, in addition to identifying which brands are vulnerable to raids. Let's return to a typical commitment profile to illustrate this, staying with the soft drink example from the USA (Figure 2.12)

Because the 'attraction of competitors' is one of the underlying measures used to create the segments, we are able to look at the shallow and convertible users of any brand and identify to which competitors they are attracted, and to what extent. In Figure 2.12, it can be seen that Pepsi users are most likely to be attracted to Dr Pepper, Seven-Up and Coke. If they defect from the brand, these are the brands they are most likely to defect to.

Similarly, it is possible to identify the competitive brands which will provide the richest source of new recruits. Pepsi is most likely to acquire new recruits from Coke and Diet Coke. The chart summarizes the potential for retention and acquisition, as well as which competitors are likely to gain or lose from brand share changes in the near term. The extent to which switching will actually take place will be a function of relative market strength, in terms of the brand's relative power in terms of market equity in the marketplace.

Commitment is a very precise measure of who is winning the battle for the mind. While winning that battle is an important part of what makes for valuable brands, it does not absolve the marketer from attending to the rest of marketing's basics, such as pricing, packaging and distribution.

> **"Commitment is a very precise measure of who is winning the battle for the mind."**

# Most often versus the repertoire model of commitment

The commitment of consumers can be measured either to all the brands they use in the category, or only to the 'most often' brand. Obviously, if you look at the commitment of consumers who use the brand most often, you would expect this to be higher than the commitment of *all* users of the brand, some of whom will only use the brand occasionally. The brand that

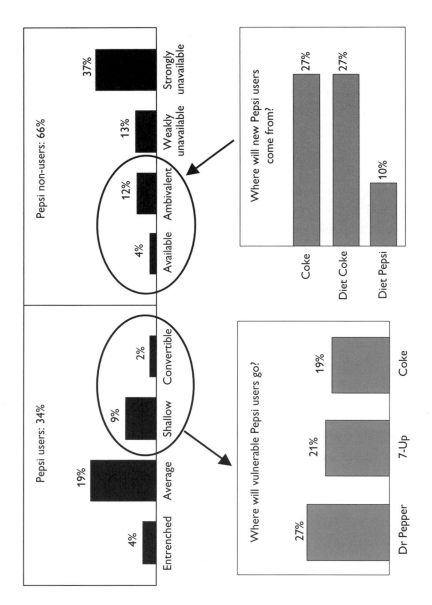

**Figure 2.12** *Who gets what, and from whom?*

*Source:* Market Facts, 1991 Soft Drink Study.

is most difficult to dislodge is the one in the position of being used most often. When brand shares change, they typically do so with brands at the periphery of the repertoire most likely to be affected. Some of the time consumers contract their repertoires, simply dropping brands at the edge of their repertoire and focusing their purchases on fewer brands. One market which provides an example of this has been retail clothing in South Africa. Over the past ten years, the amount of clothing retail chains shopped at by consumers has shrunk by about 30%.

> **"The commitment of consumers can be measured either to all the brands they use in the category, or only to the 'most often' brand."**

It is possible to identify the position a brand occupies in the consumer's repertoire. Is it the most often brand, or is it used but not most often? In each case, the degree of commitment to the brand can be accurately determined, enabling the appropriate marketing strategy to be put in place.

# Marketer's summary: using commitment-led marketing

This feels like a good time to pause and summarize, as this is the bedrock of our analysis.

- We segment users according to commitment.
- We segment non-users according to availability.
- Users are segmented into:
  1. Entrenched ⎫
  2. Average    ⎬ Committed
  3. Shallow    ⎫
  4. Convertible ⎬ Uncommitted
- Non-users are segmented into:
  5. Available  ⎫
  6. Ambivalent ⎬ Open
  7. Weakly unavailable   ⎫
  8. Strongly unavailable ⎬ Unavailable

- This segmentation is produced for all the brands in the market, enabling the marketer to determine the vulnerability or otherwise of all brands in the market.

There is a strong correlation between segmentation according to commitment and availability, and subsequent defection or acquisition of consumers in these segments. Hence, this segmentation provides insight into the future of the brand, allowing the marketer to take appropriate action. By understanding commitment, we understand what is in the consumer's mind. This understanding enables us to manage the relationship appropriately. For example, advertising will usually be inappropriate for reaching uncommitted consumers, or those unavailable to the brand. If these segments are the focus of marketing strategies, other elements of the marketing mix need to be harnessed in order to reach them more effectively. If the marketing challenge is to acquire new users for the brand, it is important to understand the degree of availability that exists, as this will impact on the way in which consumers are enticed to try the brand.

Without knowing what is in the mind of consumers, we run the risk of wasting massive amounts of marketing funds. Commitment gives us the insight we need to formulate effective and profitable marketing strategies.

The key learning points for marketers contained in this chapter are:

- Customer satisfaction does not correlate well with future behaviour. Customers can switch and dissatisfied customers will often not switch.
- Poor sales do not necessarily mean that the brand health is weak. Poor sales could well be because of poor distribution and low visibility in the marketplace, rather than brand intrinsics.
- Strong sales do not mean that the brand is healthy. Many brands do not enjoy strong commitment from their consumers, but are held in place by high visibility, a strong presence of point of sale, excellent distribution and competitive pricing.
- Not all consumers are available to your brand. The size of the segment of unavailable consumers is far larger than most marketers think, with many brands effectively operating in less than 50% of the market.
- Markets are typically more inert than marketers think they are.

- One of the reasons why consumers do not switch when they are dissatisfied is that they feel that the alternatives are just as bad as the brand they are using, or even worse.
- The more ambivalent the consumer is about which brand to choose, the more likely it is that the final brand choice will be delayed until the last possible moment. For these customers, point of sale stimuli are very important.
- By identifying those most likely to leave the brand, as well as those most likely to be acquired by the brand, the marketer is able to quantify the size of the fluid centre of the market. It is from this 'fluid centre' that share change will come in the near term.
- When brand switching takes place, it tends to happen with brands on the periphery of a consumer's repertoire, rather than with their 'most often' brands. In order for a brand to be really secure in a repertoire, it will typically need to occupy the 'most often' position.
- For most packaged goods categories, the size of the segment of available consumers is depressingly small.
- For mature brands, the most frequent reason for unavailability to the brand is that consumers are happy with what they are using.
- If there are more uncommitted consumers than committed consumers, a consolidation strategy is called for, rather than an acquisition strategy.
- The commitment of consumers needs to be nurtured. If committed consumers are ignored for long enough, their relationship with the brand will eventually deteriorate, impacting negatively on sales.
- Advertising is relatively ineffective at reaching unavailable consumers, as they are among those least likely to 'see' and 'like' any advertising for the category. Do not rely on advertising to cure too wide a range of marketing problems.

## References

1. Hofmeyr, J. (1990) The Conversion Model – a new foundation for strategic planning in marketing. New Ways in Marketing and Marketing Research, 3rd Emac/Esomar Symposium, Athens.
2. Hofmeyr, J. (1995) Is satisfaction enough? Using the Conversion Model for customer retention and acquisition. Measuring Customer Satisfaction Conference, London, February.

3.  Reichheld, Frederick F. (1996) *The Loyalty Effect*. Harvard Business School Press, Boston, MA.
4.  Walker, C. (1995) How strong is your brand? *Marketing Tools*, January/February.
5.  Ehrenberg, A.S.C. (1972) *Repeat-Buying: Theory and Applications*, 2nd edn. Charles Griffin and Company, London.

# 3

# A General Theory of Commitment

*How to measure commitment with just a few questions*

It may seem strange to think of the world's religious geniuses as producers of commercial goods or services. Yet it is clear that they were among the world's greatest marketers. Marketers envy the levels of commitment that they see in religion. The ideal customer, a marketer will tell you, is not merely one who buys your brand again and again. It is one who acts as an 'advocate' or 'missionary' for the brand. And one of the worst things you can do as a marketer is to make a customer so angry that he or she stops using your brand and then acts as a missionary against it.

So marketers should recognize that there is something in religion and the way it works that captures what marketing is trying to achieve. The title of a recent best-seller about the history of Coca-Cola, *For God, Country, and Coca-Cola*, says it all.[1] The twentieth century has seen many marketing battles for the hearts and minds of consumers, fought with an intensity which religious people would recognize.

This chapter is about how commitment develops – and about how conversion takes place – no matter what the brand or product category. It is derived from an understanding of commitment and conversion in religion, but applied to marketing.[2] It is our simple introduction to the theory which lies at the heart of our approach to commitment-led marketing. Once you understand the theory, you will realize that commitment can be measured by asking just a few simple questions. The questions are:

- How happy are you with <whatever it is>?
- Is this relationship something that you care about?

- Is there any other <whatever it is> that appeals to you?
- If so, how different is the one <whatever> from the other?

It may not be obvious how these questions can be used to measure commitment. The pages that follow will make it clear.

## How to measure commitment: the first step

**?** *Suppose we wanted to establish how committed someone was to their marriage, to their choice of political party, to the make and model of car they drove, or to the brand of laundry detergent they use. What questions would we have to ask?*

And suppose we had to keep the questions the same, no matter who we were talking to or what we were talking about. What would the questions have to be? According to the theory, there are just a few.

The first question is obvious: how happy are you?

Suppose you are married. How happy are you with your marriage? Does it satisfy all the needs and values that you have when it comes to marriage? Or how happy are you with your car? Is it everything that you look for in a car? Are the brands of laundry detergent you use regularly good enough?

People bring a complex range of needs, desires and values to every decision that they make. No matter what you are choosing – a job, a car or a toothpaste – you will tend to become attached to it if it works for you, and the longer it continues working for you, the more committed you will tend to be. The meeting of these needs and values with your experience of whatever it is that you have chosen creates the first dimension by which we measure commitment. We call this dimension *needs–values fit*. Needs–values fit is a measure of the extent to which a choice, any choice, satisfies all the goals and motivations, needs and values that a person may have when it comes to that choice.

> **"People bring a complex range of needs, desires and values to every decision that they make."**

The relationship between needs–values fit and commitment is easy to describe (see Figure 3.1): broadly speaking, the better the fit, the more

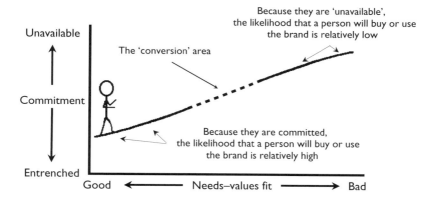

**Figure 3.1**  *The relationship between needs–values fit and commitment*

committed a person will tend to be. If a gap opens up between what someone is looking for and what they are getting, then they will tend to become less committed. Dissatisfaction and unhappiness are among the ways our emotions tell us that our choices are not working. Eventually a point may be reached where commitment has been eroded completely. Then, if at all possible, we will drop that choice and convert.

Because of its importance, marketers devote significant resources to trying to measure the needs and values that people have in a market. They put people in rooms and watch them talk about brands from behind one-way mirrors. They go into people's homes to watch them use brands. They devise long lists of brand attributes and then measure their brands against those lists. They go to all this effort because it is not easy to answer the question: what do people want?

Let's take a very ordinary and nearly universal activity – washing clothes. What does a householder want? 'Clean clothes', is the obvious answer. Yet when you look at it carefully it turns out to be a lot more complicated than that. How about 'harmony in the household'? Or 'pride in the way the children look'? Or 'time to do other things than wash clothes'? For many years, Unilever, the maker of Persil in the United Kingdom, has marketed Omo, one of its most widely used international brands, with a single-minded focus on 'taking pride in being a good housewife'. In places like Brazil, Omo is expensive and many people cannot afford it. Yet so effective has Unilever been that householders *aspire* to wash their clothes with Omo.

*When we understand how complex the needs–values mix can be, we have to ask ourselves the question: can needs–values fit really be measured with one question?*

Let's see.

## Why one question is better than many when it comes to needs–values fit

The fact that consumers may be different in what they want in a market does not affect the question we have to ask if we want to find out whether or not they are happy. Omo, for example, is the brand for people who say: 'I need a partner in being a good householder – and Omo is that partner when it comes to washing clothes'. Skip, another Unilever brand for automatic washing machines, is for people whose attitude is more like 'just get my clothes clean and don't wreck my automatic washing machine'. Two brands, very different sets of motives. No matter. The starting point for measuring commitment can be the same: to what extent does Omo (or Skip) satisfy your needs and values when it comes to washing clothes?

The question also does not have to be changed because one person may have different motivations in different markets. For example, someone who says: 'I buy Skip because it gets my clothes really clean and it doesn't wreck my automatic washing machine' may also be a person who says: 'I drive BMW because it has superb engineering – I enjoy driving – and it makes me feel good about myself'. They are completely differently motivated in each market. Yet, it doesn't matter. In both cases we can establish needs–values fit with just the one question.

It doesn't even matter that what a person looks for in a particular market may change over time. Ten years ago, frequent flyers expected very different things from an airline than they do today. Still, we only need one question to tell whether or not they are happy. Their answer may change over time, but that's fine. It just tells us that needs–values fit is dynamic. And so is commitment.

But the most important reason for measuring needs–values fit in a general way doesn't have to do with the fact that it is complicated and dynamic. It has to do with the fact that it is obscure. No matter how thorough marketers have been, they can never be sure that they have compiled a complete list of all the needs and motivations that are operating in their market. And the main reason for this is that, no matter how willing people may be to tell marketers what motivates them, there always comes a point where people are simply unaware of some of their deeper motivations. The paradox is that, despite the fact that people find it hard to tell us about all the things that motivate them in a market, they do not find it hard to tell us, in a general way, whether or not they are happy with what they have.

We have a friend who is a committed owner of Toyota. We know that when he replaces his Toyota with a new car, it is likely to be another Toyota. In part we know why our friend is so committed: it's because he thinks Toyotas are exceptionally well-engineered cars that don't cost a lot. But we also suspect that there are deeper reasons for our friend's devotion to Toyota. We think these may have to do with his personality – he doesn't buy cars to show-off. But we are not sure about this because when we talk to our friend about his devotion all he does is give rational reasons: they are well engineered and not expensive. The fact is that our friend is incapable of telling us what his more deeply emotional reasons are. Yet – and this is crucial – even though he doesn't know exactly what the 'everything' is, he can tell you in a flash without too much introspection that Toyota is *everything I look for in a motor car*.

Let's summarize:

- First, in every market, people may differ from each other in what they look for.
- Second, a person may look for different things in different markets.
- Third, what a person looks for in a particular market can change over time.

Despite all this diversity, there is only one question that we need to ask if we want to begin to establish how committed people are to the choice they have made, and that is: how happy are you? We are good at answering this simple question even though we may find it difficult to articulate all the reasons why. It turns out that needs–values fit, a complex and dynamic psychological dimension involving many underlying factors, is easy to measure because of the way the mind works.

# Why making people happy (or even ecstatic) is not good enough

The idea that satisfying consumer needs and values is the way to build commitment has been a powerful force in marketing. Companies in service industries have invested millions of dollars in trying to find out what customers want and how 'satisfied' they are. And then they have invested further millions in trying to change their products and services in an attempt to exceed expectations or, at least, eliminate any perceived gaps between what people want and what they are getting.

> **"Needs–values fit, a complex and dynamic psychological dimension involving many underlying factors, is easy to measure because of the way the mind works."**

But if 'satisfaction' were the only factor involved in determining commitment, then satisfied customers would never defect, while dissatisfied customers always would. But we know that's not true. The classic counter-example is provided by the car market – in survey after survey, high percentages of people report that they are 'very satisfied' with the car that they drive. Yet repurchase rates remain stubbornly below 50%, no matter what the level of satisfaction. And studies of defectors in, for example, banking, show that up to 20% of the people who have switched banks were perfectly satisfied with the bank from which they switched.[3]

In Figure 3.2 you will see an example of the relationship between conversion and satisfaction, which comes from a study that we did some years ago among customers of banks in Canada. Although there is a relationship, it is not very strong. Why did one in ten people who appear to have been perfectly satisfied with their bank switch within a year? And why did four out of five who were clearly very dissatisfied, not switch?

> **"If 'satisfaction' were the only factor involved in determining commitment, then satisfied customers would never defect."**

[?] *Our understanding of commitment came precisely from trying to answer this question:* why is it that people stick to choices that clearly make them unhappy?

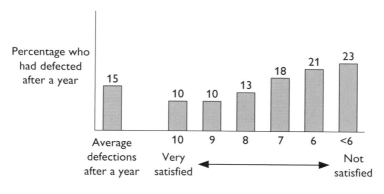

**Figure 3.2** *Conversion rates at different levels of satisfaction*

Commitment in situations in which personal needs and values are being violated is a ubiquitous phenomenon. We see it in religion, we see it in social and political organizations, we see it in personal relationships – and we see it in markets. Why do people put up with it?

Let's illustrate our answer to this question by looking at three kinds of choice: personal relationships, brands of coffee and bath soap. We know this is a strange conjunction of choices, but it will serve to make the point.

Let us imagine a woman who has just got married. It could be any country in the world. It takes some devotion to the relationship to learn to live with a person. Suppose it doesn't work out very well. Suppose the person she has married turns out not to be 'everything she was looking for' in a partner. Perhaps he attacks her self-esteem. Perhaps he is unfaithful. Whatever the case, it is generally true that people will first try to fix a personal relationship that is in trouble before giving up. And the reason is obvious: when the choice we have made is important to us, i.e. when the stakes are high (for whatever reason), then we will be willing to tolerate dissatisfaction. And the more we care about the relationship, the harder we will try and the greater the dissatisfaction we will tolerate.

The factors that create barriers to conversion in the case of marriage may be many and varied. In some cultures, the social pressures that a woman is under are so great that, no matter how desperately she wants to leave, she cannot. Sometimes she may be under no social pressure to stay, but the relationship is backed by a long and happy history which makes it hard to leave. The memory of what it used to be like creates an emotional barrier which prevents conversion. No matter, the barriers create a situation in which dissatisfaction is tolerated in preference to conversion.

Now let's take coffee: around the world, people wake up with a jolt to the brain – literally. Our intake of legal stimulants first thing in the morning is high and it is a feature of life in many cultures. Caffeine seems to be the most widely-used stimulant in this endeavour, and tea and coffee are the most widely-used delivery mechanisms.

Suppose your preference is for coffee. And suppose that a long time ago you settled on Nescafé – it was 'everything you looked for' in a brand of coffee. So you settled into the uncomplicated habit of buying Nescafé regularly. Buying Nescafé solved one of life's little problems. If we asked you to rate Nescafé on a scale from one to ten where ten meant 'it was perfect', you would probably say it was perfect. And if we asked you today, you might still say 'it's perfect'.

But every now and then you shop and Nescafé is out of stock. Let's suppose that while you really do prefer Nescafé to other brands, it's not something that you're obsessed about. So you're a little disappointed, but not enough to complain. You buy something else in a small pack to tide you over.

Sometimes you visit friends who don't have Nescafé. When they offer you coffee you accept whatever they've got. So what if the taste is different – it's not a big deal. And because it's not a big deal, you don't mind switching. You switch without too much concern, even though Nescafé satisfies all your needs and values when it comes to coffee. You switch because what brand of coffee you drink isn't *that* important.

Now let's take bath soap. We have a friend who, when it comes to soap, really doesn't care. She pays so little attention to soap that she often doesn't know which brands are in her bathroom. Yet, when we ask her how satisfied she is with the brand she's currently using, she'll say, 'it's fine!'. But if we were to replace that brand with a different one tomorrow, she wouldn't mind for a moment. She *would* know that it was a different brand – colour and smell would almost certainly tell her. So her contentment is not due to the fact that she thinks all brands are the same. She doesn't. But she doesn't care about the differences.

When it comes to personal relationships, unhappy people may not switch; when it comes to brands of soap, happy people may. The more important a relationship is to a person, no matter what the relationship is with, the more willing that person will be to tolerate dissatisfaction in favour of trying to fix it. By contrast, when a relationship doesn't matter, then even the perfectly satisfied consumer can switch on a whim. Soap doesn't matter to our friend – she makes no effort. Nescafé may matter a little more to you – you make a little more of an effort. Personal relationships tend to matter to people a lot – they make a big effort.

 *We have now arrived at a second question that must be asked if we want to know how committed someone is. And the question is: does this decision matter to you – do you care?*

> **"The more important a relationship is to a person the more willing the person will be to tolerate dissatisfaction in favour of trying to fix it."**

Unless you care, you can never really be committed. The more you care, the greater your potential for commitment. The levels of commitment that we see in religion arise precisely because religion is something that really matters to many people. We call this dimension *involvement*.

The effects of involvement can be pictured as shown in Figure 3.3. Put simply, the higher the level of involvement, the greater will be the willingness to tolerate dissatisfaction before switching takes place. For any given level of needs–values fit, low involvement increases the probability of conversion while high involvement decreases it. People who are involved are willing to tolerate significant levels of dissatisfaction. People who are not involved, are capable of switching even when satisfied.

> **"The levels of commitment that we see in religion arise precisely because religion is something that really matters to many people."**

# How involvement works – when it matters you try to 'fix' the relationship

Many people would probably argue that it is unfair to compare commitment to religion or a personal relationship with commitment to a bar of soap, and that the levels of involvement found in religions or in personal relationships just are not repeated when it comes to consumer goods. Let's examine this criticism carefully.

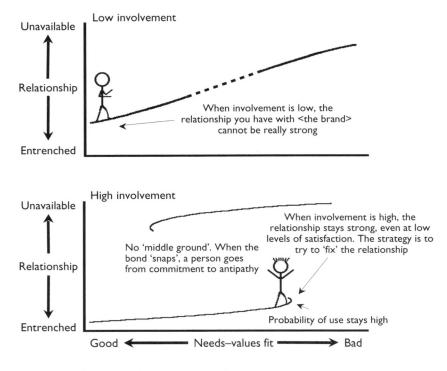

**Figure 3.3**  *The impact of variations in involvement on commitment*

There is a great illustration of the impact that involvement has on commitment and the willingness to convert in a *Harvard Business Review* from the 1990s.[4] It comes from banking. A customer had been banking with a particular bank for many years. He and the bank manager went to the same church. He believed in the virtues of loyalty when it came to banking. In short, he cared about the relationship.

When the bank closed the branch that was most convenient to him he shifted some of his business to a more convenient, new bank, but left most of it with his original bank. After some time, he was approached by the new bank with an offer to consolidate all his business. Because he cared about the relationship, however, he didn't just switch. The first thing he did was go to his original bank manager and ask if they could match the product. Only when his original bank said 'no', did he switch. From start to finish, this conversion process took three years. And at every point, this customer gave his original bank an opportunity to fix the relationship rather than just leave.

## Because it mattered to them, people stuck with Coca-Cola

Let's look at the 'cola wars' of the mid-1980s. Pepsi put a lot of pressure on Coke with a series of 'Pepsi challenge' adverts. In these adverts people were stopped in the streets and invited to taste two colas without knowing which was which. They were asked which one they preferred. Invariably people chose Pepsi. The reason for this was that Pepsi is sweeter, and it's a physiologically based fact that people will generally choose what is sweeter.

What happened next tells us just how important the dimension of 'involvement' is. When told that they had just chosen Pepsi, die-hard Coke drinkers refused to give up Coke. There was absolutely no physiological basis for this refusal. They had just experienced Pepsi as better on every non-emotional dimension. In addition, it would have been easy for them to switch – in the USA Pepsi is just as easy to find as Coke and it tends to be cheaper. The only possible explanation for this behaviour was emotional. Consumers had obviously developed an emotional relationship with Coke. Their emotional involvement was enough to create barriers to conversion.

The Coke story didn't stop with Pepsi winning the blind taste tests. The Coca-Cola Company was so spooked by the challenge that it eventually gave in. It developed and launched 'new' Coke. Roger Enrico, the CEO of PepsiCo at the time, was so excited about this that he wrote a book called *The Other Guy Blinked*.[5] But consumers revolted. They insisted that the Coca-Cola Company bring back 'classic' Coke. Consumers didn't desert the brand. Because they cared, they gave the brand a chance to fix things.

This example illustrates two very important facts about involvement.

- First, whether it be religion, personal relationships, banking or Coke, the primary strategy of the involved person is to try to fix the relationship rather than to leave. Involvement delays conversion by creating a situation in which the costs of leaving are seen to be greater than the costs of tolerating dissatisfaction.

- Second, there is no reason why marketing cannot create involvement, no matter what the product or brand. If marketers can create involvement around Coke and Omo, they can create involvement around anything.

We often hear marketers complain that theirs is a low-involvement market. Sometimes we have even heard them say that there is little point in doing research in their market because most consumers are uninvolved. But our research shows that there are no markets in which there are not at least some people who think that brand choice is important. There is therefore no such thing as a low- or high-involvement market.

> **?** *The proper question to ask is not: is mine a low- or a high-involvement market? Rather, it is: how many people are involved in* this *market?*

---

**"There are no markets in which there are not at least some people who think that brand choice is important."**

---

> **?** *This leads to the third point: if involvement is possible in any market, then the critical task for the marketer is to answer the question: how can I make people more involved in the choice of my brand?*

Our answer to this question is to draw attention to a key element of what we believe to be the contract between marketers and consumers: *if you take consumers seriously as people (and not just as 'consumers') they will take your product or brand seriously, no matter what it is.*

Let's summarize. So far we have two questions. The first is: *how happy are you with the brand?* The second is: *do you care?* Real commitment requires both that you be happy and that you care. If you don't really care, then it's easy to switch even when you're happy. If you do care, then you may be willing to tolerate dissatisfaction before switching.

## How you can become more committed, even as you become more dissatisfied

Social psychologists, particularly those involved in trying to understand processes of institutional change, have noticed with amazement that many people become increasingly opposed to change the more dysfunctional their institutions become. Early theories of cognitive dissonance would have led to the prediction that as an institution or organization fails, so people should seek alternatives or be willing to change. That doesn't happen. Why? To illustrate this we will use a political example. At times it may seem far from consumer markets, so we will be brief.

## An example of how involvement can develop

We have friends who bought their first house in South Africa in the late 1970s. At the time they were not very committed to South Africa – their needs–values fit was low. So why did they buy a house? They bought a house because it was cheaper to pay back a mortgage than to rent. They were perfectly prepared to leave the country if the situation got too bad, leaving an unpaid debt to the mortgage provider in their wake. That's how uncommitted they were.

Sometime between 1980 and 1984 our friends began to care more about South Africa. So when widespread civil disobedience broke out in 1984 and the country became ungovernable, they didn't emigrate. Instead they joined a liberal white political organization whose aim was to try to get white South Africans to change their attitude to apartheid. In terms of needs–values fit, the country was an even worse place to live in than before. Yet because of their involvement they became more committed. Eventually they were so committed that they were involved in clandestine meetings with the African National Congress.

In eight years, our friends had gone from a state of low-level discomfort and poor commitment to the country, to a state of deep discomfort yet high commitment. They had become intensely committed even as they had become intensely dissatisfied. The first step on the path to that intense commitment was that they began to care. And the more they cared, the harder they worked to make a small contribution to 'fixing' things. By the end of 1988, emigration was almost unthinkable to our friends.

In the real world, there are many situations in which involvement goes up as needs–values fit goes down. In these situations the theory of commitment predicts that as long as involvement rises fast enough, the effect will be to strengthen the relationship between the person and the

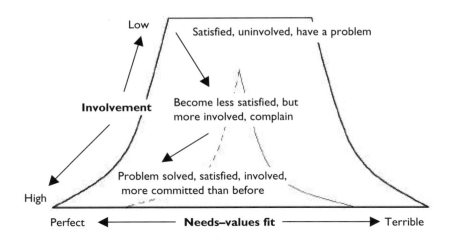

**Figure 3.4** *A simple model of service failure recovery*

choice they have made rather than to weaken it. People can then become more rather than less committed to their choices, even as their choices became more dysfunctional. This process is illustrated in Figure 3.4 and it helps to explain a phenomenon in marketing involving recovery from service failures.

Marketers often say that people who have had a problem fixed can end up being more committed than they were before the problem occurred. In service industries – banks, airlines, hotels – some customers just 'disappear' when something goes wrong. But it can happen differently. Suppose you start as a relatively uninvolved but satisfied frequent flyer of British Airways. According to our theory, your commitment to British Airways would be shallow. One day you hit a problem: you arrive for a flight and your booking has not been recorded.

You don't go to another airline. Rather, the problem increases your involvement and you make a fuss. The British Airways staff respond immediately with generosity and good grace. They find you a seat and give you a voucher for a discount on any future local flight. Here's the process: you start off with shallow commitment. Then there's a problem. The problem increases your involvement. So, even though you're dissatisfied, you're more involved. You complain. Suppose the problem gets fixed – then dissatisfaction decreases but involvement may stay higher. So –

satisfaction is up, involvement is higher – and you're more committed than you were when the process started.

If a problem is followed by a recovery which increases the customer's involvement, and the increased involvement is sustained, then as long as the customer is satisfied, commitment will be higher than before. The process is captured in Figure 3.4.

## How much you care affects how you convert

Many white South Africans have emigrated in the past twenty years. Obviously, they did not become more committed as they became more dissatisfied. Rather, they must have reached a point where they couldn't stand the stress anymore and 'snapped'. This short section is about how conversion happens when you snap.

### Conversion by snapping

We talked earlier about bath soap. Suppose someone really didn't care which brand of soap ended up in their bathroom. They were uninvolved. Yet they could be perfectly content. Their commitment to any one brand of bath soap would then be shallow. Offer them something else and they would probably switch without giving it a second thought. In fact, the conversion process can be so casual when involvement is low that we have found people – the uncaring ones – who switch back and forth from brand to brand without being able to tell us which brands they are using. That is how conversion happens when involvement is low. It is casual and undramatic – sometimes the fact that you are flip-flopping between brands hardly registers.

Now take a situation of high involvement. For this example we will revert to personal relationships. Some evolutionary psychologists tell us that when it comes to choosing to live with someone, our ideal is probably serial monogamy. That is to say, given power and freedom, men and women would probably settle on having one partner at a time, but would like to be able to swop every now and then. This may make personal relationships seem careless. Of course, they aren't – involvement is high.

So let's take a relationship. According to our theory, when a personal relationship gets into trouble, people will tend to respond by trying to fix it. They talk about things, adjust their behaviours, make small compromises and so on. If successful, then a sense that the relationship 'accommodates or satisfies needs and values' may be maintained. Otherwise dissatisfaction will set in. One or other partner will move towards conversion.

Suppose a person's dissatisfaction with the relationship continues to increase. For the sake of telling the story, we will suppose that we are describing a woman. We fast-forward to the situation shown in Figure 3.5. She is deeply dissatisfied with the person she has chosen to live with. But she is also highly involved and has therefore been trying to save the relationship. It is not broken yet, but she is critically close to the conversion threshold.

The first thing to notice from the chart is that a very small increase in her unhappiness would be enough to take her over the threshold. It could be anything – even a trivial irritation. Whatever it is, if it causes a negative change in needs–values fit she will be tipped over the threshold. This is the phenomenon of 'the last straw that breaks the camel's back'. It is a phenomenon in which the event which causes conversion may seem minor compared to the impact – a relationship that is decisively broken.

The second thing to notice is that the event that 'breaks the camel's back' can be quite different from what drives the woman to the threshold in the first place. This is why, for example, when people are close to 'the edge' in a relationship, they tend to dig up old grievances whenever they argue. Arguments that occur close to the threshold of conversion are not just about the event that may have started them. They are about trying to save the whole relationship. Either partner may argue that ancient grievances are 'ancient history'. But the fact that they are ancient history is precisely the point – it is the history that drives people to the edge and as such, the history is totally relevant.

The third thing to notice is that when a relationship snaps under conditions of high involvement, it is anything but casual. If you are pushed to conversion in a situation that means a lot to you – a job, a person, a country – it will be an emotionally charged event. Which leads to the fourth thing: there tends to be no middle ground. When someone converts from a situation of high involvement then they are unlikely to lapse into a state of indifference. They will tend to go from trying to save the relationship to being overtly angry and unavailable.

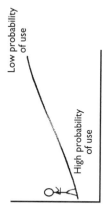

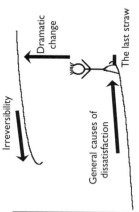

**Low involvement:**

**If we don't care, we drift: the strength of commitment varies in a casual way**

**High involvement:**

**The phenomenon of the last straw . . .**
What causes the changes may seem trivial, and differ from what took you to the edge

**The process is not casual; it is dramatic**
From trying to fix things to unavailable

**Irreversible: go far to win back . . .**

**Missionary against the brand . . .**

**Figure 3.5** *How involvement affects the way commitment changes*

And this, in turn, leads to the fifth thing about these processes: they are relatively irreversible once conversion has taken place. When involvement is low, a person can drift back and forth casually, from one thing to another, without being concerned. When involvement is high, if the relationship breaks it becomes infinitely more difficult to fix. If a person is driven to the point where they finally snap and walk out, asking that person back will take more than just promising not to allow 'the last straw' to happen again. It will take negotiating to remove a whole lot of the stresses that drove that person to the edge in the first place. When marriages finally break, they tend to stay broken.

The last thing to notice is that it is especially when conversion takes place from high levels of involvement that we get consumers who become 'missionaries' against the brand. Once a person has given up on the relationship, they have no reason to restrain their anger. This is the process behind bitter and messy divorces, employees who have nothing good to say about their previous employer, or customers of banks who switch and tell everyone possible how bad their previous bank was.

It is surely in a marketer's interests to create involvement in their brands. Involved consumers remain committed, even when dissatisfied. But it is also clear that the consequences of failure when involvement is high are very negative. As the brand manager, you may be given a chance to make the consumer happy before they go, but if they do go before you rescue the relationship, it will do your brand a lot of damage.

> **"It is especially when conversion takes place from high levels of involvement that we get consumers who become 'missionaries' against the brand."**

Let's summarize what the process of 'snapping' looks like:

- First, a small increase in dissatisfaction can be the catalyst to change. This is the phenomenon of the 'last straw that breaks the camel's back'.
- Second, the decision will come as a culmination of factors which go back in time, many of them different from whatever happened to be the 'last straw'.
- Third, the process requires high involvement, for it is only when involvement is high that a person will hold out in a way which causes a relationship to 'snap'.

- Fourth, there tends to be no middle ground. Because it is an emotional process, people tend to go from committed to unavailable.
- Fifth, the process tends to be irreversible. Once a person has given up on a relationship it takes a lot to get them back.
- Finally, a consequence is the 'missionary effect' – a person who has 'snapped' will tend to become a missionary against <whatever> once they're gone.

## A third question: what about the alternatives – how do you like them?

We have dealt extensively with needs–value fit and involvement, the first two dimensions of what creates commitment. And we understand now that satisfied customers can convert if they are not involved, while dissatisfied customers will tend to delay conversion, as long as they are involved. We have used a mixture of illustrations from religion, politics, personal relationships, coffee and bath soap to explain all of this. And we have pointed out that while religion, politics and personal relationships may seem far from the world of brands, great brands like Coca-Cola are built on significant levels of consumer involvement.

So let's return to the paradox with which we started – high levels of satisfaction in the motor car market tied to low levels of loyalty. It doesn't take much thought to realize that we have not accounted for this paradox. Clearly, it's not a problem of needs–values fit – at least, not obviously. Most people say they are satisfied with the car they drive. It is also surely not a problem of involvement – most people tell us that the decision about which car to buy is important. So the problem lies elsewhere. It may seem remote, but the easiest way to clear this up is to think about the job market.

One of the paradoxes of employee satisfaction surveys is that it is often the most satisfied senior employees who are most at risk of leaving. Yet it ought not to be a paradox. Excellence and commitment often go together in the employment stakes. And that is precisely the problem, because it is when you are doing a good job that you attract the attention of head-hunters. So let's imagine that you're doing a great job, and that you enjoy your work, and that you are committed to the company for which you work. One day a head-hunter knocks on your door and confronts you with an offer: more money, a step up the corporate ladder, but a less prestigious company.

According to the theory of commitment, the effect of the offer will be immediate and two-fold:

- The attractions of the new job will tend to undermine your satisfaction with your existing job.
- But you will become ambivalent rather than dissatisfied, because of the things that you like about your current job.

Let's look at this in more detail. Your new job offer involves a better salary and more power and responsibility. If this appeals to you then you will probably look at your current job and your current company and feel that you could be doing better for yourself. So – you become a little less satisfied with what you've got.

But that doesn't mean that you will jump. Your potentially new company is not so prestigious, you probably have many working friendships where you are, and you may be part of your company's recent history and be able to look back to business battles fought and won. These things are not easy to leave behind. So we get the conjunction of positives and negatives – things that attract and things that repulse – a state of ambivalence.

Literally, when faced with an attractive alternative while at the same time having reasons not to switch, our minds are split in two. When the regular buyer of a brand is ambivalent, they are no longer as committed as they used to be. The presence of an attractive alternative undermines commitment. But it need not lead directly to conversion (Figure 3.6).

## How repertoire behaviour arises as a consequence of ambivalence

Although it may seem like a jump from jobs to shampoo, our behaviour as consumers in the shampoo market provides a rich vein of material for understanding behaviour under conditions of ambivalence.

Over the years, shampoo marketers have done a superb job of slicing up our minds so that it is not possible to want only one shampoo. There's

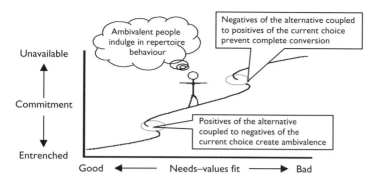

**Figure 3.6** *The impact of an attractive alternative*

shampoo for greasy hair and shampoo for dry hair. There's shampoo which is supposed to nourish the scalp – beer, honey, eggs, wheat germ, mineral salts.

There's shampoo for when you suspect that all that artificial hair-curling you have been doing has done damage to your hair. So you give your hair a dose of the 'fixes damaged hair' shampoo. But you don't need to use it all the time. So when you think your hair has had enough of that, you can revert to the one with egg in it. And when you've had enough of that, you use the honey and wheat germ shampoo for a while. Then, of course, there's the shampoo that has to be used once in a while to strip off everything that's been left behind by all the other shampoos you've been using.

Hair is a powerful motivator when it comes to beauty in almost all cultures. And being attractive to members of the opposite sex, whatever people may say, remains a powerful motivator of what most people do – especially when they're in the market for a partner. Shampoo marketing tries to tap into this complex web of motivations.

The market for shampoo provides us with just one illustration of the way in which marketers create ambivalence by appealing to a variety of different needs and values that consumers think they have. Consumers' minds have been sliced into pieces by sets of motivations which cannot be satisfied by one brand choice – repertoire behaviour is the natural outcome.

A mind divided by ambivalence and its attendant, repertoire behaviour, are ubiquitous in consumer markets. Think, for example, about the market for what children drink. Parents around the world prefer their children to drink healthy stuff – milk, fruit juice etc. Children around the world prefer to drink sweet stuff with bubbles in it – carbonated soft drinks. Parents around the world are also budget conscious. The stuff that children really like tends to be more expensive. But parents around the world are not averse to giving their children a treat. So they are involved in a complex juggling act – the divided mind and its attendant, repertoire behaviour. Parents try to satisfy both themselves and their children by buying both what's good and what's a treat.

> **"A mind divided by ambivalence and its attendant, repertoire behaviour, are ubiquitous in consumer markets."**

**[?]** *Work, shampoo, drinks – whatever the case, a third question we have to ask if we want to know how committed someone is, is:* are there are any alternatives in the frame and if so, how do they rate?

To the extent that a consumer's world is surrounded by alternatives that they find attractive, to that extent commitment will be undermined and the probability of repertoire behaviour increased. As long as there are no competitors in the frame, the person is in a position to be committed.

We are now in a position to understand the paradox of high satisfaction coupled to low commitment in the motor car market. When people buy a new car, they actively compare all the makes and models that are available to them. It is the 'attractive alternative' car that undermines commitment to the make and model they are about to replace. It's not the lack of satisfaction with the car currently owned.

## How different are your options?

We come, at last, to the fourth question: how different are your options?

Throughout this chapter we have used what people may feel are unfair examples to illustrate a principle. We used politics and personal relationships to illustrate the principle of involvement – and there may have been a question as to whether it is appropriate to do so when marketing deals with far more mundane things like soft drinks, laundry detergents, banking services and shampoos. But we argued that, when we look carefully, we see

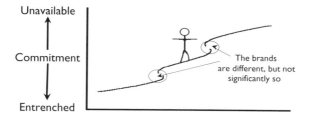

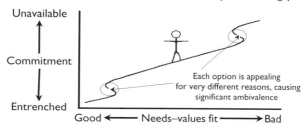

**Figure 3.7** *Ambivalence can be slight or considerable*

that involvement can be high in even the most mundane of product markets.

Now people may feel that it is unfair to compare the market for shampoos with the jobs market when it comes to ambivalence. Surely these are different kinds of choice?

The answer to that question is 'yes'; they are – and that leads to an important feature of ambivalence and a fourth question. The feature is this: *the things that cause you to be ambivalent can vary in terms of how different they are from each other*. When you have to choose between one of two jobs, you may feel that a gulf separates them. By contrast, most people probably feel that choosing between two shampoos involves options which do not involve a gulf of difference. So an important question when someone is faced by competing options is: how different are they?

We illustrate the effect of the difference between alternatives in Figure 3.7. When two options are very different, the extent of ambivalence or indecision is much greater than when they are similar. At its worst, the mind can be consumed by indecision. The importance of this difference is that it impacts on the level of satisfaction at which commitment will be undermined. Broadly speaking: *the more different an attractive alternative is, the higher the level of satisfaction at which it will undermine commitment.*

**?** *Hence the fourth and final question:* if you are attracted to something else, how great is the ambivalence to which it gives rise?

## How ambivalence works – some examples of ambivalence in action

Ambivalence is the spontaneous outcome of a situation in which alternatives are attractive but there are reasons to preserve existing relationships. If there were no inhibiting factors, then an attractive alternative would result in rapid conversion. That situation is rare. Mostly, attractive alternatives cause ambivalence. Given the choice, people who cannot resolve two competing options will indulge in repertoire behaviour. They will satisfy each subset of needs in a market with a brand chosen to fulfil those needs. This is what happens in the shampoo and children's drinks market. But there are situations in which a person cannot have it both ways. Under most conditions, the job market is one. Let's have a look at the dynamics of decision making when only one option can be chosen.

The new job offers more money, a move up the corporate ladder, and possibly an exciting challenge – more responsibility and the offer to take a less prestigious company and make something of it. The old job offers a great place to work, friendships, a sense of history and certainty. Which one will win? According to the theory, *the one which is seen to fulfil the needs and values that matter to you most.* If friendships, history and certainty mattered to you most, the old job would win. If money, opportunity and new challenges mattered most, the new would win.

But suppose you really cannot make up your mind. How are you likely to behave?

- To start with, it is likely that you will delay the decision while you try to find a way to reconcile the competing needs and values that each option satisfies.
- One attempted 'resolution' might be, for example, to go to your current employer and tell them about the new job offer in the hope that they will offer you incentives to stay.

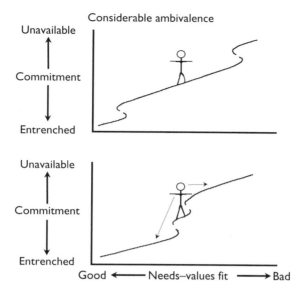

Considerable ambivalence

Unavailable
Commitment
Entrenched

Unavailable
Commitment
Entrenched

Good ◄─────── Needs–values fit ───────► Bad

Which job will you take? The more ambivalent you are,
the longer you will delay, the more unpredictable your decision will be,
and the more subject it will be to last-minute influences

**Figure 3.8** *A situation of forced choice*

- A second strategy would be to go on an intensive information gathering exercise in an effort to arrive at a decision about which one of the options stacks up best in terms of your needs and values, so as to eliminate the other.

But what happens if you are completely stuck and incapable of making a decision either way. Let's examine how this process goes (see Figure 3.8).

According to the theory, someone in this situation will behave in three distinctive ways:

- First, they will delay making a final choice for as long as possible; literally, indecision continues to consume the mind.
- Second, during the delay they will gather up as much information as possible about each option in case they have to make a choice.
- Third, if they are completely undecided, then the decision they finally make will be determined by factors operating right at the time the decision is taken.

When a person really cannot decide which of two options to choose, then small and insignificant factors operating at the point of decision will make the difference one way or the other. But what this in turn means is that the closer someone is to the middle of the surface, the harder it will be to predict what they will do. Not only will it be hard for us. The person themselves will be hard pressed to tell us which way they intend to jump.

It may be helpful to illustrate this with another example: suppose that when you get home in the evening after a long day at work, you like to pour yourself a drink. Now, let's also suppose that it always used to be a glass of red wine. But recently, you have discovered the joys of whisky. And so, increasingly, whisky is taking the place of red wine. You really enjoy both, for quite different reasons. Whisky, the way you drink it, with a lot of water and ice, is an exceptionally clean and meditative drink. Wine, by contrast, is more complex with more flavours – it's more sensational in the mouth.

Let's suppose that because you like them both so much, you're never sure exactly which one you're going to want when you get home. It really depends on which impulses have a minute advantage when the moment comes for you to decide. And even then, sometimes when you sit down to enjoy your drink, you realize that you've made the 'wrong' choice. You would actually have enjoyed the other one more.

Often in the above sorts of situation, the market-leading product or brand will be at an inherent advantage over other choices. It is more likely than others to have been advertised the night before. And it is more likely to occupy a favourable position in store. The smaller the product or brand in terms of market share, the less attention it will get in-store. The stronger, then, must be the active desire with which our consumer wants to buy the smaller brand, in order for him or her to overcome the market obstacles that stand in the way.

Let's draw together our analysis of ambivalence:

- First, to the extent that there is ambivalence and that forced choice can be avoided, repertoire behaviour is the natural behaviour of a person.
- Second, how much energy – or, in the consumer case, how much of the personal budget – will be devoted to each alternative will be a function of the extent to which each of the alternatives appeals or shapes up in the tug-of-war.

- Third, if the appeal of an alternative is strong enough, then commitment can be undermined even at high levels of satisfaction with the current choice.
- But fourth, to the extent that the current choice is also appealing, the trajectory to complete conversion will be long and potentially traumatic.
- And finally, the closer people are to the middle, unable to decide, the more unpredictable their behaviour will be. It is worth repeating: not only will we not be able to predict what they will do, they themselves may not know.

## How to tell if someone is committed with a few questions

So, there we have it – a few simple questions:

- How happy are you with <whatever>?
- Is this something that you care about?
- How do you rate the alternatives?
- If the alternatives rate, how different are they from each other?

The mind of the *perfectly committed* person is easy to describe:

- They are happy with what they've got
- It's something that they care about
- None of the competitors rate

When a person is in this state of mind, the likelihood that they will continue to use their current choice is very high.

The uncommitted person, by contrast, can be close to a switching threshold in a number of ways. First, they may not care. Even if happy, this means that they will be uncommitted. The likelihood that they will continue to use their current choice will be relatively high if they are happy, but it would not take much to get them to switch.

Second, the uncommitted person may be uncommitted because they are dissatisfied. This is the way in which the commercial marketing research industry mostly understands the conversion process – make the person unhappy and the likelihood that they will buy or use something else rises. But as we have seen, this need not be the case – if rising dissatisfaction is coupled to increasing involvement, commitment may actually increase. Commitment only decreases if involvement does not increase – then the likelihood that the person will continue to buy or use the brand, decreases.

And finally, people may be uncommitted because they are attracted to more than one possibility and therefore cannot make up their minds. The full discussion of how this works is contained in the last few sections of this chapter.

## Revisiting satisfaction and commitment

Before we leave this chapter, let's revisit satisfaction and commitment. We have already shown a graph of the defection rates at different levels of satisfaction for banking customers in Canada. What we should do now is look again at those results once we have taken into account the additional factors which we argue underpin real commitment. When we analysed the defection rates using commitment we got significantly better prediction rates (see Figure 3.9).

As we look in more detail at the relationship between our theory of commitment and actual consumer behaviour, we will expand on the above story in greater detail. But for the time being, what you have read above is enough to lay down the basics.

# Marketer's summary: commitment – what it is and how it works

## How to tell if a person is perfectly committed to something

Three conditions must be true for a person to be perfectly committed to anything:

- They must be happy with <whatever>
- The relationship must be something that they care about
- There must be nothing else that appeals to them

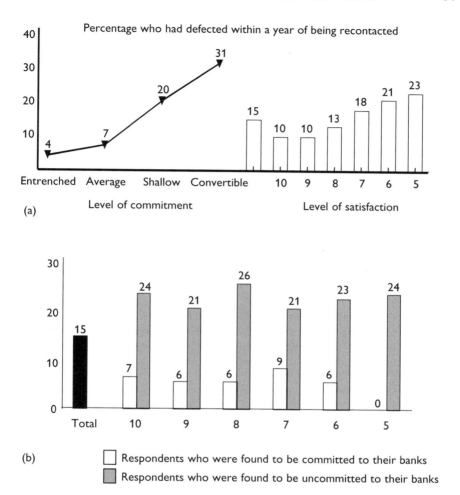

**Figure 3.9** *(a) A comparison of commitment and satisfaction measures. (b) How the measure of commitment helps to identify who is or is not at risk at every level of satisfaction*

No matter what we are talking about – personal relationships, jobs, brands of laundry detergent – it is easy to establish whether or not these three conditions apply: simply ask. Because of the way the mind works, simple questions are good enough to get reliable measures of these complex dimensions.

Commitment is possible when people are dissatisfied as long as the relationship is something that they care about. This is because someone who cares about a relationship tries to fix it when things go wrong.

## The ways in which people can be uncommitted

There are also three ways in which people can be uncommitted:

- They don't care which product or brand they use
- They are so dissatisfied that it doesn't matter how much they do care
- Something else appeals to them, causing ambivalence

When you are dealing with consumers who are uncommitted because they don't care, you either have to give them something to care about, or you have to manage them through superior distribution or point-of-sale activity.

Dealing with consumers who are uncommitted because they are dissatisfied is easy: identify and remove the causes of dissatisfaction. You can also solve the problem by increasing their involvement, but that is not an ideal route to go if it fails to address the causes of dissatisfaction.

There are three options open to you when dealing with people whose low commitment is due to the fact that they are attracted to other products or brands:

- First, you can try to improve your brand performance on the dimensions which attract people to the competitors.
- Second, you can identify your competitive advantages and try to make those the most important drivers of product or brand choice.
- Third, you may recognize that the battle cannot be won by your brand and so create a 'look-alike' (i.e. move to a portfolio approach) to retain business.

## The effects of ambivalence

Ambivalence arises whenever a competitor brand appeals to a person. Ambivalent consumers indulge in repertoire behaviour if possible. If repertoire behaviour is not possible, then a consumer who is ambivalent will:

- Delay the decision about which brand to use for as long as possible.
- Be swayed by factors operating right at the point where they have to decide.

- Choose the brand which satisfies the needs and values that matter to them most.

The more ambivalent a consumer is, the more unpredictable their behaviour will be when finally forced to choose, not just to observers but even to themselves.

The dilemmas that arise from ambivalence are nicely illustrated by family life. Consider the question: can you be committed to more than one person? When it comes to the person with whom you choose to live, the answer ought to be 'no'; when it comes to your children, the answer ought to be 'yes'.

# References

1.  Pendergast, M. (1994) *For God, Country and Coca-Cola: The Unauthorized History of the Great American Soft Drink and the Company that Makes It.* Collier Books.
2.  Hofmeyr, J. (1990) The Conversion Model – a new foundation for strategic planning in marketing. New Ways in Marketing and Marketing Research, 3rd Emac/Esomar Symposium, Athens.
3.  Keaveney, S.M. (1995) Customer switching in service industries: an exploratory study. *Journal of Marketing*, April.
4.  Reichheld, F.F. (1996) Learning from customer defections. *Harvard Business Review*, March/April.
5.  Enrico, R. and Kornbluth, J. (1986) *The Other Guy Blinked: How Pepsi Won the Cola Wars.* Bantam Books, New York.

# 4

## Answers to Some Old Questions

*Clearing up confusion about loyalty and brand equity*

Having loyal customers is generally thought to be a good thing. In what has since become a widely quoted study, Bain and Co. found that 'it costs five times more' to win a new customer than retain the customers you already have.[1] Researchers have also claimed that a small cut of 10–15% in the rate at which customers defect from your brand can increase profitability by up to 60%.[2] But how do you define and measure 'brand loyalty'? Let's begin by looking at a brief history of the concept.

## Brand loyalty: a brief history of the idea

Back in 1923, some of the world's great brands were already respectably old. Coca-Cola had been around since 1886, Sunlight soap since 1884 and Levi's since 1853. Clearly, marketers already knew something about how to create long-lasting brands. Yet it was not until 1923 that the first attempt to define brand loyalty was made. That definition, due to a marketer called Copeland, is deceptively simple: a brand-loyal person is anybody in a market who buys your brand 100% of the time.[3]

In 1923 the range of choices available to consumers in most countries was a fraction of what it is today. Even so, there were many people in every market who could not be classified as loyal using that definition. So marketers began to work with the concept that every market has two kinds of consumer: those who are loyal and those who are switchers. This way of looking at consumers was common by the late 1940s. It has remained one of the most enduring concepts in all of marketing. Yet, while it is easy to recognize that people may differ in their degree of loyalty to brands, its far more difficult to arrive at generally accepted methods for identifying who is loyal and who is a switcher.

One of the most widely used methods is the 'share of requirements', which emerged in the USA in the 1950s. Put simply, the degree of a person's loyalty to a brand is measured by looking at what 'share' of that person's 'requirements' in a category, are filled by that brand. So, for example, if a person buys Levi's seven times out of ten when buying jeans, then Levi's has a 70% 'share' of that person's 'requirements' when it comes to jeans. Similarly, if someone buys Coca-Cola five times out of ten in the soft drinks market, then Coca-Cola has a 50% 'share' of their 'requirements' for soft drinks. Identifying who is 'loyal' is then simply a matter of agreeing how many times a person should buy Levi's or Coke to be classified as 'loyal'. Most marketers are happy to work with a cut-off point somewhere around 67%. So, a person who buys Coke 67% of the time or more would be considered brand loyal to Coke. People who buy Coke less would be called 'switchers'.

The problem with 'share of requirements' is that people do not always buy a brand because they want to. Sometimes they buy it because it is the only brand available. Other times it may be the only brand they can afford. This raises a serious question: should people who buy a brand 67% of the time because it is the only brand available, be lumped together with those who buy it as often, but because they want to? Most marketers would answer 'no', which is why the most widely used definition of brand loyalty is: a brand loyal person is someone who expresses a 'biased behavioural response over time' in favour of a particular brand 'as a result of psychological evaluative processes'.[4]

Put simply, brand loyalty is the tendency of someone to buy a brand again and again because they *prefer* it over others. The definition insists that somebody must really want the brand before we can consider them as loyal.

> **[?]** *This brings us to the heart of the issue: how can we recognize people who buy a brand again and again because they really want to?*

And what shall we call those who buy it again and again, even though they do not want it strongly?

There are more questions:

- What about all those who do not buy any brand repeatedly – the switchers? We tend to think that they switch across brands regularly because they have no real attachment to any one brand.
- If it is possible for people to buy a brand repeatedly even though they are not attached to it, isn't it also possible that people may not buy any one brand repeatedly, yet still be attached to the brands they buy?
- Finally, what about language? There is so much confusion because we do not have any consistent way of referring to all these different types of consumer. Wouldn't it help if we could develop a common language, once and for all?

# The difference between loyalty and commitment

Let's begin by getting some language issues out of the way. The fact that people can buy a brand loyally and yet not be attached to it had already been proven back in 1969.[5] So marketers have known for a long time that there is a difference between what they call *behavioural* and *attitudinal* loyalty. Buying a brand repeatedly but without attachment is behavioural but not attitudinal loyalty. On the other hand, someone who buys it both repeatedly and with attachment is both behaviourally and attitudinally loyal.

Given that the foundation for what we measure is the world of religious commitment and conversion, it has always been natural for us to use the word 'commitment' rather than 'loyalty'. No one has ever said to us 'no – what you really mean is "attitudinal brand loyalty" as first mentioned by Day in 1969'.

So it is that since the late 1980s we have been using the word 'commitment' to refer to what many marketers before had called 'attitudinal loyalty'. The word 'committed' replaces the term 'attitudinally loyal'. And because 'attitudinal loyalty' need never be used – we've got 'commitment' instead – we don't need the word 'behavioural' anymore. Loyalty is always going to be behavioural; 'attitudinal loyalty' is always going to be 'commitment'.

Our proposal therefore is that we allow the word 'loyalty' simply to stand for what marketers, in any case, have mostly used it for: to refer to consumers who buy one brand repeatedly. A committed person is one who is strongly attached to a brand. They need not be the same thing. It is possible to be committed to a brand and yet seldom buy it. It is also possible to buy a brand again and again, but not be committed. When the two are combined, we get committed loyalty. If there is no commitment, then what we have is (merely) loyalty.

> **"It is possible to be committed to a brand and yet seldom buy it. It is also possible to buy a brand again and again, but not be committed."**

## How not to measure commitment

**?** *Accepting this view allows us to recognize loyalty easily: someone for whom a brand forms a high share of their requirements, say 67%, is loyal to that brand. But that doesn't mean that they are committed. How can we recognize committed loyalty?*

One common measure, still widely used, is that of 'purchase intent'. Marketers ask consumers how likely they are to buy a particular brand each time they go shopping. If the answer is something like 'definitely', then that is taken as an indication that the person may be loyal and committed. Someone who says, for example, 'When I buy a soft drink for myself, I almost always buy Coke', is taken as loyal and committed to Coke. But what if the reason they 'almost always buy Coke' is that it is the only brand that's always available? Although it is still widely used, the question is a poor indicator of commitment.

A second, widely used, measure is 'consideration'. Someone who says: 'Coca-Cola is one of only one or two brands that I would ever consider buying', is taken to be loyal and committed. But this too is flawed. And we can tell how it's flawed by looking at what happens with premium brands like Marlboro, Levi's and Coke in poor countries.

In many countries there are poor people whose favourite cigarette is Marlboro. But it's too expensive for them, so they mostly buy some cheaper brand. Think about what happens when we ask them what they would consider buying. Some are realistic. So Marlboro isn't on the list because they can't afford it. Others are truer to their wishes. So Marlboro is on the list. In both cases we have people who are strongly attached to Marlboro. But we get two completely different answers because of the way they treat the question.

The critical problem with measures like these is that they are mere indicators. They are like a thermometer which can give us an indication that someone may be sick, but cannot tell us why. And even when it comes to giving us an indication, they are not always accurate. Now that we have a theory of commitment we can be much more precise. We can both establish whether or not someone is committed, and if they aren't committed, we can tell why.

A person is committed to a brand if they are happy with it, involved in the brand choice and not attracted to any alternatives. This is an accurate and reliable way to measure the presence of commitment. And it is easy to measure. Just ask the following questions:

- How do you rate your brand in terms of your needs and values?
- Is the decision about which brand to use in this market important to you?
- Are there any other brands that appeal to you?

> **"We can both establish whether or not someone is committed, and if they aren't committed, we can tell why."**

Our proposition when it comes to loyalty and commitment is therefore simple: loyalty can be measured in the old fashioned way using 'share of requirements'. Commitment needs to be measured using the dimensions outlined in the theory of commitment and embodied in the above questions.

# A simple framework for understanding what people buy

Committed loyalty is obviously the ideal state. As marketers, we aim to have as many consumers as possible buy our brand *with enthusiasm* every time they have to buy some brand. In other words, we aim to have as many 'committed

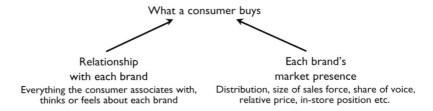

**Figure 4.1**   *A simple framework for understanding what people buy/use etc.*

loyalists' as possible. We achieve committed loyalty when consumers are happy with our brand, care about the brand choice, have no interest in competitors, and, crucially, if there are no impediments like availability or affordability which prevent consumers from acting on their enthusiasm. Early in its history, the Coca-Cola Company formulated a slogan which captured this perfectly. Coke, they said, should always be 'within an arm's length of desire'. They understood how important it was that Coke should be both desired and available. So seriously did they take the issue of availability, in fact, that they invented the stand-alone soft-drinks' fridge.

> **"Loyalty can be measured in the old fashioned way using 'share of requirements'. Commitment needs to be measured using the dimensions outlined in the theory of commitment."**

The Coke example provides us with a simple framework for understanding what makes people buy what they buy. We show this framework in Figure 4.1. Only two forces are involved. The first is everything that is in a person's mind about the different options that are available to them. Within this landscape of brands, people develop desires of varying strengths – a person becomes psychologically attached, in a positive or negative way, to each brand. This is the 'relationship' that a consumer has with each brand. And obviously, the stronger the positive relationship that a person has with a particular brand, the more likely it is that they will buy it.

But the other force that clearly drives what people buy is the *market presence* of a brand. It helps the Coca-Cola Company nothing if everybody wants Coke but it is unavailable, or if it is priced at such a level that it seldom gets stocked because it is unaffordable. Distribution, relative price, the extent to which a brand is advertised – these are all elements of a brand's 'market presence'. Market presence, in other words, is everything about the brand that is *external* to people's minds. Great brands combine both a strong presence in people's minds and a strong presence in the marketplace. These are the conditions which lead to lots of committed loyalty and they establish a simple framework for understanding what drives people to buy what they do.

## Loyalty without commitment: how it happens

Our framework for understanding what causes people to buy what they do helps us to understand some of the more perplexing behaviours that we see in markets. One of these is loyalty without commitment. Clearly, having committed loyalists is the marketing ideal. But having consumers who are loyal even though not committed is not a bad second choice. It's better than nothing. Let's spend some time, therefore, looking at how loyalty without commitment arises.

### Microsoft: you have to use it because everyone else does

For our first example we choose Microsoft. Microsoft's 'Office' suite – Word, Excel, PowerPoint etc. – is by far the dominant brand in its market. But it has not achieved its overwhelming dominance purely by consumer choice. It has done so by what are known as network effects. These arise whenever the likelihood that a person will be forced to use a particular product rises for every other additional person already using the product. With products like these, it is easier to use what other people are using – it eliminates problems of incompatibility, for example. So, as more and more people started using Office so more and more of the remainder were pushed into doing so, whether they liked it or not. And when any of these consumers want to upgrade their software, they buy Office again – a case of loyalty without commitment. This is loyalty by compulsion, created by overwhelming market presence.

### Political choices: you don't like any of them!

For a second example of loyalty without commitment we go to politics. During the 1992 presidential campaign, our business partners in the USA researched the levels of commitment that voters had to presidential candidates. Commitment levels were very low, yet many voters felt that the decision about who to support was very important. We found a similar situation when we researched party political preferences in the UK in 1995. Voters chose a party persistently and loyally because they thought it was important to do so even though there were no parties that they liked. They were loyal, not committed.

## 'Developed world' brands like Marlboro are sometimes too expensive

For a third example, think about the cigarette market in emerging markets. As in many emerging markets, there is quite a sharp distinction in South Korea between premium brands and local brands. One of the best-known premium brands is Marlboro. The problem is, while many smokers are strongly attracted to it, they cannot afford to buy it. So they choose one of the best local, cheaper brands instead – and they smoke it loyally. This doesn't mean that they never smoke Marlboro. They do, but only every now and then. In the case of the local brand therefore, there are smokers who are loyal but not committed. In the case of Marlboro, they are committed, but not loyal.

From the above examples we see that the most obvious way in which loyalty without commitment occurs is when there is a systematic external reason why consumers cannot get the brand they want. If they nevertheless have to choose something, then they may settle on a second or third best choice, without being committed to it. The three examples alluded to here – applications software in the PC market, voter choices in the political market, premium-brand choices in emerging markets – are caused by three different kinds of external reality:

- Network effects
- The lack of a decent choice
- Affordability and distribution

In each case, the problem is that commitment is constrained by some external reality.

> **"Loyalty without commitment occurs when there is a systematic external reason why consumers cannot get the brand they want."**

# Loyalty without commitment, but by choice

When loyalty happens without commitment because people have no choice, then we feel somehow that it is 'cheating'. If people could, they would be both committed and loyal.

**?** *We have to ask therefore, if there are any situations in which people are not committed to a brand and yet buy it loyally* by choice?

As it happens, the answer to this question is 'yes'. And we can explain it by the theory of commitment.

Let's return to Figure 4.1. According to this chart, what people end up buying is a function of both what brand they want most and which brand has the greatest market presence. Now obviously, if someone cannot get the brand they want, then they may be more or less forced into a situation in which they buy an alternative brand again and again (i.e. loyally), even though they are not committed to it.

**?** *But there is an alternative scenario: what if this is a market in which the consumer doesn't want* any *brand in particular?*

When we looked at politics in the USA and the UK, we saw a situation in which consumers actually did want a brand. They wished there was a political party or candidate for whom they could vote with enthusiasm. So that was not a situation in which voters didn't want any brand. Nevertheless, we can get people who use a brand loyally by choice and yet without enthusiasm. It has the potential to happen among consumers *who are uninvolved.*

**?** *How do people who are uninvolved behave in a market?*

Using our model, we see that the relationship side of what drives people to buy what they do will not play any role. Being uninvolved, they are indifferent – they have no relationship with any brand. But this need not mean that their behaviour will be completely haphazard. The 'market presence' side of things will still be in play. And they will tend to buy whichever brand is easiest, cheapest and most convenient. But this, in turn, will tend to be the local, market-leading brand. And since market leadership tends to be quite stable, market forces will tend to push uninvolved consumers in the direction of the local, market-leading brand again and again – in other words, you will get loyalty without commitment.

Our research shows that almost all markets have consumers in them who are completely uninvolved in the brand choice. To take just one example, in the Netherlands over 30% of all householders have no real interest in which brand of laundry detergent they buy.[6] As a result, many of them loyally buy the local market-leading brand without enthusiasm. In a sense, brands with a strong market presence herd uninvolved consumers into being unconsciously loyal.

## Consumer preferences and market forces: how they interact

We have already argued that the ideal consumer, from a marketing point of view, is one who is committed and loyal.

This is most likely to happen if the consumer has a strong relationship with one brand and no others (the 'mind' piece), and if, in addition, the brand with which they have a strong relationship has a strong market presence (the 'market' piece). But what happens if one or other of the forces is missing?

 *What happens if a particular consumer has no strong brand preference, or if a particular brand has no strong market presence? Let's explore this question.*

> **"Brands with a strong market presence herd uninvolved consumers into being unconsciously loyal."**

We argue that market forces will tend to be the dominant factor driving brand choices among consumers who have no strong brand preference because they are uninvolved. But there is another situation in which consumers have no clear preference for one brand. And that happens whenever they cannot make up their minds which of a selection of brands to buy. This in turn happens whenever consumers are ambivalent. The broad principle here is: when a consumer has no strong preference for any brand, then they will tend to buy the brand with the greatest presence in the local market. And there are two circumstances under which that is most likely to occur:

- First, when they don't mind which brand they buy because they don't care.
- Second, when they cannot make up their minds because they are equally attracted to more than one brand simultaneously.

> **"When a consumer has no strong preference for any brand, then they will tend to buy the brand with the greatest presence in the local market."**

Either way, the brand with the greatest local market presence has a better chance than others of being bought.

## Sometimes a consumer will 'climb mountains' to find their brand

The reverse situation is one in which a person strongly prefers one brand over others, but which has a weak market presence. For example, we have a friend who drinks a brand of beer in South Africa called Lion lager. Over the years Lion's market share has dwindled – and with it, Lion's market presence. It is seldom advertised, it is hard to find in bottle stores, and it is never bought when people organize social gatherings. That does not deter our friend. Because she is committed to Lion she goes out of her way to find it. She makes a note of bottle stores that regularly stock Lion. And when she goes to parties, she sometimes takes Lion with her. The principle here is: the more committed a person is to a brand, the less relevant the brand's market presence.

It is almost impossible to escape the presence of Coca-Cola. Anyone who travels a lot will be aware of this. You land in a city like Istanbul. You're sitting in the cab on the way from the airport, a little concerned about the way your cab driver seems to be pushing his small car beyond safe engineering limits. You look out of the window at the city-scape and what do you see? Plastered across the top of one of the tallest and most prominent buildings in the city, the logo for Coca-Cola.

You go to Zagreb. Your hosts take you for a tour of the city. What do you see when you get to the central city square? Plastered across the top of one of the most important buildings, the logo for Coca-Cola. And if you came to South Africa and drove into Johannesburg from the airport, what would you see again? The logo for Coca-Cola.

On TV, if you were to watch South Africa play cricket against England, you would see that the ground is often surrounded by billboards for Coca-Cola. Then if you watched South Africa play soccer against France – Coca-Cola again. Whether you like it or not, Coca-Cola is a brand that never lets you out of its sight. It's global market presence is massive and quite astonishing.

> **"The more committed a person is to a brand, the less relevant the brand's market presence."**

We capture the interaction between brand relationships and market power in Figure 4.2. Now that we have this model, it's worth revisiting the example of Coca-Cola. Coke, as a brand, has always had a massive market presence. The point about this is that the brand is always given a chance. Committed consumers can get it whenever they want to. And uncommitted consumers will be nudged to buy it even though they are uncommitted. This is why a brand's market presence is so important. When relationship factors are weak, market presence takes over. Invariably this works out to be the local market-leading brand – in the soft-drinks market, Coke.

In its most brutal form, big brands are associated with loyalty without commitment wherever store owners confront practical limits to what they can stock. A small-town grocery owner cannot stock all brands. It is common sense for the store to stock market-leading brands. That way the store owner will keep most of the customers happy. Those who are not happy will still buy the brand because it's the only one they can get – loyalty without commitment. However, the fact that it mostly involves the uncaring or ambivalent consumer means that the bigger a brand, the more

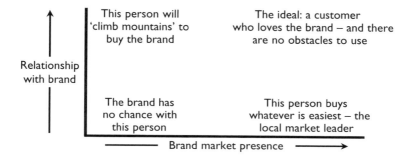

**Figure 4.2**  *How the 'mind' and the 'market' interact*

likely it is that it will be used by loyal but uncommitted consumers. This, in turn means that loyalty without commitment is found most in the consumer franchise of market-leading brands.

*Loyalty which is commitment driven is relatively impervious to changes in the market power of brands, loyalty without commitment is found mostly in market-leading brands.* Clearly, brand management requires fundamentally different strategies for managing these two kinds of loyalty.

- Managing committed consumers has to do with reinforcing their beliefs about the brand and maintaining the desires that drive the brand.
- Managing uncommitted, uncaring consumers has to do with strengthening the brand's market presence.

## Going from loyalty and commitment, to equity

How should brand equity be defined? And how can the value of a brand be measured? That brands are valuable is no longer disputed. For a while in the early 1990s, when store brand sales were growing in the Western economies, the trade press delighted in stories about the death of brands. By that time we had been using commitment-led marketing for a number of years. The value of strong brands was very obvious to us. We were not surprised, therefore, when the wheel turned in a few years and great marketers became heroes of the world's business press.

Intel took the microchip at the heart of the PC and turned it into a branded product. We remember very clearly the late 1980s when we first started talking about commitment. PC makers didn't think they could use our approach because, they said, PCs are 'commodities'. Whether a PC was made in Taiwan or California didn't matter. Neither did what brand it was. As long as it was IBM compatible and worked, the buyer would not care. Commitment-led marketing could not be useful for products like these or so marketers told us!

Now the situation is quite different – even we, relatively sophisticated computer users, are nervous of buying a PC that doesn't have 'Intel inside'! The key is the phrase 'as long as it works'. We know that all our software will work with an Intel microchip. We know, from the problems that we have had, that conflicts between hardware and software can be troublesome. So we do not want to take the risk of buying a PC powered by a chip which might be incompatible with the software we are using. We don't know if we're being stupid or intelligent in this – frankly, we don't understand the whole thing well enough to know. And that is precisely the point – because we don't understand, we are swayed by public opinion and market leadership. We go for PCs with the microchip that everybody uses, assuming that it must be all right because it's been widely tested – and that tends to be the market leader, in this case, Intel.

When you think about it, it is not surprising that PCs should have become branded. They are complex machines which demand high-tech and highly skilled production environments. Their inner workings are not understood by the average user. This combination – a complex machine whose inner workings are not understood by most of its users – is absolutely tailor-made for branding.

What are brands for if not to signal to potential customers that the product can be bought with confidence? The fact that there could ever have been a time when marketers thought computers and their contents could not be branded shows how little branding is understood.

The fashion for arguing the death of brands was in full flight by 1993. Yet, by 1996, brands had made a spectacular come-back. There can be few people in the marketing world who do not know about Roberto Goizueta, the former CEO of the Coca-Cola Company, who is widely credited with having taken a moribund and rather aimless Coke marketing machine in 1981 and turning it into the most widely known brand in the world. By 1996, with the benefit of hindsight, it was possible to see that the Coca-Cola Company had been building shareholder value almost continuously since 1981. In the life of Coca-Cola there was never really a serious threat to the brand. The death of the brand was merely a figment of journalists' imaginations.

Nowadays branding is taken so seriously that even corporations for which there may be no directly measurable benefit spend millions of dollars each year on branding. Think of General Electric's 'we bring good things to life' – for a company like GE, a brilliant slogan and a brilliant campaign. The advertising shows things that most of its viewers would never buy – for example, jet engines. Many of the people around the world who see these adverts will probably never fly. Yet GE believes that the spending is justified.

 *And that brings us back to our starting point – how, if at all, can the value of a brand be measured? How can we establish that the money spent on marketing will pay back in terms of value added to the brand? How should brand equity be defined?*

Let's look at some of the issues involved.

## A framework for understanding brand equity

Every year InterBrand, a company that makes money out of placing financial values on brands, publishes its list of the world's most valuable brands. For the past number of years, brands like Coca-Cola and Marlboro have topped the lists. We do not know how widely used the services of InterBrand are, but it would not surprise us to find that it is the most widely used brand valuation company in the world.

The basis for InterBrand's system is a combination of a number of factors, including:

- The average of some years of the brand's profits
- Brand market share
- Advertising expenditures
- The stability of the brand's product category, both locally and internationally.

In the past the problem with the InterBrand approach was that it relied heavily on historical data – and that made it unstable.[7] The instability of the InterBrand measure came starkly into view when IBM first stumbled, some years ago. In 1992, InterBrand rated IBM as one of the top five most valuable brands in the world. Yet, in 1993 it dropped IBM just about to the bottom of a list of 290 brands. Then, in 1994 when it became clear that it had over-reacted, InterBrand placed IBM back in the top ten!

Whatever we may think about the apparent instability of InterBrand's approach, it should be clear from these difficulties that placing a value on a brand is not easy. So we prefer to take a different tack. Rather than talk about how to establish what a brand is worth, we prefer to focus on what it takes to make the brand valuable in the first place. Building brand value is at the heart of marketing. So let's look at how we might define the components that go to make valuable brands.

# Defining the value components of brands

Broadly, brand equity is easy to define: it is the value that is added when a product is sold branded as compared with its value when sold unbranded.[8] When less is gained by branding than what it costs to brand a product, then a brand has negative value. Strictly speaking, there is nothing which is not branded. Even the most minimally packaged product is branded in a way – it's just that the branding is minimal. Companies value high-equity brands because they contribute substantially to profits. But people also value high-equity brands – because they help to remove uncertainty when buying.

> **?** *Although it is easy to formulate an informal definition of brand equity (as above), its much harder to unpack the elements that go to make up valuable brands. And when we say 'elements' here, we do not mean simply 'how can we recognize a valuable brand?'. We mean: what are the factors (or 'causes', if you like) that make brands valuable?*

One of the problems with the InterBrand approach is that it used to look mainly at manifestations of value – market share and the like. It does not answer the question: how did the brand become valuable in the first place? Our framework for understanding the forces that drive customer or

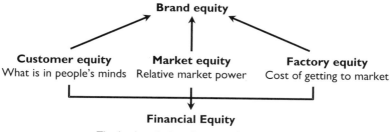

**Figure 4.3**   *A simple framework for understanding brand equity*

consumer choice argues that there are just two general forces that shape what people use or buy (see Figure 4.1):

- First, how strongly they are psychologically attracted to or repulsed by each option, i.e. the relationship they have with each brand.
- Second, the relative market power of each brand, i.e. its strength of distribution, share of advertising spending, relative price and so on.

Let's consider the first: take all the people in a market. Look at what's in their minds about the choices they have in that market. Then take the sum of all that mental stuff – what we will have is an overall measure of the strength of various brands in people's minds.

Now take all the factors that are external to a consumer's mind but which incline them to buy a brand, for example, advertising presence, sales force. What we have in these factors is an overall measure of the brand's market power. Put the two together, and we have a simple and elegant framework with which to begin to understand brand equity.

We call the 'relationship' side of things a brand's customer or consumer equity. In a formulation proposed by Keller, this is 'all the associations, thoughts and feelings' that a person has about a brand. It is one element of brand equity.[9] The second element is the 'equity' equivalent of what we call the 'market power' of the brand and we refer to it as the brand's 'market equity'. We complete the picture by drawing attention to the importance of cost. Great 'factory' processes are the third plane in which value can be added. Hence what we call 'factory equity' (Figure 4.3).

## The secret of Coca-Cola: great market equity combined with great consumer equity

The Coca-Cola Company may be struggling at the moment, but that does not mean that Coke has suddenly become less than a great brand. Great mainstream brands like Coca-Cola combine both a strong position in the minds of many consumers and a strong market presence. In other words, they tend to have both high consumer equity and high market equity. Their market power is one reason why they can sometimes continue to maintain high market share even if commitment is relatively low. Store brands, on the other hand, are an example of market equity exceeding consumer equity in local environments – they sell because they are cheap and are prominently displayed at the point of purchase. Rolls-Royce would probably qualify as an example of a brand with great consumer equity and relatively low market equity. It is not available everywhere; if you want one, you have to go and get it.

Many marketers might suppose that we would now be done with what gives a brand high equity. But that would be a mistake, as can be seen in Figure 4.3. It would ignore the importance of costs in determining the financial equity of brands. Think again: you might be managing a brand whose position in people's minds is very strong – high customer equity. In addition, your brand may have an all-pervasive presence in the marketplace – high market equity. But you still need to be able to sell it for more than it costs to get it to market. Most of the time when marketers discuss brand equity they ignore this third component.

## The secret of Dell: equity is created in the 'factory'

Dell computers is a great brand with very high equity in the computing world. But its equity is not due only to the force with which it occupies consumers' minds. To a significant degree, what enabled Dell to build its equity was the process it engineered to get computers to people. Dell created a great 'factory'. And this factory allowed it to custom-build top-quality computers at speed and cheaply for its customers. Efficiency in the factory allowed it to respond to customer needs in a unique and superior way. Customers repaid it by giving it strength and prominence in their minds.

So, the full framework for understanding where brand value can be created consists of three elements:

- Customer equity
- Market equity
- Factory equity

Obviously, value can be added to a brand within any of the three. Before about 1992, Intel did not have much customer equity. Most people did not know what brand of microchips were in their PCs. Since 1992, however, it has added customer equity to the list of what makes it valuable. In so doing it has encouraged a situation in which buyers of PCs feel just that much more comfortable about their purchase if it bears the sticker 'Intel inside'.

And in so doing, Intel has created a situation in which the people who make PCs are that much more inclined to put Intel inside, and the people who sell PCs have been encouraged to stock a good range of PCs with Intel inside.

## Most marketing research fails to integrate attitudes with behaviours

Marketing research – the industry which provides information to marketers – is strangely split between those who focus on attitudinal research and those who focus on behavioural research. Attitudinal research folks concentrate on the customer equity side of things. Behavioural research folks concentrate on the market equity side of things. We now see that management consultants like McKinsey have made fortunes concentrating on the factory equity side of things. It has always seemed strange to us that the three should be so thoroughly divided, because it is clear that marketers need to focus on all three. And it should be obvious that an opportunity exists for a service which builds models to integrate all three.

Commitment-led marketing is about focusing on customer equity, and so it would be true to say that our particular speciality is understanding the 'customer equity' part of what makes a brand strong. Yet, increasingly we are finding that the more we know about customer equity, the more important it is to understand market equity, factory equity and the relationship between all three. As responsible marketers, we should never recommend actions to build brand value that cost more to implement than the value that they add. That is why it is essential that marketers and their advisers think about factory equity.

> **"The more we know about customer equity, the more important it is to understand market equity, factory equity and the relationship between all three."**

## The single most important question a marketer can ask

**?** *The single most important question a marketer can ask every day is: where should my scarce resources be spent today to build the value of my brand most cost effectively?*

Should I be spending money on advertising, or on increasing my distribution? Should I invest in building customer equity or market equity? What weight should I give to each? And which element of each should I choose to invest in? What if I should be doing neither? What if the single best thing I could do would be to invest in new processes which reduce costs in the factory? Where should the money go?

## Brand strength and steady-state markets

We should not leave the topics of commitment, loyalty and brand equity without discussing the phenomenon of 'double jeopardy'.[10] Double jeopardy is the well-documented relationship between brand size and other brand performance measures. Put simply, the more users a brand has, the better it tends to perform in terms of all brand performance measures. So a brand gains 'doubly' when it gains new users – not only will more people be buying it, but all those who buy it tend to do so with more loyalty (in our sense of the word 'loyalty').

This is a remarkable fact. It allows marketers to make strong predictions about a brand's penetration, repurchase rate, price elasticity and size in the average consumer's repertoire merely from knowing its market share. It even allows marketers to predict how well the brand will perform on a variety of attitudinal measures.[11] So robust is this relationship, that scanner-panel data shows that there may be no such thing as a 'niche' brand.[12] In other words, the real world does not appear to contain many small brands whose sales are due mostly to a small group of highly loyal buyers.

The problem with 'double jeopardy', real as it is, is that it only applies to steady-state markets – in other words, markets in which brand market shares are relatively stable. But market shares can change. And sometimes they change rapidly. Back in 1994 we documented a case in which a market-leading brand of beer lost over 50% of its market share in little over six months.[13] We were fortunate to catch a shift in consumer commitment to this brand about three months before its share slide began. The point is: markets can become unstable. And when they do, double jeopardy breaks down and brand performances change. One way to think about marketing is to think of it as a conscious attempt to destabilize markets in ways which favour one's own brands.

Because of their sheer size, market-leading brands always have a great many uncommitted consumers. Yet many of them manage to sustain remarkably high levels of market share for many years. The phenomenon of double jeopardy celebrates this fact. But how does it happen?

It happens, we suggest, through the phenomenon of loyalty without commitment. It is the market presence of market-leading brands that sustains their sales and hence their market shares, even among consumers who are uncommitted.

> **"One way to think about marketing is to think of it as a conscious attempt to destabilize markets in ways which favour one's own brands."**

For a good example, let's look at Levi's in the USA. Levi's used to be so dominant in the USA that many retailers could not afford to be without a full range of Levi's – styles, fits and sizes – in case they lost a sale because they didn't have what a particular lover of Levi's wanted. But this in turn meant that so much shelf-space had to be devoted to Levi's that it was not possible to stock much of anything else. Consumers who were uncommitted to Levi's would find themselves in a position where Levi's was available in the style and fit they wanted, but nothing else was. As long as they were not particularly concerned to buy another brand, they would then buy Levi's.

Did this mean that Levi's was invulnerable? Not at all. The crucial point is that any increase in the marketing aggression of competitors would have the potential to make an immediate impact on any consumer who may have been uncommitted to Levi's. In other words, market-leading brands can always be attacked if a way can be found to tilt the balance of market power – what we have called market equity. And as long as competitor aggression was sustained and increasing, Levi's sales share of the jeans market would decrease.

Levi Strauss & Co. have recently received a lot of adverse editorial about their management of the jeans market. But any aggressive increase in the distribution and share of voice of a brand like Tommy Hilfiger would have *had* to undermine sales of a brand like Levi's. Apart from anything else, Tommy Hilfiger's marketing changed the relative balance of Levi's market equity. And this would immediately have put pressure on sales among uncommitted Levi's consumers. As the editorials make clear, eventually a point was reached where retailers no longer had to stock such a full range of Levi's – or where they discovered that they had to offer choices other than Levi's to make sales.

The rule is: all other things being equal, when the number of a brand's uncommitted consumers exceeds the number of non-consumers who are available to it, any increase in the marketing activity of competitors will lead to a decline in sales. To the extent that the new balance in relative market presence is maintained, the decline in sales will become permanent unless commitment is increased. In the case of a market-leading brand, this will result in a slow loss of market share, at first not distinguishable from background noise, but eventually so apparent that retailers might start to withdraw support for the brand.

> **"When the number of a brand's uncommitted consumers exceeds the number of non-consumers who are available to it, any increase in the marketing activity of competitors will lead to a decline in sales."**

## Shifts in market share can be as inevitable as the ebb and flow of tides

What has happened to Levi's classic blue jeans reminds us of an ancient legend: there was once a king called Canute whose subjects believed that he could do anything. He did not think that this was a healthy state of affairs. Like a good marketer, he was aware of the dangers of exaggerated expectations among his subjects. But nothing he said could persuade his subjects that he was not omnipotent. Eventually, to make the point, he asked his subjects to seat him at the sea's edge while the tide was out. He then demonstrated that he had absolutely no power to stop the tide from coming in.

Sometimes marketers are faced by fundamental shifts in consumer tastes. Tidal shifts are hard to stem when they run against your brand or product category. Whatever Levi's might have done wrong – and the press has certainly not hesitated to climb into brand management – when we look at situations like this they sometimes have an air of inevitability about them. It takes enormous courage under these conditions for marketers to make the radical shifts in strategy that may be needed if they are to keep abreast with where consumers are heading and so preserve their revenues.

## Marketer's summary: understanding loyalty, commitment and brand equity

Loyalty and commitment

Loyalty – the behavioural propensity to buy a brand repeatedly – differs from commitment – the strength of the consumer's psychological attachment to the brand. *Committed loyalty* is the ideal state. But it is possible for a brand to be bought loyally without commitment. This happens in two ways:

- By force of circumstance – when consumers cannot buy the brand that they want, and so loyally buy a second or third best brand.
- By choice – when consumers don't care what they buy, and so loyally buy the market-leading brand by default.

Many consumers in many markets are both *uncommitted* and *disloyal*. Our tendency when confronted by such consumers is to think that we must make them committed by making them enthusiastic about the brand.

But the fact that loyalty can exist without commitment means that there are other options:

- Uncommitted, disloyal consumers can be managed either by making them enthusiastic about the brand or by mobilizing market forces in favour of the brand.
- Consumers who are committed and loyal should be managed by maintaining both their beliefs about the brand and the importance of those beliefs.
- Consumers whose loyalty is based on market factors need to be managed by maintaining a strong brand presence because they are market driven.

### Adding value to brands: the components of brand equity

The most important question a marketer can ask is: what can I do to add value to my brand most cost effectively? There are three points at which value can be added:

- In the factory (i.e. factory equity): what Dell did when it created super, cost-effective production and product delivery processes.
- In the marketplace (i.e. market equity): what Coke does by its domination of the city-scape in many countries.
- In the minds of consumers (i.e. consumer equity): what Intel did when it capitalized on consumers' need for reassurance when buying computers.

Sometimes marketers are faced by tidal shifts in consumer tastes or market circumstances. At times like these it takes extraordinary courage and vision to make the revolutionary changes to brand management that may be required to preserve the value of the brand.

# References

1.  Reichheld, F.F. (1996) Learning from customer defections. *Harvard Business Review*, March/April.
2.  Reichheld, F.F. (1993) Loyalty based management. *Harvard Business Review*, March/April.

3.  Jacoby, J. and Chestnut, R.W. (1978) *Brand Loyalty: Measurement and Management.* Wiley, New York.

4.  Jacoby, J. and Kyner, D.B. (1973) Brand loyalty vs repeat purchase behaviour. *Journal of Marketing Research*, February.

5.  Jacoby, J. and Chestnut, R.W. (1978) Ibid.

6.  Based on market research conducted in 1998 by NIPO, one of the foremost marketing research agencies in the Netherlands.

7.  Simon, C. and Sullivan, M. (1992) The measurement and determinants of brand equity: a financial approach. *Journal of Marketing Science.*

8.  Leuthesser, L. (1988) Defining, measuring, and managing brand equity. Published in the summary of the Marketing Sciences Institute conference, Austin, Texas.

9.  Keller, K.L. (1993) Conceptualizing, measuring, and managing customer-based brand equity. *Journal of Marketing*, January.

10. See, for example, Ehrenberg, A.S., Goodhardt, G.J. and Barwise, T.P. (1990) Double jeopardy revisited. *Journal of Marketing Research*, July.

11. Ehrenberg, A.S. (1991) Politicians' double jeopardy: a pattern and exceptions. *Journal of the Market Research Society*, **33**.

12. Fader, P.S. and Schmittlein, D.C. (1993) Excess behavioural loyalty for high-share brands: deviations from the Dirichlet model for repeat purchasing. *Journal of Marketing Research*, November.

13. Hofmeyr, J. and Bennett, R. (1994) Double jeopardy and consumer commitment. *Canadian Journal of Marketing Research*, **13**.

# 5

## The Impact of Commitment on How People Behave in Markets

*Proven results from over 2800 studies worldwide*

In the previous chapter we set out our approach to questions like the definition of brand loyalty and brand equity. We showed how loyalty without commitment and commitment without loyalty happen. We developed a simple model to explain what people end up buying in any market and explored the implications. In this chapter we take our analysis further, using hard empirical data from the more than 2800 studies commissioned worldwide which use our measure of commitment.

## The customer equity profile of two brands in France

We analyse how strong a brand is in the minds of people by using 'commitment–availability' profiles like those in Figure 5.1. These profiles can be thought of as quantifying the consumer equity of a brand. In this case we are looking at the profiles of two laundry detergent brands in France. Ariel is a market leader, used by about 45% of all consumers regularly. The other, Le Chat, is a small, 'environmentally friendly' brand, used by about 15% of all consumers.

Some people may feel that the first picture is unreasonable. After all, how many brands achieve that level of regular usage these days? The answer, surprisingly, is many. By Lloyds TSB's own reckoning, it has 18 million customers in the UK, a country of some 55 million people. A great many men in the USA own at least one pair of Dockers casual pants. And in most countries that we have looked at, there are strong and dominant

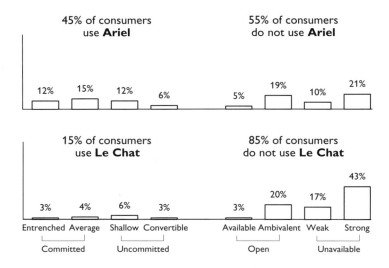

**Figure 5.1**   *The customer equity profile of two brands of laundry detergent in France measured using the theory of commitment*

regional brands: Singha beer in Thailand, Omo laundry detergent in South Africa, Maruti cars in India.

So, let's have a look at what we have learnt about the relationship between commitment and human behaviour in markets, starting with these two brands.

**?** *What can we predict people will do when we know how committed they are to the brands they buy?*

# Commitment affects how much of a brand people buy

We begin by looking at the impact that commitment has on how much of a person's business you get. We have seen hundreds of examples from projects in which measures of brand commitment were combined with measures of what people actually do. Sometimes the combination is based on what people say they do. Increasingly, however, marketers are combining commitment with behaviour as recorded in customer databases. Across all these studies, we have consistently found the following relationship: as commitment increases, so loyalty (defined as share of requirements) increases.

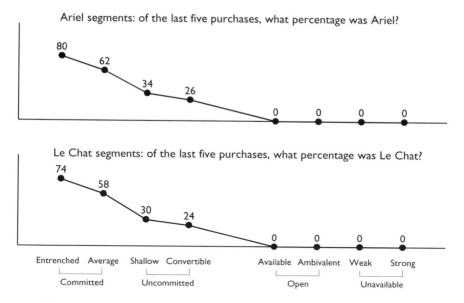

i.e. 80% of what 'entrenched' Ariel buyers buy regularly is Ariel. But only 26% of what 'convertible' Ariel buyers buy regularly is Ariel.

**Figure 5.2**   *The relationship between loyalty (measured as 'share of requirements') and commitment as measured using the theory of commitment*

In Figure 5.2 you will find a graphical representation of this rela-tionship for Ariel and Le Chat. The chart shows that the stronger a person's relationship with Ariel or Le Chat, the more of it they are likely to buy as a percentage of all the laundry detergents they buy. This is an exceptionally robust relationship. No matter what the brand, product category or country, when commitment is measured as we measure it, the more committed a consumer is to a brand, the bigger the 'share' of that consumer's 'requirements' the brand will fill. We have seen it for cooking oils in India, beer in the USA, petroleum brands in Hong Kong, jewellery shopping in South Africa – in short, everywhere.

One of the reasons for linking commitment and consumption in this way is that it enables marketers to quantify what they can gain by driving up commitment to their brands (or, conversely, what they will lose if commitment falls). Let's look again at Figure 5.2: we can say that a person's consumption of Ariel will go up by 80% if the Ariel brand manager in France can get that person to go from 'shallow' to 'average'. Consumption of

**Table 5.1**   *Commitment and its impact on 'share of wallet' (19 countries, 2 product categories)*

| | Strength of commitment to brands being used* | | | |
| --- | --- | --- | --- | --- |
| | Entrenched (%) | Average (%) | Shallow (%) | Convertible (%) |
| *Product 1* | | | | |
| Country 1 | 88 | 78 | 48 | 32 |
| Country 2 | 92 | 82 | 60 | 32 |
| Country 3 | 82 | 70 | 40 | 30 |
| Country 4 | 74 | 60 | 62 | 44 |
| Country 5 | 90 | 88 | 58 | 36 |
| Country 6 | 92 | 82 | 70 | 44 |
| *Product 2* | | | | |
| UK | 68 | 70 | 36 | 34 |
| Netherlands | 70 | 68 | 56 | 44 |
| France | 76 | 52 | 30 | 24 |
| Germany | 66 | 50 | 28 | 18 |
| Poland | 70 | 56 | 32 | 28 |
| Romania | 80 | 74 | 36 | 28 |
| Turkey | 88 | 60 | 40 | 26 |
| India | 80 | 66 | 36 | 12 |
| Australia | 94 | 70 | 52 | 30 |
| Canada | 84 | 60 | 44 | 28 |
| Mexico | 94 | 84 | 50 | 30 |
| Brazil | 76 | 78 | 36 | 26 |
| Colombia | 68 | 52 | 32 | 20 |
| **Mean**[†] | 81 | 69 | 45 | 30 |

In each market the 'share of requirement' was calculated for a 'mid-range' brand, i.e. not the market leader, but also not a small brand.

\* Interpretation: in Country 1, 88% of what 'entrenched' consumers buy in this market is the brand to which they are entrenched.

[†] The 'mean' is the simple, unweighted mean within each level of commitment across both product categories and all countries.

Ariel goes up by 208% among people who move from 'convertible' to 'entrenched'. The reverse is also true. When an 'entrenched' consumer becomes 'convertible', the impact on sales is usually severe.

These kinds of results are not unusual. Table 5.1 quantifies the impact that commitment has on share of requirements in two product categories across 19 countries.

> **"Linking commitment and consumption enables marketers to quantify what they can gain by driving up commitment to their brands."**

# Why not use 'share of requirements' as a surrogate for commitment?

> **?** *Two questions come to mind. The first is: but isn't this obvious? Surely we* should *find that these relationships exist? The second is: if the relationship between 'commitment' and 'share of requirements' is so close, why use 'commitment' at all – why not revert to the old 'loyalty' approach using share of requirements by itself?*

Our answer to the first question is: of course it's obvious – but it wasn't when we started. We measure commitment using a purely psychological method. The fact that we have found this very robust relationship between behaviour and commitment helps to validate our approach, but it wasn't obvious originally that we would find it.

The more interesting question is the second: if there is a close relationship between commitment measured psychologically and 'share of requirements' measured behaviourally, why bother with the psychological? Why not return simply to 'share of requirements' and stick with loyalty?

By now the reason for this should also be obvious: loyalty and commitment are not the same thing. The former is about behaviour. The latter is about the psychological relationship that underpins behaviour. When people are committed, they tend to be loyal. But there are many ways in which people who are loyal, are not committed.

The problem with allowing 'share of requirements' to represent commitment is that it can give you a very misleading picture of the health of your brand. We will prove this using real-world data taken from a project in a developing country.

> **"When people are committed, they tend to be loyal. But there are many ways in which people who are loyal, are not committed."**

## Why it is dangerous to use loyalty as a surrogate for commitment

For the sake of client confidentiality, we have disguised this as a study of liquor consumption in Taiwan. Figure 5.3 shows the commitment–

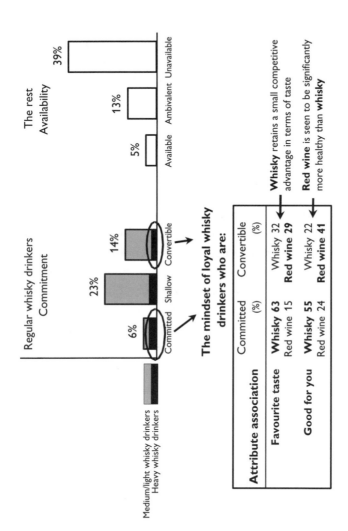

**Figure 5.3** *Close to a third of the heavy (i.e. loyal) whisky drinkers were identified as 'convertible'. The analysis of imagery shows that the identification is accurate*

availability profile for whisky. The numbers are *real*, although the country and product category have been disguised. According to our results, 43% of all spirits drinkers regularly drink whisky, and 6% are committed. But 37% are uncommitted (i.e. shallow or convertible).

> **"Allowing 'share of requirements' to represent commitment can give you a very misleading picture of the health of your brand."**

This marketer divides regular whisky drinkers into those who are 'heavy', 'medium' and 'light' drinkers of whisky. In this way, his company aims to identify and distinguish low-value from high-value whisky drinkers. When we combined his volume approach with our measure of commitment, however, we found that 62% of his high-value (i.e. heavy) whisky drinkers were uncommitted. A full 32% were convertible. In other words, at least a third of the volume from heavy whisky drinkers was at risk.

We showed these results to the marketer and were immediately confronted with a challenge: prove it – prove that high-value whisky drinkers whom you say are at risk, actually are.

So we had a look at what was in the mind of these high-value, uncommitted whisky drinkers (see Figure 5.3). It was very clear that they had a bad opinion of whisky on some key dimensions. In particular, they were attracted to wine because of its perceived health benefits. We were therefore able to:

- Quantify the amount of heavy volume at risk – 32%.
- Identify the source of the risk – wine.
- Identify the reason – wine is seen to have health benefits.

The phenomenon of loyalty without commitment is one of the most dangerous that a marketer can face. At an aggregate level, commitment will correlate with loyalty. But at the micro-level of the individual consumer, there will always be loyal consumers who are not committed. Typically, we have found that they can make up to 20–35% of a brand's heavy users. This is why loyalty cannot be used as a surrogate for commitment. Without a measure of commitment these people would be impossible to identify – and that volume could melt away without warning.

> **"The phenomenon of loyalty without commitment is one of the most dangerous that a marketer can face."**

## How a brand's market presence impacts on share of requirements

We have shown that there is a relationship between commitment and loyalty: the more committed someone is, the more likely they are to be loyal. This relationship is so robust that we can use it to help marketers predict the impact that changes in commitment will have on sales at an aggregate level. But we have also shown that, despite the relationship, 'loyalty' behaviourally defined cannot be used as a surrogate for commitment. This is because doing so prevents marketers from identifying high-value customers or consumers who are actually at risk.

What, then, about Ehrenberg's claim, that all measures of brand strength merely reflect a brand's penetration?[1] How does this impact on our view?

In 1994, we published research which showed that when commitment is measured properly, big brands are not always healthy and small brands can be.[2] In other words, commitment is not a phenomenon that conforms to 'double jeopardy'. Still, we are supporters of the work of Ehrenberg and his colleagues. Let's look at why.

Figure 5.4 comes from research that we conducted for a beverages company in the early 1990s. In order to preserve client confidentiality, we have disguised both the category and the brands by inventing a set of fictitious brand names. Imagine that we are talking about carbonated beverages. Figure 5.4 shows a distinctive pattern. The elements of that pattern are:

- The bigger the brand, i.e. the more 'weekly drinkers' it has, the greater the share of requirements it gets from each of its 'weekly' drinkers. This is the relationship Ehrenberg expects to see and it is one of the reasons why he challenges the concept of brand loyalty so vigorously. As he is fond of saying, there are no strong or weak brands, only big or little ones.

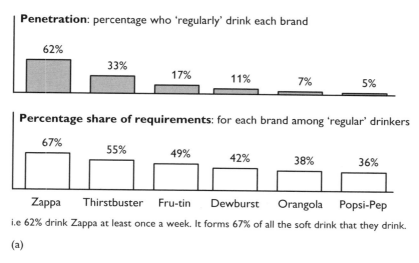

i.e 62% drink Zappa at least once a week. It forms 67% of all the soft drink that they drink.

(a)

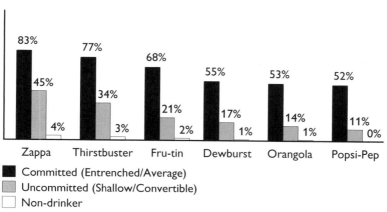

■ Committed (Entrenched/Average)
▨ Uncommitted (Shallow/Convertible)
□ Non-drinker

i.e. 83% of what committed consumers of Zappa drink is Zappa. 45% of what uncommitted consumers of Zappa drink is Zappa. 4% of what the rest drink is Zappa.

(b)

**Figure 5.4** *The interaction of double jeopardy with the commitment segments. (a) Penetration and its relation to 'share of requirements'. (b) Commitment and its relation to 'share of requirements'*

- The relationship between brand size and 'share of requirement' carries through *at every level of commitment* and not just at the aggregate level of weekly consumption. Entrenched users of the bigger brands consume more of their brands than entrenched users of the smaller brands. The pattern is maintained through 'average' to 'convertible' levels of commitment.

- The rate at which a brand's share of requirements falls in relation to commitment is much greater for small brands than for big brands. In other words, the bigger the brand, the less volume it loses to competitor brands as commitment declines. Uncommitted consumers of big brands are more likely to continue drinking their brand than uncommitted consumers of small brands.

## Why small brands consistently lose volume among their uncommitted consumers

Marketers of small brands cannot but help losing sales among their uncommitted consumers. Here's why: what consumers do depends on both how they feel about a brand and how big the brand is. Let's take one of the small brands in Figure 5.4, say Orangola. Because it is small, it is likely to be prejudiced in the market. It will not get as much advertising as a big brand like Zappa. And it is less likely than Zappa to be supported by the trade. That would not worry committed drinkers of Orangola. They would overcome all sorts of hurdles to get at the brand. They would shop where it was in stock. They wouldn't care if it wasn't advertised. They would take their own stock of it to social gatherings in case the host hadn't thought to buy Orangola.

> **"The rate at which a brand's share of requirements falls in relation to commitment is much greater for small brands than for big brands."**

But now think about Orangola's uncommitted drinkers. Some of them drink it regularly, but don't really care when they cannot get it. Others also drink it regularly, but are uncommitted because they also like other brands. Either way, if they walked into a shop and Orangola wasn't available, they wouldn't really mind buying something else. After all, they're uncommitted. Similarly, if they were at a party they wouldn't mind drinking something else. And because Orangola has a low market share, this happens all the time.

The net effect is that committed users of Orangola make an effort to buy and drink it as much as they can even though it is difficult to do so because it's a small brand. Uncommitted users of Orangola often find that it's unavailable but they don't care because they're uncommitted. So they drink something else.

## Why marketers of big brands retain sales among their uncommitted consumers

The situation is completely different when it comes to a popular brand like Zappa. In this case, the uncommitted consumer, i.e. someone who really doesn't care which brand they drink, is likely to find that Zappa is almost always available. Certainly, it is more likely to be available than smaller brands like Orangola. And since the uncommitted consumer isn't too concerned about which one they drink, Zappa will tend to be drunk more.

Let's look at a brand like Zappa in greater detail: what is its market situation? Consider Figure 5.5. This brand has a 62% penetration. A very large percentage, 40%, are committed drinkers of Zappa. This means that every retailer knows that four out of ten people walking into their store will ask for Zappa. If Zappa isn't stocked, there is a chance that the retailer would lose the sale.

What all of this adds up to is that committed consumers of brands, whether those brands are small or big, will try to devote most of their category consumption to those brands. The share of requirements that a small or big brand gets from its entrenched users will tend, therefore, to be quite similar.

By contrast, uncommitted consumers of a small brand will find that the scales are often tipped against them. Unlike the committed consumers, however, they wouldn't mind so much. So they drink something else without too much concern. Uncommitted consumers of big brands find the opposite: the scales are tipped in favour of the big brand – it's easy to get hold of and so they end up drinking it.

Basically, big brands retain sales from their uncommitted consumers more easily than small brands. What drives big brands among their uncommitted consumers is their market power. They are more heavily advertised, more generally available and more regularly endorsed. So real is this phenomenon of brand market power, that, as Fader and Schmittlein have pointed out, big brands get consumed even more than Ehrenberg's purely statistical model would predict.[3] The main reason is that retailers prefer to stock popular brands when shelf space is limited.

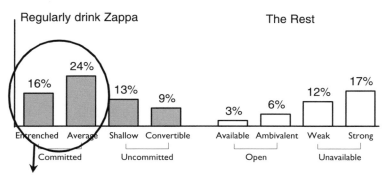

**Because four in ten soft drink drinkers are committed to Zappa:**

- it must always be in stock
- it must be available at all social gatherings
- it need not be advertised as heavily to achieve sales

**Figure 5.5**  *The committed customers of a brand 'pull' it through the market*

In the USA, many men are probably committed to Dockers, a brand of casual pants produced by Levi Strauss & Co. This means that many men, when they walk into a store, are probably thinking: 'Where are the Dockers?' But customers come in all shapes and sizes, and so many retailers have to devote quite a lot of shelf space to Dockers, just to make sure that committed Dockers customers can get what they want. This in turn reduces the space available for other brands – and ensures that uncommitted consumers of all brands are more likely to buy Dockers than anything else.

Someone who is uncommitted to any brand of casual pants has a reasonable chance of finding a pair of Dockers that fits. Uncommitted users of smaller brands are much less likely to have that chance.

# Market power: its impact on defection and recruitment rates

One of the ways in which a marketer loses sales is when people become uncommitted and start buying a brand less – and this is what we have been looking at in the last few pages. But another is when people simply stop buying the brand altogether. Low commitment therefore hits a marketer in two ways:

- First, the brand gets less of a consumer's or customer's current business.
- Second, the likelihood of complete defection is much higher.

The first study we ever did using our approach to commitment-led marketing was for a bank. The first ever validation study we did involving a test of the link between commitment and complete defection was done some six months after the banking study. We re-contacted people who had been interviewed in that study to see what they had done in the meantime. The validation was successful – people who had been identified as convertible were significantly more likely to have switched to another bank than those identified as entrenched.

Validations of this kind are the toughest kind of test to which attitudinal models can be subjected. But we have found them to be so reliable that we often design and act on studies on the basis that our approach will continue to be predictive. So, for example, we use our measures to recruit people for focus groups. Suppose a private banker wants to find out why some customers are uncommitted – we will use our key questions to recruit people. It never disappoints – invariably people recruited in this way are so uncommitted it can be quite hair-raising to have to listen to them.

So, what we can say with confidence is that, at every level of commitment, a person identified as more committed will have a significantly lower likelihood of defection than someone identified as less committed. The same goes for 'availability': at every level of availability, a person identified as more available will be significantly more likely to start using a brand than someone identified as less available (see Figure 5.6).

But the relationship between commitment, availability and subsequent defection or recruitment behaviour is not independent of the 'double jeopardy' phenomenon. Figure 5.7 shows this. Taken from packaged goods studies in South Africa and the USA, it shows that bigger brands both retain their uncommitted customers and recruit their available non-consumers more easily than smaller brands.

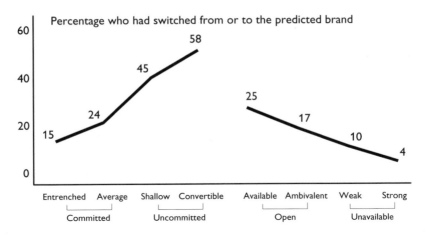

i.e. 15% of those who had been entrenched had defected from the brand.

**Figure 5.6**  *A validation study showing the percentage within each segment who had switched from or to the predicted brand*

Percentage who were found to have stopped or started using the predicted brand

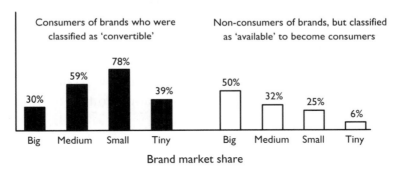

i.e. A year later, 30% of the convertible users of 'big brands' (share > 20%) had converted compared with 78% for 'small brands', and so on.

**Figure 5.7**  *Defection and recruitment rates as a function of brand size*

Put simply, the rate at which uncommitted customers or consumers defect is a function of brand size. Similarly for acquisition. The reasons why this should be so are the same as the reasons why uncommitted consumers of small brands consume less of their brands than uncommitted consumers of big brands.

## Why brand size impacts on the acquisition of new users

Consider two brands – one, a small brand with low market share, say, 1%; the second a large brand with a large market share, say, 33%. Now imagine that among the non-users of both of them, some 5% were available to become users.

In both cases, the 5% available would have to find the brand to start using it regularly. But the 5% available to the small brand would have to work a lot harder to find it than the 5% available to the big brand. The big brand will always tend to be in stock and easy to find; the small brand will not be. The big brand is likely to be more regularly advertised; the small brand will not be. The big brand will have a market presence which makes it easier for available non-users to become users.

> **"What drives big brands among their uncommitted consumers is their market power. The rate at which uncommitted customers or consumers defect is a function of brand size."**

The same thing happens on the user side of the line: big brands are at an advantage in retaining uncommitted users because they win the battle to make the sale more easily at the point where purchase decisions are made.

## Why uncommitted big brand users are less likely to defect

Let's illustrate this situation with an example from the soap-powder market: suppose we had a consumer who regularly used Radion, a rather small brand in the UK. This consumer would constantly be facing marketplace disincentives to buy the brand – stores which don't sell it, limited advertising, few in-store reminders, limited shelf space. If their commitment to Radion weakened, then their determination to buy it would weaken. At some point the effect of the marketplace disincentives to buy would be strong enough to push them towards an alternative – say, Ariel, one of the biggest brands in the UK.

Now let's consider Ariel. In this case, there would be constant marketplace incentives to buy the brand. It's available everywhere, easy to find and the pack is recognizable. It is involved in a heated battle with Persil for market supremacy which means that there is a lot of marketing activity around it. If our consumer became uncommitted, there would still be plenty of market pressure favouring Ariel. Unless our consumer actively wanted something else, this market pressure would incline them to continue buying Ariel.

But now suppose this consumer stayed uncommitted to Ariel for a while. The main competitor to Ariel in the UK is Persil. Unless our consumer actively disliked Persil, they might be quite willing to start buying Persil in addition to Ariel. Promotions, advertising the night before – a whole range of in-market activities could tip the scales in Persil's favour every now and then. This person would then start flip-flopping back and forth between these two brands as a function of the in-market activity of each one.

Now, we know that the relationships that people have with brands are not static. This means that, in time, our consumer's commitment to Ariel could recover. And that is the point: Ariel's market presence will have ensured that this person continued to buy Ariel even when uncommitted – and in this way 'bought time' for the Ariel brand. The time 'bought' would give the brand a chance for commitment to recover. So, because big brands are able to win the battle for the undecided mind more easily than small brands, they are able to retain sales among uncommitted users for longer and so increase the chances that commitment will recover and that defection will be prevented.

## Brand size is irrelevant when it comes to defections among committed consumers

Now let's compare defection rates among committed consumers. Our longitudinal studies have shown that committed consumers do defect, given enough time. That this should be so is obvious – the relationship that someone has with a brand need not be static. But the rate at which committed consumers defect is a fraction of the rate at which uncommitted consumers defect. An interesting question arises: do we find the same 'big brand – little brand' effect when we look at the defection rates of committed consumers as exists among uncommitted consumers?

The answer is in Figure 5.8 and it's 'no'. Our framework for understanding what people do or buy predicts that the more committed a person is to their brand, the less influential market factors will be in driving brand

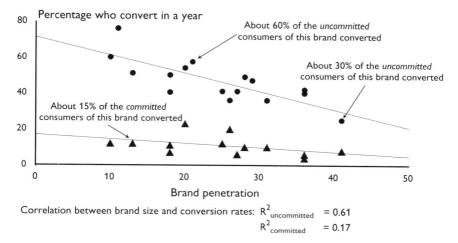

**Figure 5.8** *A comparison of defection rates among committed and uncommitted consumers*

purchase behaviour. It therefore leads us to predict that the effect of brand size on defection rates should be lower, the higher the levels of commitment we look at. As Figure 5.8 (from a longitudinal study conducted in the USA) shows, this is indeed the case.

## Summary: the two ways in which commitment impacts on sales volume

Our findings about the relationship between commitment and defection are very similar to our findings about commitment and share of requirements. In both cases, a decrease in commitment hits smaller brands harder than bigger brands. Smaller brands lose more business as a person becomes uncommitted, and they are more likely to lose that person altogether. Bigger brands retain their uncommitted consumers for longer; and they retain a greater share of the business of their uncommitted consumers.

This difference between smaller and bigger brands all but disappears when we look at committed consumers. Because market factors play a lesser role in what committed consumers buy, the amount of business that a brand gets from its committed consumers is high, irrespective of brand size. And the length of time that a brand continues to get that business is also relatively independent of brand size.

These differences add up to a potent link between commitment and brand value. Because of the relationships, we are able to quantify sales gains or losses very precisely as a function of changes in commitment. And because the difference is greater with small brands than with big brands, the sales 'kick' you get from an increase in commitment to a small brand can be very dramatic. In our experience, the lifetime value of a person who shifts from being convertible to being entrenched can rise by anything up to 100 times. Big brands also gain significantly, but by less. In Chapter 7 we show you how to use these results to attach a lifetime value to consumers as a function of their commitment to your brand.

## The relationship between commitment and price

Lower defection rates, more business — these are just two ways in which we have shown over the years that a brand benefits from commitment. A third benefit is in price. The first time we had strong evidence that there might be a relationship between the strength of a person's commitment to a brand and the price they would be willing to pay for it was in a study done for a beer manufacturer in Canada. The manufacturer was concerned that cheaper brands from the USA would be marketed aggressively in Canada. So they did what is known as a brand–price trade-off study coupled to a measure of commitment. The analysis quantified the sales losses that would result at various levels of discount for the imported brands. The commitment analysis then showed how this would vary as a function of commitment.

The analysis showed that brands from the USA like Budweiser would indeed impact on consumption of Canadian brands, and the deeper the discount, the bigger the impact. But it also showed that the impact of discounting would be significantly greater among uncommitted consumers of the Canadian brands (see Figure 5.9).

Four levels of relative price are shown, from a situation in which brands from Canada and the United States are at parity, to a situation in which the brand from the United States can be bought some 25% cheaper than the client brand. The rates at which drinkers of Canadian brands would defect to the competitor are shown at each level of discount for entrenched and convertible consumers. At every level, the rate at which

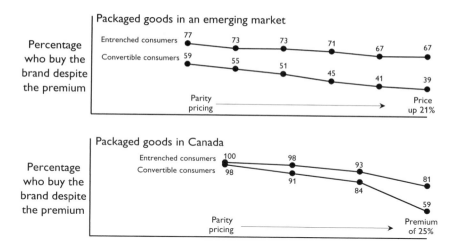

Percentage who buy the brand despite the premium

Packaged goods in an emerging market

Entrenched consumers 77 73 73 71 67 67
Convertible consumers 59 55 51 45 41 39

Parity pricing → Price up 21%

Percentage who buy the brand despite the premium

Packaged goods in Canada

Entrenched consumers 100 98 93 81
Convertible consumers 98 91 84 59

Parity pricing → Premium of 25%

i.e. In the emerging market, when a brand was priced at parity with a particular competitor, 77% of its entrenched consumers chose the brand. When the brand was priced at a 21% premium, 67% of the entrenched consumers still chose the brand.

**Figure 5.9** *The relation between commitment and the willingness to resist competitive discounting*

defection takes place is significantly greater among convertible drinkers. In short, the more committed consumers are, the more they will be prepared to pay for the brand.

This is not an isolated result. In addition to the results from research in Canada, Figure 5.9 shows the results from similar research done in an emerging market for packaged goods. Again, we found the same relationship – committed consumers are willing to pay more for their brands.

# What to do when you find loyalty without commitment

In this chapter so far we have looked at numerous examples of the relationship between loyalty and commitment, ranging from laundry detergents in France, to what we called 'alcoholic beverages in Taiwan'. We have proven that, while there tends to be a relationship between commitment and loyalty, not all loyal people are committed.

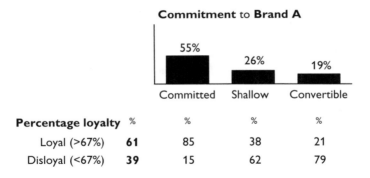

| Percentage loyalty % | % | % | % |
|---|---|---|---|
| Loyal (>67%)  **61** | 85 | 38 | 21 |
| Disloyal (<67%)  **39** | 15 | 62 | 79 |

i.e. 85% of the committed customers of Brand A are loyal (i.e. they buy it more than 67% of the time). This compares with only 38% of the shallow customers who are loyal.

**Figure 5.10**  *The relation between commitment and loyalty in a market for gasoline*

---

> **"Committed consumers are willing to pay more for their brands."**

Using a commitment-led marketing approach, it is possible to identify these loyal but uncommitted consumers. The ability to do so is obviously critical to marketers wishing to identify high-value consumers who may be at risk. This goes for marketers in service industries with large customer databases like banking, airlines or retailing, and it goes for marketers of packaged goods wishing to ensure that their market leading brands retain a high market share.

 *But what kind of action should we take when we find these people?*

In this section we begin to answer this question.

Figure 5.10 comes from a study for a brand of gasoline conducted in an emerging market. In this case, because it really is a gasoline study (unlike the 'whisky in Taiwan' example), we have preserved client confidentiality by changing the numbers and disguising the brands. But the relationships shown reflect the truth of what is embodied in the original study.

Brand A is a premium brand. We established that 55% of its regular users were committed. A further 26% were shallow and 19% convertible. As expected, there was a relationship between loyalty and commitment –

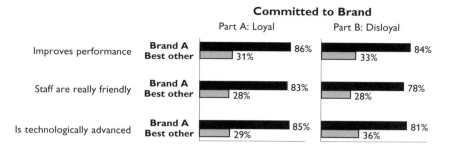

i.e. 86% of the loyal committed customers of Brand A say that it improves performance;
84% of the disloyal but committed customers of Brand A also say so.

**Figure 5.11**  *Disloyal but committed customers of Brand A rate the brand just as highly as loyal committed customers*

the more committed, the more loyal. But there were also committed customers who were disloyal, and many uncommitted customers who were loyal. What does this mean for marketing?

We begin by looking at what is in the mind of these different groups. Figure 5.11, part A tells us how *committed loyal* customers rate Brand A; part B tells us how *committed but disloyal* customers rate it. The key point is this: whether loyal or disloyal, both groups of committed consumers rate the brand equally highly. But this must mean that the reason Brand A loses sales among the latter group has nothing to do with what they think about the brand. And since their attitude to the brand is not the problem, the problem must be that their purchases are depressed by market factors.

Now we look at the uncommitted consumers of Brand A. A sizeable number of them are loyal. There are various ways of looking at the size of the loyal group among them. They are 31% of all the uncommitted, or 23% of all loyal customers, or 14% of all current customers. No matter which way you look at them, they represent a sizeable percentage of Brand A's sales. Now look at what's on their minds. As Figure 5.12 shows, they do not rate Brand A as highly as committed customers. They are loyal, but uncommitted. In this case we have to answer the question: why, then, are they buying Brand A? The answer is: it's the flip side of the same coin. Although uncommitted, they continue to buy Brand A because of its market power.

In the first case (Figure 5.11), market factors are obviously interfering with the ability of committed consumers to buy what they want to buy. In

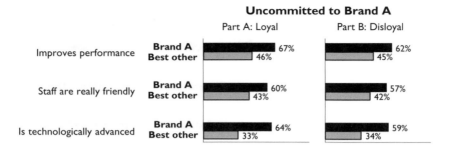

i.e. 67% of the loyal but uncommitted customers of Brand A say that it improves performance; 62% of disloyal uncommitted customers of Brand A also say so.

**Figure 5.12**  *Loyal but uncommitted customers of Brand A rate the brand almost identically to disloyal uncommitted customers*

| Low ─────── Commitment ─────→ High | | |
|---|---|
| **Task: improve brand image** | **Task: maintain** |
| These customers are loyal, but their image of the brand is poor | These customers have a good image of the brand and buy it a lot |
| **Task: leave for last/ignore** | **Task: remove market hurdles** |
| These customers are both disloyal and have a poor image of the brand | These customers have a good image of the brand, but do not buy it much |

*High ↑ Loyalty ─ Low* (left axis)

**Figure 5.13**  *A framework for deciding what sort of marketing response is appropriate for different customer groups*

the second case, market factors are ensuring that uncommitted consumers continue to buy a brand to which they are uncommitted at levels higher than their attitude would suggest. These results lead to a decision framework which we call the 'knowing what to fix' grid (see Figure 5.13).

When we find a case of loyalty without commitment we can almost always be sure that our brand is being bought for reasons which have as much to do with market factors as what they think about the brand. In order to retain the business of these people we therefore have to 'fix' what they think about the brand – or continue to ensure that our brand is dominant in terms of key market factors.

By contrast, when we find commitment without loyalty we can almost always be sure that there is nothing that we have to do to change the way these consumers think about the brand. In this case, therefore, what the marketer must do is identify the market barriers which prevent these people from acting on their desires. In our experience the barriers will most commonly turn out to be distribution or price. Once that is understood, it is relatively easy to initiate marketing activity aimed at removing the barriers to further consumption.

## Driving up frequency: the differences between rich and poor people

Sometimes we have worked with marketers who are more interested in frequency than in loyalty (although many marketers confuse the two). So, for example, marketers of beverages may define their goal as to increase the percentage of people who drink their brand at least once a day, or once a week – whatever. Marketers of this kind often talk about 'drivers of consumption'. And their particular interest is in trying to understand the drivers sufficiently well to drive up the frequency of consumption.

In Figure 5.14 you will see the results of research that we conducted in two different countries, one relatively wealthy and one relatively poor. In this case we analysed the relationship between commitment and frequency for a market-leading brand, rather than commitment and loyalty. As we would expect, frequency rises with commitment, and at every level of commitment there are some people who drink the brand very frequently and others who drink it rather infrequently. What are these numbers telling us about what we should do?

Look again at the pattern: a striking feature of the results is that uncommitted consumers in both countries drink the brand with about the same low frequency. Remember, in both countries this is a big brand, so it is not impacted by variations in brand size.

Now look at how often committed consumers drink the brand in each country. There is a big difference: in poor countries, frequency is depressed among committed consumers. As we show in Figure 5.15, this is not due to

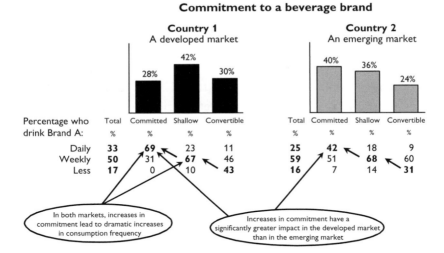

**Commitment to a beverage brand**

i.e. In the developed market, 69% of the committed drinkers drink the brand daily. This falls to 23% among shallow and 11% among convertible drinkers. In the emerging market a much lower 42% of the committed drink the brand daily.

**Figure 5.14** *The variation of frequency with commitment in two countries: one a developed market and one an emerging market*

what they think about the brand. In fact, even though they are consuming the brand relatively seldom, they still rate the brand better than heavier volume drinkers who are uncommitted. In addition, they rate it just as highly as the higher frequency committed consumers from wealthy countries. The problem therefore, is affordability, rather than access or image. The reason why the pattern is not repeated among uncommitted consumers is that, whether rich or poor, they do not want the brand anyway.

A number of marketing predictions follow from this:

- The gains that can be achieved by driving up commitment are significantly greater among rich than among poor people – because poor people cannot consume more even if they want to.
- Driving up frequency among the poor will have less to do with motivating them harder than with making the brand available in affordable 'chunks'. We see this in mainland China, for example, where Procter & Gamble sell personal care products like shampoos in single-serve sachets.

**Research into laundry detergents in two countries**

| France | | India | |
|---|---|---|---|
| **Attributes ranked by importance** | | **Attributes ranked by importance** | |
| Preference | Usage | Preference | Usage |
| High quality | Has a good smell | *Value for money | High quality |
| Gets clothes clean | Gets clothes clean | Gets clothes clean | Gets clothes clean |
| At any temperature | High quality | Removes stains | Cleans all types |
| *Has a good smell | At any temperature | Cleans all types | Use in hard water |
| Works on whites | *Rinses completely | *Soft on hands | Removes stains |
| Gentle on clothes | Gentle on clothes | *Preserves colour | Value for money |
| Clothes smell fresh | Works on whites | Gentle on fabrics | Gentle on fabrics |
| Value for money | Clothes smell fresh | *Use in hard water | *Lathers well |
| *Doesn't irritate skin | *Value for money | *High quality | *Leaves fresh scent |

## Comment

The * denotes attributes which vary significantly across the two lists. Many more attributes vary in their importance to consumers in India than in France. Quite simply, in France there are more consumers who can buy what they want. In India, both affordability and distribution will play a role in separating 'usage' from 'desire'.

Notes: The Jaccard coefficient was used to determine the relative importance of attributes.
To determine importance in relation to preference, 'brand for me' was the dependent variable.
To determine importance in relation to usage, brands bought the last five times were the dependent variables.

**Figure 5.15** *What is associated with brand usage is more likely to coincide with what is associated with brand preference in wealthy than in poor markets*

- When analysing what drives consumption, the poorer the country or the people that we are looking at, the greater will be the difference in the result of the analysis depending on what is chosen as the dependent variable.

If we look at actual usage, the drivers of consumption will depend more on what is affordable than on what people want. If we look at preference, the drivers of consumption will depend on what people want rather than on what they actually consume.

We have often been struck by the marketing anomalies created when strategies are forged for brands in poor countries by marketers in rich countries. We know of global brands whose management in the USA, for example, have little sense of the ways in which poverty impacts on what people buy. They use behaviour as their guide in countries where consumers cannot afford to buy the brands to which they are committed. Brand strategies are then based on a wrong sense of what drives brand preference. And there is little understanding that trying to amplify desire for a brand will do little to move brand volumes. The brands that people actually buy only coincide with the brands they want to buy in countries where consumers are sufficiently wealthy to follow the course of their desires.

## Marketer's summary: the relationship between commitment and behaviour

How commitment impacts on a brand's revenues

The higher a consumer's commitment to your brand:

- The more of their category spending you will get,
- And the less likely they are to defect, which means
- You get their category spending for longer.

The fact that sales vary systematically with commitment means that you can calculate the impact that changes in commitment will have on the sales of your brand. You can therefore calculate the potential return you can get from your marketing spending. The effect is usually dramatic: many times the marketing spend.

Small brands benefit more from an increase in commitment than big brands. This is because big brands retain a greater share of the spending of their uncommitted consumers than small brands and hold onto those uncommitted consumers for longer. The market power of big brands causes these effects.

Committed consumers are willing to pay anything up to 30% more for your brand. This means that the more committed users your brand has, the more you should resist the temptation to increase your sales through special offers or discounts.

### Why share of requirements cannot be used as a surrogate for commitment

There appear to be loyal but uncommitted customers or consumers in every market. They can form up to 30% of a brand's loyal users. By measuring commitment we can:

- Identify these people and quantify exactly how many of them there are;
- Understand the reasons why they are uncommitted;
- Devise strategies to prevent them from defecting to competitor brands.

Without a measure of commitment these people would be impossible to identify – and the volumes they represent could just melt away without warning.

### A simple strategic grid for marketing decisions

*Committed loyalty* is the ideal, but you cannot get more business than you are already getting from a committed, loyal person – unless, that is, they are prepared to increase their category spending. The marketing imperative is therefore: promote the category to these consumers.

*Commitment without loyalty* happens when market barriers prevent people from buying the brands to which they are committed. The most common barriers are price and availability. The marketing imperative: identify the barriers and remove them if possible.

*Loyalty without commitment* happens when market factors encourage people to use brands they would rather not be using, or when people don't care what brands they use. If you have people like this using your brand:

- Manage them by ensuring the continued market dominance of your brand;
- Recognize that they do not rate your brand highly and fix the problem.

## References

1. Ehrenberg, A.S. and Scriven, J.A. (1994) Brand loyalty: now you see it, now you don't. *Marketing and Research Today*, May.
2. Hofmeyr, J. and Bennett, R. (1994) Double jeopardy and consumer commitment. *Canadian Journal of Marketing Research*, **13**.
3. Fader, P.S. and Schmittlein, D.C. (1993) Excess behavioural loyalty for high-share brands: deviations from the Dirichlet model for repeat purchasing. *Journal of Marketing Research*, November.

# 6

## Why Advertisers Cannot Ignore Commitment

*What is already in the mind determines what gets seen*

## We got it wrong

It has now been proven beyond any reasonable doubt that many of the traditionally accepted theories about how advertising works have been wrong. As a result of this incorrect conceptualization, much of the investment in advertising by marketers has been wasted.

By adopting the philosophy of commitment-led marketing, we can quantify just how much is wasted in an advertising campaign. Typically, particularly for smaller brands, the wastage in national advertising campaigns is significant, usually exceeding half of the adspend.

In tandem with the incorrect conceptualization of the advertising process has been the incorrect evaluation of the effectiveness of advertising. Over the years, many 'creatives' in advertising agencies have come to loathe marketing researchers who evaluate their advertising, feeling that many campaigns have been incorrectly condemned to the trash heap. Our research shows that, in many cases, the creatives were right. The researchers got it wrong.

In this chapter we will discuss the traditional thinking of the past, pointing out some of the fallacies. After that, we propose an alternative model of advertising, as well as suggesting more appropriate ways of testing the effectiveness of advertising. We then outline how advertising planning should take place, taking the commitment of consumers into account.

We also discuss some of the issues surrounding advertising currently being debated by academics and practitioners, exploring their arguments and giving our views on the current debate.

Usage of a brand is the key to effective advertising, with those users who are committed to the brand being most likely to see and like advertising for the brand, as well as interpret the message in a positive way. There is a circularity in advertising which has not been fully recognized before, either in the conceptualization of advertising or in the measurement of its effectiveness. In this chapter the impact of usage and commitment on advertising will be clarified, as well as pointers given on how to plan an advertising strategy more effectively, taking commitment into account. We need to begin with the traditional thinking on advertising, exposing flaws in the logic that has traditionally been applied, before developing an alternative approach.

## Linear models of advertising

In the past, linear models of advertising were prevalent. Even today, it is probable that models such as the AIDA model of advertising are still being taught to many marketing students. The AIDA model dates back to 1898,[1] when it was developed as a model of personal selling, only being adapted later for advertising. The AIDA model suggests that consumers pass through hierarchical levels of:

- Awareness
  ↓
- Interest
  ↓
- Desire, and finally
  ↓
- Action (a sale!)

The AIDA model is typical of hierarchical models, which rely on the assumption that advertising is something that works *on* consumers. Consumers move up a hierarchy, beginning with awareness, before developing an interest in the brand. This interest is transformed into a desire to purchase and, finally, to action.

Advertising has traditionally been regarded as something that is capable of *persuading* consumers to try a brand for the first time, and of having a measurable impact on sales. Notwithstanding this, many advertising researchers only measure the awareness of advertising, as a surrogate for advertising effectiveness. They confess that they are not sure how to measure higher levels of the hierarchy with validity, but will argue that awareness of advertising is a necessary condition for the advertising to have any effect at all, and hence use this as their yardstick for success.

An additional complicating factor is the difficulty of extricating the effects of advertising from other factors which impact on sales. For this reason, the net effect of advertising on sales is usually difficult to quantify, unless a controlled experiment is conducted, which is usually impractical for everyday purposes. If one were to conduct such an experiment, all marketing variables would have to be held constant in two regions which are identical, with the only variable in the marketing mix allowed to vary being advertising weight. It is extremely difficult to find regions which match exactly, as well as being able to control all variables other than advertising to ensure that the differential effect of advertising is being correctly measured. So, most marketers are stuck with a measure of ad awareness to evaluate the effectiveness of their advertising, sometimes together with a measure of 'liking'. Pre/post measures of persuasion, although popular in the USA in particular, have yet to gain global acceptance in terms of their validity.

Despite the popularity of hierarchical models of advertising, few, if any, researchers have been able to provide convincing evidence that these hierarchical models exist. Although appealing conceptually, they remain elusive in terms of their validation.

One of the more provocative, effective speakers on marketing platforms is Don Schultz of the Medill School of Journalism at NorthWestern University, Chicago. We first heard Don speak at a conference in San Diego at the 1994 Attitude Research and Behavioral Research Conference, where he delivered a paper entitled 'Attitudinal segmentation is dead!'.[2] At one point in his presentation, he delivered a scathing attack on traditional communication models and challenged anybody in the packed audience to come up with proof of a hierarchy of effects in advertising. Nobody took up his challenge.

Other researchers have come to similar conclusions, albeit looking at the problem in different ways. John Deighton of Harvard University, together with Caroline Henderson and Scott Neslin, investigated the impact of advertising on sales, using scanner panel data.[3] Scanner panels record the actual behaviour of a panel of consumers, in terms of their purchases. Their advertising consumption is monitored via meters attached to their television sets. Using this data, the ads to which they have been exposed on television are recorded, together with their purchasing patterns, which can then be correlated to examine the impact, if any, of advertising on brand choice.

> **"Despite the popularity of hierarchical models of advertising, few, if any, researchers have been able to provide convincing evidence that these hierarchical models exist."**

Deighton *et al.* found that advertising appeared to do little to change the repeat purchase probability of those who had just purchased the brand. They concluded that it appeared as if advertising was *reminding* those who had not recently bought the brand of its existence and attributes. Those who had bought the brand recently did not need this reminder. An important finding of their research was the need to incorporate advertising/ usage interactions in models of advertising effectiveness. Without these interactions, there was an implicit assumption that the effect of advertising was the same on somebody who had just bought the brand as it was for somebody who had just bought another brand. The evidence that they gathered in their experiment suggested that this was not the case.

Agreeing with these researchers is Andrew Ehrenberg of the South Bank University, London. Ehrenberg, one of the most respected research academics internationally, talks about the 'nudging' effect of advertising, rather than the persuasive effect of advertising.[4] To replace traditional hierarchical models, he proposes what he calls the ATR model of advertising, as follows:

- Awareness
    ↓
- Trial
    ↓
- Reinforcement/Reassurance

He suggests that advertising plays a role in promoting awareness of a brand, after which trial takes place. Advertising nudges consumers towards their next purchase, providing a measure of reinforcement for brand choice. However, he does not believe that advertising is 'persuasive' in the strong sense.

None of these researchers subscribes to a linear model of advertising or a hierarchy of effects.

# Where advertising works best

Our fascination with advertising started independently of our interest in commitment. In the late 1980s, a client approached us to help her understand what appeared to be a contradiction in research results. A TV campaign was being flighted for an established deodorant brand with a rather small market share. Prior to flighting the commercial, it had been exposed (in its finished form) to focus groups. The reaction of these focus groups had been positive. In terms of marketing objectives, the brand manager was satisfied that the advertising agency's execution of the ad was on brief. Subsequent to launch, sales were satisfactory, but the marketing team was still unsure just how effective the ad campaign had been.

> **"Advertising nudges consumers towards their next purchase, providing a measure of reinforcement for brand choice."**

Quantitative research was commissioned in order to measure the relative impact of the commercial (post-launch) compared to other commercials in the same product category. The results of this research indicated that the effectiveness of the campaign, based on ad recall, was below the norm for the category. The research supplier recommended that a significant amount of additional funding be invested in the campaign, in order for it to achieve the norm.

So, there was a conundrum. Qualitative research findings, as well as actual sales, indicated that the campaign was satisfactory, but the quantitative research findings disagreed. The question was: which research was right – the qualitative research, which was in line with the marketing team's gut feel, or the quantitative research, conducted after the launch of the commercial, which indicated that it was relatively ineffective at reaching its target audience?

The methodology which was used for the quantitative research consisted of interviewing a random sample of 100 housewives every week, over a period of six weeks, beginning in the second week of the campaign.

The questions asked were simple. The respondent was asked whether she recalled seeing a TV commercial for the brand 'recently', and if so, the content that could be recalled. She was also asked how much she 'liked' the commercial.

Central to the research supplier's approach was the contrasting of the noting or awareness scores for the commercial against the norm for the category. It was on this criterion that the effectiveness of campaigns was judged. The six data points (from six weeks of data collection) were used to fit a mathematical model, which related awareness of the advertising to the advertising spend, as well as the weekly decay rate in awareness. Using this simple model the researcher was able to calculate the amount of additional funds that would have to be spent in order for ad awareness to achieve the norm for the product category. Here is the form of the equation that was used:

$$\text{Ad Awareness}_t = a + b \times \text{GRPs} + c \times \text{Ad Awareness}_{t-1}$$

The equation shows that ad awareness in week $t$ is a function of a base level of awareness that exists in the absence of gross rating points (the coefficient $a$), plus a multiple of GRPs (coefficient $b$), plus a carry-over of ad awareness from the previous week (represented by the coefficient $c$). Using the equation, different amounts of GRPs can be compared in order to ascertain the degree of ad awareness that is likely to be achieved. The impact of the commercial is largely measured by the coefficient $b$, which quantifies the increase in advertising recall per gross rating point.

Here is an example of how the equation is applied, using hypothetical values for $a$, $b$ and $c$. In practice, the model would produce these coefficients:

$$\text{Ad Awareness}_t = 10 + 0.2 \text{ GRPs} + 0.9 \text{ Ad Awareness }_{t-1}$$

Hence, if GRPs were at a level of 20, and, in the previous week, 30% of consumers were aware of advertising for the brand, then advertising for the current week would be predicted to be:

$$\begin{aligned}
\text{Ad Awareness}_t &= 10 + 0.2 \times 20 + 0.9 \times 30 \\
&= 10 + 4 + 27 \\
&= 41\%
\end{aligned}$$

The research supplier's recommendations to increase campaign support were duly accepted. More funds were invested in a second campaign burst, in an attempt to boost the noting scores. During the second flighting, the same quantitative research methodology was used. However, the campaign still failed to achieve the norm for the category.

We were asked to examine all the relevant data and to provide an explanation. Our initial investigation sent us off on an intellectual wild goose chase. The commercial was one with low copy but a high image content. It was dreamy in feel. Branding was not overtly strong. This, we thought, was the problem.

Because the quantitative research prompted awareness of the commercial by mentioning the name of the brand to the respondent tele-phonically, the visual images which would have served as a better cue for advertising recall were absent. It was for this reason that the commercial was underperforming in terms of (prompted) recall. We could think of no other explanation. A visual prompt would have been significantly better than a simple verbal prompt, resulting in recognition, rather than recall.

Butch expended a significant amount of intellectual energy on researching the impact of low-copy versus high-copy commercials on noting, and subsequently presented a paper entitled 'In the mind, out of sight'[5] at our local research industry conference. However, he was not entirely comfortable with his explanation, which relied very much on left brain/right brain theory, which had not been fully validated. That aside, the analysis did not solve the problem of determining just when a low-copy television commercial, high in image, would be judged effective.

It took a couple of years for a more convincing explanation to present itself. We had undertaken a major usage and attitude study for a local retailer. The results of the study had not been flattering for our client. Some time after the study, the marketing director called and said, 'You'd better take another look at those results of yours. We have just com-missioned another study, with far more positive results'.

We asked him to send us the results of the other study, so that we could find out what was causing the difference. When we received the report from the competitive company, we went through the usual steps of examining the questionnaire and sample design. Although the sample design was supposed to produce a representative sample of all shoppers, the sample that had been achieved was strongly biased.

Whereas in reality only about 5% of all shoppers were regular customers at our client's stores, the fieldworkers had somehow managed to recruit a sample of respondents of whom more than 50% regularly shopped there.

As a result, all of the measurements regarding the client's retail chain were inflated and dramatically more positive than the findings from the representative sample of shoppers that we had initially interviewed. This was the first time that the impact of usage on research results had struck us so forcefully. Users of a brand react more positively to any question about the brand than do non-users.

Immediately, we remembered the conundrum of the past. The correct explanation was now blindingly obvious. The deodorant brand had a very small share of the market. Because it had a small share, random samples of housewives would include relatively few brand users. This would automatically depress all scores for the brand. It was almost impossible for a small brand to achieve the norm for the category. For a large brand, however, beating the norm for ad awareness was relatively simple, as a large brand would have the advantage of having far more users in a random sample, biasing their results positively. This was the first time that we fully recognized the impact of usage on advertising effectiveness and evaluation.

# The relationship between brand usage and advertising effectiveness

Few researchers appear to comment on this fact in the research literature. Apart from the paper by Deighton *et al.*, already alluded to, one of the few is David Stewart, who, in a paper entitled 'Advertising in a slow-growth economy',[6] argued strongly for the conceptualization of advertising as being primarily effective for users of a brand, rather than having any impact of note on non-users. However, the basis for his stance is more related to the difficulty of mature brands growing in mature economies than anything else.

Many marketers have yet to recognize the impact of brand usage on advertising testing. We continually encounter marketers who have commissioned studies in which advertising campaigns have been incorrectly condemned by the research supplier. If you are using quantitative advertising techniques to measure the effectiveness of your advertising, using representative samples of consumers to whom the commercial has been exposed, these are the implications:

- The bigger your brand share, the more users of your brand you will have in the sample, and hence the higher the liking and noting scores will be for the campaign.
- Users of a brand are more likely to recall advertising for the brand than are non-users.
- In the same way, users of a brand are more likely to 'like' the commercial than are non-users.

> **"Many marketers have yet to recognize the impact of brand usage on advertising testing."**

Figure 6.1 shows a typical example of this type of finding.

When it comes to recall, our research has indicated that, on average, brand users are approximately 50% more likely to recall the brand's advertising than are non-users.[7] This is something which is easy for marketers to investigate in research studies that have been carried out in the past. If you do have data measuring the effect of your advertising, ask the research supplier to analyse the reaction to the advertising within user and non-user segments. In most cases, you should find notable differences. We do come across campaigns that have the same effect across all consumer segments. However, these campaigns are in the minority.

> **"Brand users are approximately 50% more likely to recall the brand's advertising than are non-users."**

So, what about small brands? Small brands, with a share less than the average for the product category, will typically underperform advertising norms for the category. Having fewer users, they will have fewer respondents in any randomly selected sample of respondents. Accordingly, as they have fewer players on the home team, they will achieve lower

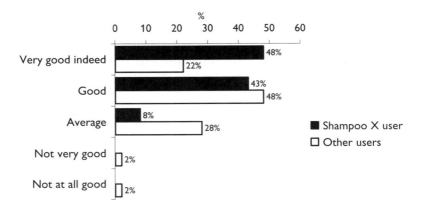

i.e. 48% of shampoo X users thought that shampoo X advertising was 'very good indeed' compared to only 22% of users of other brands.

**Figure 6.1**  *Overall reaction to shampoo X ad*

noting and liking scores. These lower scores can be completely independent of the execution of the commercial, simply reflecting the make-up of the sample interviewed.

Table 6.1 presents a recent example from the detergent market in the UK showing the relationship between the brand used most often and ad recall. For each brand, it is clear that users of the brand are more likely to be aware of the advertising than are users of other brands.

> **"Small brands, with a share less than the average for the product category, will typically underperform advertising norms for the category."**

It can be seen in the table that 41% of consumers who use Ariel powder most often are aware of its advertising. However, only 29% of consumers who use Surf powder most often are aware of the same advertising. One of the most striking examples of the impact of usage is found when examining the effectiveness of the advertising for Surf powder: 47% of consumers who use Surf powder are aware of the advertising for their brand, compared to only 23% of consumers who use Persil powder most often.

If one were to create two identical TV commercials, for two different brands in the same category, the brand with the higher brand share would achieve the higher advertising effectiveness scores, if liking and noting were the criteria for success.

**Table 6.1** *What percentage of customers using a brand of laundry detergent most often are aware of the brand's advertising?*

| Avertising awareness | Most often usage | | | | | |
|---|---|---|---|---|---|---|
| | Ariel powder % | Ariel liquid % | Bold powder % | Daz powder % | Persil powder % | Surf powder % |
| Ariel powder | 41 | 30 | 33 | 32 | 28 | 29 |
| Ariel liquid | 23 | 39 | 22 | 22 | 20 | 17 |
| Bold powder | 46 | 41 | 55 | 42 | 47 | 40 |
| Daz powder | 46 | 50 | 45 | 60 | 48 | 49 |
| Persil powder | 24 | 21 | 23 | 24 | 30 | 20 |
| Surf powder | 27 | 29 | 28 | 24 | 23 | 47 |

*Source*: RSBG/Taylor Nelson Sofres non-proprietary study, 1999.

# Making sense of nonsense

Much of what we are saying here might be obvious to some readers. To prove that it is not obvious to everybody in the advertising industry, here is an anecdote.

When Butch taught mathematical statistics, he used to show the graph shown in Figure 6.2 to his first-year students. The graph shows the relationship between the number of babies born and the number of lamp-posts in the world, going back for many years. We cannot remember where this example was originally gleaned from, but it is safe to assume that, over the years, this sort of relationship would exist. The learning point of the graph was that it appeared that the number of babies born every year depended on the number of lamp-posts. The number of babies is shown on the vertical axis, which is the axis traditionally used for the dependent variable. So, babies depend on lamp-posts. Hence, it would seem that an easy way of dealing with population explosion is to go out one night and cut down all the lamp-posts. With no lamp-posts, all births would cease immediately. This obviously nonsensical example was used to teach students the concept of spurious correlations. It is fairly obvious that as populations get bigger year by year, more babies are born and more lamp-posts are put up in residential suburbs as they develop. The learning point of this exercise was to instil a cynical approach to relationships where causality was being inferred. In statistics, it is not possible to prove

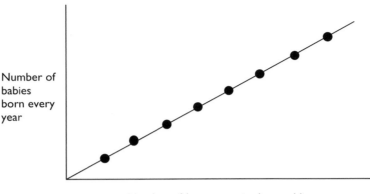

**Figure 6.2**  *The relationship between babies and lamp-posts*

causality from simple charts such as these. However, causality is often inferred.

> **"If one were to create two identical TV commercials, for two different brands in the same category, the brand with the higher brand share would achieve the higher advertising effectiveness scores, if liking and noting were the criteria for success."**

As human beings, we have an amazing ability to make sense out of nonsense. For babies and lamp-posts, it is obvious that we are dealing with a nonsensical example. However, the world of marketing provides us with a more up-to-date example which would appear to fall into exactly the same trap, this time provided by a paper presented in New York in 1998.[8] This paper was presented to specially invited guests, with the objective of presenting the views of experts on advertising. One of the findings of this paper was that ad likeability is a good predictor of advertising recall. Figure 6.3 is one of the key charts from the paper, used to validate the researcher's point of view.

In this paper, the liking and noting scores of more than 10 000 commercials were analysed. It was found that there was a strong correlation between ad recall and ad liking. From this finding, it was deduced that liking *causes* awareness (reminiscent of lamp-posts causing babies). Representative samples of consumers were interviewed and asked which TV

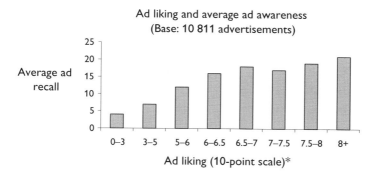

**Figure 6.3**   *The supposed relationship between 'liking' and 'awareness' of a brand*

Source: Du Plessis (1998). Reproduced by permission of Telmar Group Inc.

commercials they recalled having seen recently, prompted via the brand name, as well as how much they liked these commercials. They were not asked whether they were users of the brands for which they were questioned. The results of the research thus become predictable. Notwithstanding the impressiveness of having tested thousands of commercials, those brands which enjoy a high brand share *automatically* produce higher liking *and* noting scores, because they will have more users in the sample. The more users in the sample, the higher the noting score will be as users are more likely to 'see' advertising of 'their' brands. Equivalently, the more likely it is that the liking score will be high, as users are more likely to 'like' the commercial than are non-users.

Although the paper quite correctly identifies a correlation between liking and noting, the inference that there is a causal relationship is impossible to justify without usage being taken into account as a significant contributor to awareness and liking scores.

> **"Brands which enjoy a high brand share *automatically* produce higher liking *and* noting scores."**

We remain unconvinced that the more likeable the advertising, the higher the ad recall. If researchers did want to prove this hypothesis showing a *causal* relationship, they would have to examine the reaction of users and non-users of the brand separately, in line with our findings, and the recommendations of Deighton *et al.* To ignore usage when evaluating advertising recall and liking scores makes the findings highly questionable.

# The impact of prior experience on the decoding of communication

The OJ Simpson case provides us with an excellent example of how our prior experiences impact on our decoding of information. For many months, just about every American citizen watched TV incessantly, enthralled by the OJ Simpson case. The question on everybody's lips was: 'Guilty or not guilty?'.[9]

At the conclusion of the trial, perceptions as to OJ Simpson's guilt were absolutely clear cut. African Americans said 'Not guilty', while white Americans said 'Guilty'.

Although all Americans were exposed to exactly the same set of stimuli, the processing of the information was very different, dependent on the beliefs and experiences already resident in their minds, according to their experience with the justice system in America.

Advertising is no exception to this rule. Your prior experience of the brand affects the way in which the message is received and decoded. If you do not know what the prior relationship is that the consumer had with the brand, which is usually dependent on experiences with the brand in all its facets, you are unable to evaluate the effectiveness of your communication.

Brattish children provide another nice example of the way in which we see the same thing completely differently. We have all been exposed to situations where a small child wreaks havoc in somebody else's sitting room, threatening to demolish everything in sight, while the parents look on adoringly. Adults who are not related to the child see the situation very differently. They see a child who needs disciplining, in the firmest possible way. The parents on the other hand, view everything that the child does with intense pride, and see the child's antics as proof of his or her energy, brilliance, entertainment value and so on.

> **"If you do not know what the prior relationship is that the consumer had with the brand, which is usually dependent on experiences with the brand in all its facets, you are unable to evaluate the effectiveness of your communication."**

Again, we have the same stimulus – a child behaving in a certain way. We see exactly the same thing, but the way in which we process what we are seeing depends on our prior relationship and experiences.

## So, how does advertising work?

A little digression is in order here, before describing the conceptualization of advertising that we believe to be correct.

Western thinking favours linearity and attempting to understand causality. In contrast, Eastern thinking favours circularity and the acceptance of interaction, without necessarily attempting to extricate causality. An example of this stark difference in conceptualization can be found in the concept of time. In the West we conceptualize time as being linear. We are writing this in 2000. Last year was 1999 and next year is 2001. 1999 will never reappear. We conceptualize time as a straight line. We stand in the present, with the past stretching behind us and the future stretching ahead of us.

In the East, this conceptualization of time is foreign. Time is not linear, it is circular. This year is the year of the dragon, which reappears every twelve years. Day dissolves into night, which dissolves into day. The seasons revolve, returning every year. We are created from universal energy and return to universal energy. Our existence is circular. All things are interrelated.

Yin-yang theory provides a handy platform for the conceptualization of how advertising works. The yin-yang symbol looks like this:

For those of you who are not sure what this symbol means, let us explain.

The symbolism of the diagram is profound. The dark shaded area represents yin, which is feminine and negative, while the light area represents yang, which is masculine and positive. The diagram illustrates that yin and yang are interrelated, and that one is always present in the other. In yang there is always yin, and vice versa. Implicit in positivity is negativity. Implicit in femininity is masculinity. You cannot extract a single element and examine it without taking the other into account. But this is what we have been attempting to do with advertising.

How do we apply this circularity and interactiveness in thinking to advertising? Here is how:

- Somebody who sees the advertising for your brand is more likely to use your brand;
- But somebody who uses your brand is more likely to see your advertising.

Usage and the 'reception' of advertising are inextricably interlinked. Our recall of advertising is related to our usage of the brand. Usage is the fertile soil in which advertising grows. The more users your brand has, the more effective your advertising will be. The effectiveness of your advertising is as interlinked with the relationship between consumers and your brand, as yin is interlinked with yang.

## How consumers filter out advertising

**?** *Why is it that users of a brand are more likely to receive the advertising message than non-users?*

> **"The more users your brand has, the more effective your advertising will be."**

Jerome Bruner[10] provides us with insight into this phenomenon. Our brains are extremely selective in what they process. Every day they are bombarded by millions of stimuli. To allow all of these stimuli into our minds would result in an 'overheating' of our brains. We simply could not cope. So, we have governing mechanisms which decide which stimuli are relevant to us. A simple example illustrates this.

We have all visited somebody who stays in an apartment situated next to a noisy road or railway line. When the first train thunders by, and the entire building shakes, our question to the occupant is always the same: 'How can you live in a place this noisy?'. And the answer is always the same: 'To be honest, I don't hear it any more'. That is the reality. They actually do not hear it any more. It is not that they have become accustomed to the noise and that they hear it, but do not mind its intrusion.

The incoming signal to the brain of the noise of the train is deemed unnecessary after a certain amount of time spent in the noisy apartment. The signal is 'cut' before it can make any impact as a stimulus.

And that's what happens with advertising. A lot of consumers 'don't hear it any more'. The commercial does not leave any trace in the consumer's mind. The signal is deemed irrelevant, and is cut off before it has time to burrow its way into our memory.

> **"So, we have governing mechanisms which decide which stimuli are relevant to us."**

As we attempt to build a new conceptualization of advertising, it is perhaps time to pause. Eventually, we will be describing the implications of this for commitment, but we are starting at the beginning in terms of constructing a model. So far we have seen that:

- A lot of quantitative advertising testing arrives at the wrong conclusions;
- Users of a brand are more likely to *recall* the brand's advertising than are non-users;
- Users of a brand are more likely to *like* the brand's advertising than are non-users.

What are the implications of this for mass media advertising? The larger your brand, the more effective your advertising will be, because there are more 'receivers' tuned to your message than if you had a small brand. Thus, a large brand spending a million dollars gets significantly more return on its investment than does a small brand spending a million dollars. Many marketers believe that their share of voice should match their share of market, when it comes to budgeting for their advertising spend. This is incorrect. The smaller your brand, the more your share of voice should *exceed* your market share. As you have fewer 'receivers' out there, you need to try much harder than the big brands if you want your advertising to achieve the same sort of results.

> **"The smaller your brand, the more your share of voice should *exceed* your market share."**

## How is advertising related to commitment?

Users are more likely than non-users to recall and like the brand's advertising. This is something which is easily verified by any marketer by examining the data from quantitative advertising tests. But we know that there are two types of users of a brand – the committed and the uncommitted.

## Advertising works best on committed brand users

Predictably, advertising is more effective among committed users than among uncommitted users. Indeed, we would argue that one of the primary functions of advertising for a mature brand is to maintain the commitment of an already committed consumer. This thinking is very much in line with Ehrenberg's concept of 'running hard to stand still'.

Figure 6.4 is an example from a study we conducted many years ago in the life assurance industry, showing how differently the same piece of communication is received by the same demographic segment of consumers, depending on the relationship they have with the brand. It can be seen that the propensity of the committed consumer to receive the advertising in a positive way is about five times that of the strongly unavailable non-user.

> **"Advertising is more effective among committed users than among uncommitted users."**

More recently, a paper was published by Rice and Bennett[11] which summarized the differences across 25 different advertising studies carried

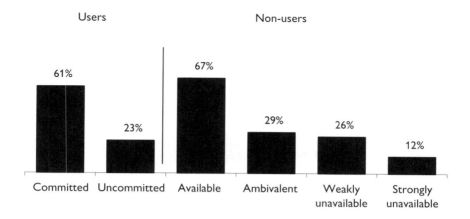

Note: 39% of the total sample liked Brand A advertising.

**Figure 6.4** *Likeability of Brand A advertising*

Source: Research Surveys Pty Ltd, South Africa.

out using the same methodology. Figure 6.5 shows some of the findings. It can be seen that 62% of committed users recall advertising for the brand to which they were committed, compared to only 46% of uncommitted users. The difference in overall reaction ('liking') is even more striking. Committed users were approximately twice as likely to 'like' the ad than uncommitted users.

Committed users of a brand often represent the majority of the net present value of the brand's revenue. Not only do they spend more on the brand, but their lifetime expectancy is far greater than that of uncommitted consumers. For this reason, it is often worthwhile formulating advertising campaigns with the single-minded objective of *maintaining* consumers' commitment. They are the foundation of the brand's continued success.

What happens when advertising is taken away? What will that do to a brand? Recently, we encountered a graphic illustration of the pitfalls of withdrawing advertising support for a successful brand. The segment of committed consumers declined from 60% of brand users in 1994 to 40% in 1998, after advertising support was withdrawn in 1995. Continuous brand health tracking showed that commitment to the brand was declining by approximately 2% per quarter. Initially, sales did not suffer.

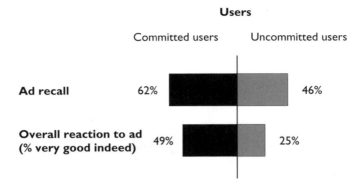

**Figure 6.5** *The responses of committed and uncommitted users to advertising*

The decline in commitment preceded the decline in sales, which inevitably followed.

> **"It is often worth while formulating advertising campaigns with the single-minded objective of *maintaining* consumers' commitment."**

In line with the research that Ehrenberg has conducted, we are convinced that successful mature brands need advertising to hold them in place. This is the way in which advertising should be conceptualized and formulated. Often, a successful campaign will result in *no* change. It will have maintained the commitment of already committed consumers.

A cynical marketer might argue that it is unnecessary to devote significant marketing support to committed consumers, as they would stay committed regardless. As we have already pointed out, this is not necessarily so.

Advertising is particularly inappropriate when a significant segment of consumers are uncommitted because of dissatisfaction with the brand. Advertising will often remind them of how much they dislike the brand, and make them even less committed. If the brand has a large segment of uncommitted consumers, the most important task is to understand the reasons for this low commitment, and then manage the relationship appropriately.

> **"Advertising is particularly inappropriate when a significant segment of consumers are uncommitted because of dissatisfaction with the brand."**

# Unavailable non-users

In the past, marketers were fond of quoting Lord Leverhulme, who said that half of advertising was wasted but that nobody knew which half. We have progressed a lot since that pronouncement. We can now accurately quantify the wastage in an advertising campaign, simply by examining the size of the segment unavailable to the brand. Following our argument outlined above, the unavailable segment represents the rocky ground of advertising. Unavailable consumers are highly unlikely to switch to the brand in the near term, regardless of the advertising content or weight. They are the least likely to see and like the advertising, and even if they are aware of it, it is unlikely to have any impact on their attitudes or behaviour.

It is not unusual for us to encounter brands for which as many as 90% of consumers are unavailable. What this would mean is that, with the current positioning of the brand, 90% of the advertising budget expended on mass media is largely a waste of money.

> **"We can now accurately quantify the wastage in an advertising campaign, simply by examining the size of the segment unavailable to the brand."**

For any brand, a certain amount of wastage is inevitable. We have yet to encounter a brand for which all consumers in the target market are available. However, we would argue that excessive wastage is avoidable, because by knowing how many people are unavailable to your brand, you are able to quantify wastage prior to making the investment.

We are often asked what marketers do as a result of the findings of studies that measure the commitment and the availability of consumers to all brands in the market. The most frequent thing is – they stop wasting money! It is not unusual to identify brands with a sizeable unavailable segment, with the result that the media budget is reallocated, and the marketing efforts realigned, in order to take this into account. In situations such as these, it is difficult to justify advertising in national mass media. It is true that sometimes we will not know what the best alternative is. But we will know that the wastage in a mass media campaign will be so high that the existence of a better solution to the marketing problem is highly probable.

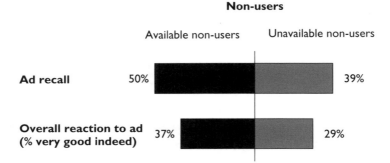

i.e. 50% of available non-users recalled advertising for the brand compared to only 39% of unavailable non-users.

**Figure 6.6**  *The responses of available and unavailable non-users to advertising*

> **"By knowing how many people are unavailable to your brand, you are able to quantify wastage prior to making the investment."**

The most difficult challenge for advertising is that of reaching the unavailable non-user. The strongly unavailables are least likely to 'see' or 'hear' the advertising. If they do see it, they are least likely to like it. They are just not interested. The brands to which they are committed satisfy their needs. Advertising is ill equipped to break through this barrier. More findings from the 25 advertising tests referred to earlier are shown in Figure 6.6, contrasting some of the responses of available non-users to those of unavailable non-users.

If advertising is relatively ineffective at changing an unavailable consumer into one who is available, what can the marketer do to increase availability among non-users? Our experience has been that forced trial (sampling) is one of the best strategies for improving the availability to the brand of these consumers.

> **"The most difficult challenge for advertising is that of reaching the unavailable non-user."**

We have already seen that usage is the key to improving the effectiveness of advertising. Hence, product sampling among non-users of the brand will improve the effectiveness of advertising significantly.

# Available non-users

The available non-user is often the consumer most receptive to advertising for the brand. However, the value of advertising to these consumers differs. In packaged goods, they typically represent only a small segment of consumers, with a comparatively low value, not justifying significant investment in communicating to them. The reason that there are very few available consumers in packaged goods categories is because, unless distribution and availability on shelf is really a problem, those who are available to the brand are already including it in their repertoires. Only a very small percentage of consumers will not yet have done so. In contrast, in a market such as the car market, it is conceivable that the available segment could be significant in size, particularly for new models which have just been launched. However, there is no way of quantifying the size of the available segment without conducting the necessary research and hence deciding the wisdom of targeting advertising at this segment.

In summary, then:

- Advertising usually works best on consumers who are already committed to the brand, and non-users who are already available to the brand.
- It is least effective among consumers who are not using the brand and who are unavailable to it. Typically, unavailability will be caused by commitment to the brands that these consumers are already using. Because of their commitment to the brands they use, selective perception will not allow the competitive advertising message to break through. Unless trial of the product can be achieved (by whatever means), advertising is unlikely to be a sound investment.

> **"Product sampling among non-users of the brand will improve the effectiveness of advertising significantly."**

# New product advertising

A question that frequently springs to mind among marketers when exposed to this thinking for the first time is: how does this tie in with new product launches? Well, it is fairly obvious that if you are launching a new brand or product, you have no users, by definition. Hence, this is the most difficult challenge in terms of marketing communication. What you should set as the objective of your launch advertising is to make consumers *aware* of your new brand, and little more. For this you need advertising that communicates clearly, putting the brand up-front, that goes for reach rather than frequency, letting consumers know there is a new brand out there. Essentially, all you are doing is publicizing the brand. Only after a significant number of brand users have been acquired does classic brand-building and brand-sustaining advertising make sense.

> **"What you should set as the objective of your launch advertising is to make consumers *aware* of your new brand, and little more."**

Too often, advertising is incorrectly conceptualized when launching a new product. It is the *brand* itself that is attractive or unattractive to consumers, not the advertising. A criticism that we would have of a lot of launch advertising is two-fold:

- First, a lot of launch advertising is too cluttered, and the brand *gestalt* is lost in the clever executional ideas embodied in the campaign.
- Second, classic brand building is embarked upon at launch, when it does not make sense, as there are no users to receive the advertising in that way. Usage of the brand is necessary for the advertising to make sense and to be properly digested.

It will often be the case that advertising, on its own, is one of the least effective and most expensive ways of getting a consumer to buy your brand for the first time. There are many instances of successful brands in which a rapid sales increase was achieved without any advertising at all. In packaged goods, the consumer is often attracted to the product purely because of the look of the pack.

As an example, when Salon Selectives, Revlon's shampoo range, was launched in South Africa, there was no launch advertising at all. But the brand proved successful. Consumers were attracted to the brand

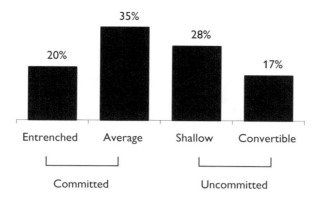

... But how does this impact on attitudes?

i.e. 20% of all Comstar's customers for local calls are entrenched customers of Comstar.

**Figure 6.7** *Commitment to Comstar*

because of the impact of the pack design of the range on shelf visibility. Its excellent non-verbal cues, as well as the way in which the range stood out on the shelf, encouraged trial in a category in which brand switching is fairly frequent. Only once a number of consumers were using the brand was classic brand-building advertising launched by the marketing team.

> "It will often be the case that advertising, on its own, is one of the least effective and most expensive ways of getting a consumer to buy your brand for the first time."

# A case study

The following example uses disguised data, with fictitious brand names. However, the findings are factually accurate.

This was a market in which there were only two major telecommunications competitors, Comstar and Telecom. Commitment to Comstar was fairly high, with 55% of its customers being committed (Figure 6.7). Committed customers tend to be insulated from competitive messages.

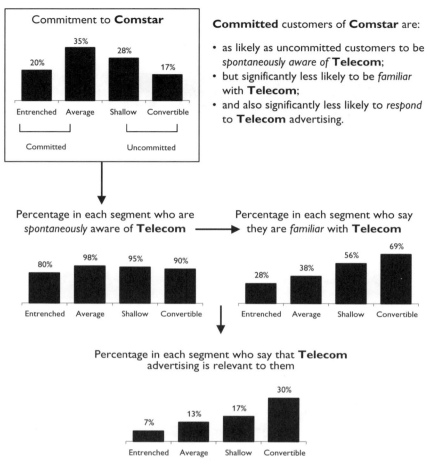

Committed customers of **Comstar** are:

- as likely as uncommitted customers to be *spontaneously aware of* **Telecom**;
- but significantly less likely to be *familiar* with **Telecom**;
- and also significantly less likely to *respond* to **Telecom** advertising.

i.e. 80% of Comstar's entrenched customers are 'spontaneously aware' of Telecom, but only 28% say they are 'familiar' with Telecom.

**Figure 6.8**  *Committed customers tend to be insulated from competitive messages*

This is illustrated in Figure 6.8 which shows how the relevance of competitive advertising increases as commitment to Comstar decreases. As commitment decreases, the decoding receptors for *competitive* information are opened up, allowing competitive messages to be recalled, and to be processed in a way more likely to make the message relevant.

Committed customers find their own brand's advertising relevant and persuasive, as can be seen in Figure 6.9. Because committed customers are unfamiliar with the competitor, they are significantly less likely than

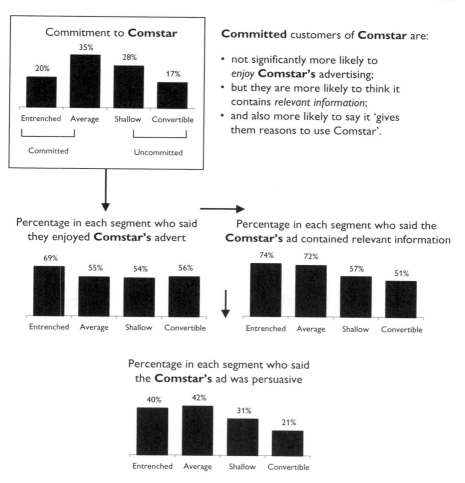

i.e. 69% of Comstar's entrenched customers say they 'enjoyed' Comstar's advertising; 74% of them say it contained 'relevant' information.

**Figure 6.9** *Committed customers find their own brand's advertising relevant and persuasive*

uncommitted customers to form an opinion about competitive prices (Figure 6.10). Committed customers are more likely to give Comstar good ratings than uncommitted customers and believe that Comstar offers value for money. This is illustrated in Figure 6.11.

This is a neat example illustrating the circularity in marketing communication. The nature of our relationship with brands, which is based on our past experiences, impacts on our propensity to receive information for all brands in the market, as well as our propensity to like what we hear. In

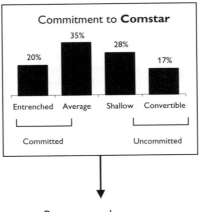

Percentage who say . . .

i.e. 44% of Comstar's convertible customers say Telecom has the lowest prices
for long distance calls and 39% of Comstar's convertible customers say Telecom has
the lowest prices for local calls.

**Figure 6.10** *Because committed customers are unfamiliar with the competitor, they are significantly less likely than uncommitted customers to form an opinion about competitor prices*

addition, the message of the communication is decoded in different ways according to prior experiences.

The case illustrates:

- How commitment impacts on brand knowledge: committed customers are less interested in information about competitive brands.
- How commitment impacts on customers' own brand's adverts: committed customers are more likely to rate their brand's adverts positively.

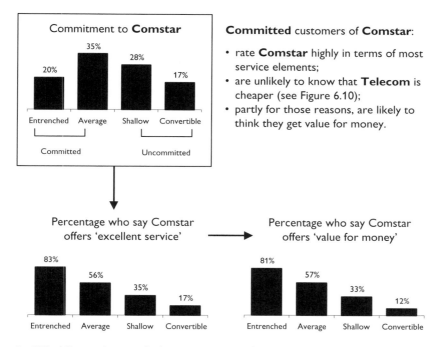

Committed customers of **Comstar**:

- rate **Comstar** highly in terms of most service elements;
- are unlikely to know that **Telecom** is cheaper (see Figure 6.10);
- partly for those reasons, are likely to think they get value for money.

i.e. 83% of Comstar's entrenched customers say that Comstar provides 'excellent service'.

**Figure 6.11** *Committed customers are more likely to give Comstar good ratings than uncommitted customers, and believe that Comstar offers 'value for money'*

- How commitment impacts on brand ratings: committed customers tend to have more positive attitudes towards their brands.

# The strong versus the weak theory of advertising

A debate which is currently of relevant interest is whether advertising conforms to what has been labelled the weak theory or strong theory of advertising. Two proponents of the theories are John Philip Jones[12] of Syracuse University, who has aligned himself with the strong theory, and Andrew Ehrenberg, who has aligned himself with the weak theory. Jones, in particular, has come under fierce attack in certain quarters in the industry. One of the best critiques of his methodology was that published by

**Table 6.2**   *The two theories of advertising*

|  | **Strong theory** | **Weak theory** |
|---|---|---|
| Main aim | Brand building | Brand maintenance |
| Consumers are hypothesized to be: | Loyals or switchers (i.e. monogamous or promiscuous) | Habitual split loyalties (polygamous, with steady ongoing relationships) |
| Brands are hypothesized to be: | Differentiated | Distinctive but substitutable (Distinguished mainly by name and pack) |
| Ad content | Aims to persuade via reasons or mood | Provides publicity for the brand: 'Here I am' |
| Timing | Mostly short-term | Mostly medium or long term |
| Process | Near-instant conversion | Awareness → Trial Reinforcement and nudging, rather than persuasion |

Leonard Lodish[13] in 1997 in which his methodologies were found to be significantly flawed, at very least giving pause to accepting some of his findings.

The difference between the strong and weak theories can be summarized as shown in Table 6.2, according to Ehrenberg.

According to the weak theory, advertising is necessary to hold the brand in place. Paradoxically, proponents of the weak theory, including ourselves, argue more vehemently for ongoing advertising than do proponents of the strong theory, who argue that advertising is persuasive and can produce sales, even if only in the short term.

Ehrenberg argues strongly that, for most brands, the pertinent issue in advertising is one of salience, rather than differentiation.[14] He argues that brands are mostly seen to be the same by their users. Supporting his view is an example from a recent banking study that we were involved in, in which three major banks in the industry were contrasted in terms of their image. Marketing researchers often present image attribute matrices showing the relevant strengths and weaknesses of the brands in the marketplace. However, they do not always examine the perspective of each brand as seen by its *users*. By looking at the data in this form, we produced Table 6.3. It can be seen that there is only a marginally negative bias in Bank A's attribute associations. Interestingly, Bank A had slightly

**Table 6.3** *How each bank is perceived by its customers*

| Staff | Bank A % | Bank B % | Bank C % |
|---|---|---|---|
| Handle queries efficiently at the branch | 86 | 85 | 89 |
| Resolve problems quickly | 75 | 84 | 81 |
| Branch staff are competent | 83 | 83 | 87 |
| Keep you informed on developments | 75 | 77 | 77 |
| Handle queries efficiently over the phone | 65 | 75 | 71 |
| Take time to offer financial planning advice | 62 | 66 | 65 |
| Provide information on how to manage a cheque account | 66 | 68 | 62 |
| Are committed to quality | 77 | 85 | 84 |

Base: users of each bank.

fewer committed users than the other two banks. That aside, the numbers are remarkably similar, supporting Ehrenberg's view. Essentially, each bank's customers see it in the same way as customers of other banks. Hence, these banks are not differentiated in terms of image. This finding has been confirmed on a broader scale in a paper presented by Jane Campbell[15] in which she found that commitment was one of the best predictors of the level of attribute association in image matrices. Putting it another way, much of the variation in the level of image attribute associations with brands is due to the relationship between users and the brands they use, rather than due to significant differences in the image of the brands themselves.

Over the years, we have been struck by the intellectual energy that has been expended by marketing departments and advertising agencies in order to find an attribute which differentiates the brand from the competition. Ehrenberg makes the strong point that, should a differentiating attribute be found and prove to be relevant to consumers, it will only be a matter of months before a competitor copies the differentiating attribute. Ehrenberg argues in favour of 'here I am' advertising rather than advertising predicated on differentiating attributes, be they image related or 'personality values'.

> **"Much of the variation in the level of image attribute associations with brands is due to the relationship between users and the brands they use, rather than due to significant differences in the image of the brands themselves."**

These are theories which 'mostly' apply. Thus, exceptions do exist, but marketers have to take cognisance of the probabilities of success in their marketing activities. For the majority of markets, we feel that it is far more likely that the weak theory of advertising will apply than the strong theory.

Ehrenberg also makes the distinction about advertising whose primary purpose is to convey information. An example of this would be the announcement of a new brand, or a functional feature which was previously not incorporated into the brand, for example, air bags. It is important to distinguish between the ability of advertising to convey information and its ability to strengthen brand image, or attempt to change the perception of brands on certain attributes. Our experience has convinced us that the task of shifting the perception of a brand on image attributes is a daunting one, and is seldom successful. When it is achieved, it will only be because of a single-minded focus on the attribute over many years.

Too often, marketing researchers recommend to marketers that they attempt to change the perception of the brand on certain dimensions or attributes. We think that a more realistic challenge would be to attempt to change the *salience* of certain attributes. It is not uncommon to find that brands have strengths on certain attributes, but that these attributes are not terribly important to consumers as reasons for brand choice. The marketing challenge is not one of changing perceptions, but increasing the importance of a dimension in the decision-making process.

Although not easy, conceptually, this approach is more likely to yield positive results than attempting to change the perception of an attribute from being a weakness to one of being a strength for the brand. Perceptions of mature brands change very slowly, if at all.

> **"Our experience has convinced us that the task of shifting the perception of a brand on image attributes is a daunting one, and is seldom successful."**

We have become pretty good at identifying what no longer works, but we still have a long way to go in terms of discovering what *does* work in terms of improving brand health. But this is what makes marketing today so intellectually challenging and satisfying on the occasions one is able to meet the challenge.

# Implications for ad testing

The implications for advertising testing are clear. If one does not know the underlying segmentation of the market, in terms of commitment and availability, quantitative advertising testing can produce completely misleading results. The larger the segment of consumers unavailable to the brand, the worse will be the advertising effectiveness scores. In the light of this, some marketers disregard the reaction of consumers unavailable to the brand to their advertising. They know that these consumers are unlikely to be acquired in the foreseeable future and, hence, their reactions to the brand's marketing activities are irrelevant. All that the unavailable consumer will do is negatively bias research results, misleading the marketer in terms of the actual effectiveness of the marketing programme.

> **"The larger the segment of consumers unavailable to the brand, the worse will be the advertising effectiveness scores."**

This approach can be incorporated into qualitative research as well. In a focus group, strongly unavailable consumers tend to react negatively to everything about the brand in question. We would recommend that they be screened from qualitative research. It is relatively straightforward to include questions designed to measure commitment and availability on the recruitment questionnaires used when selecting respondents for the focus group. An analysis of these responses will identify those consumers who are unavailable to the brand. In some cases, unavailable consumers are particularly valuable. However, focus groups with these consumers should then be conducted with them as a homogeneous group, rather than mixing them with other consumers who have a very different relationship with the brand.

Equivalently, when conducting focus groups among brand users, the distinction should be made between those who are committed to the brand and those who are uncommitted. In particular, if the reason for poor commitment is that brand choice doesn't matter, reactions obtained from this group will be misleading, in terms of recommended actions to be taken.

> **"In a focus group, strongly unavailable consumers tend to react negatively to everything about the brand in question."**

# A checklist for an advertising plan

These are the questions we recommend you answer when drawing up an advertising plan as part of the execution of your communication strategy.

## 1. Should you be advertising at all?

There are a number of things which will impact on your decision as to whether advertising is appropriate for your brand. One of the most important issues to consider is the question of wastage. If your brand is relatively small, it is highly unlikely that advertising in national media will be justified. This is because wastage will significantly exceed 50% of your advertising spend, because of the large size of the segment of consumers unavailable to your brand.

The other important criterion for deciding whether advertising is appropriate is your marketing objective. If your marketing objective is to *increase* sales, it is unlikely that advertising on its own, without any other marketing support, will achieve this. The market structure should be thoroughly examined, with reasons for your languishing share being identified. Advertising will seldom be a significant factor in improving sales, except under the circumstances where the brand has been ignored by the marketing team for some time.

> **"If your brand is relatively small, it is highly unlikely that advertising in national media will be justified."**

If you have a small brand, it does not mean that advertising is ruled out altogether. Although national media might be inappropriate, it is often the case that regional media can be used, as it is not unusual to find that small brands have regional strongholds or niche markets where they enjoy disproportionate strength. Hence, regional media or specialist media might provide the appropriate channels for advertising the brand.

## 2. What are the objectives of your advertising?

Above-the-line advertising works best at maintaining the commitment of an already committed consumer and encouraging available non-users to cross the threshold and become users of the brand, but not much else.

Having said this, the objective of 'holding the brand in place' is a vitally important one. Commitment needs to be nurtured and maintained. Your committed customer will pick up messages about the brand to which they are committed among the plethora of advertising messages with which they are bombarded daily. Having identified the messages of their brand, they are also more likely to 'like' the advertising.

In new markets, such as telecommunications or IT, available non-users soak up information about the brands and categories to which they are available. It is not unusual to find that available non-users are available to several brands. In this case, the brand that wins the battle in terms of top-of-mind awareness, as well as communicating ease of purchase in terms of convenience and price, wins the day. In these situations, heavy advertising spend is entirely justified.

> **"The objective of 'holding the brand in place' is a vitally important one."**

Advertising will seldom be appropriate for increasing the commitment of an uncommitted customer. Neither will it be appropriate for breaking down strong availability to your brand among non-users. If users of other brands are unavailable to your brand, your advertising will be screened out, having little impact.

If the ad campaign *is* noted by unavailable non-users, it is unlikely to have any effect on changing their attitudes. However, advertising accompanied by product sampling can be effective at changing the attitudes of non-users, but this strategy has to be applied in a selective way, due to the cost of executing such a programme.

> **"Advertising will seldom be appropriate for increasing the commitment of an uncommitted customer."**

## 3. Who is the target market?

Typically, media planners specify target markets in terms of demographics, as they are constrained by the databases at their disposal. In some countries, product usage is also available as an adjunct to demographics, significantly improving the effectiveness of the media plan. Ideally, commitment-led marketing dictates a policy of including measures of commitment in the media plan. This is not always easy to accomplish, but we predict that it will become increasingly easy.

In some countries, such as Australia, it is relatively easy to incorporate measures of commitment into the database used by media planners, because of the research services offered. Marketers are able to include proprietary questions in a media usage survey. TV viewership is fused with the usage of other media, as well as product usage, together with the answers to the proprietary questions of the marketer, providing the media planner with a unified single-source database. In these cases, one is able to specify the target market, not only in terms of demographics and product usage but also in terms of openness to the brand message. Hence, one can specify the target market as being committed consumers of the brand, or consumers who are, at the very least, not unavailable to it. Applying this principle results in significantly enhanced media effectiveness.

## 4. What is your brand positioning?

A key part of the brief to the ad agency will be the positioning you would like the brand to enjoy among its target audience. If the brand has characteristics which are truly differentiating, then the brief is a fairly simple process. However, it does become a lot more complicated if your brand is not, in fact, differentiated on intrinsic attributes, which is more likely to be the case.

The debate continues as to which theory of advertising is more applicable – the strong or weak theory. It is for you to decide which is more applicable to your category. If you support the weak theory, then the primary role of advertising is to hold a relationship in place. In this case, 'here I am' advertising is appropriate. What matters most is that the brand is pushed to the forefront of the advertising, with a positioning that is possibly more personality based than intrinsics-based.

However, if you support the strong theory of advertising, you would attempt to differentiate your brand by positioning it on one or other of the intrinsics of the product category. For this to be successful, it is almost essential that you are the brand leader in the category.

Visibility of the brand is the key to successful advertising. In too much advertising, the brand identity is swamped by 'clever' executions. Consumers remember the ad, but don't know which brand it was for. We believe that part of the brief to the agency should be an insistence on a strong brand identity. Given the fact that committed consumers will seek out their brand among competing advertising messages, it makes sense to have the brand identified as early in the commercial as possible. Too often, one sees commercials which are weakly branded, except for a discreet mention of the brand at the end of the commercial. These commercials will tend to be less successful than commercials in which the brand is clearly identified at the beginning of the commercial, as the identification of the brand opens the communication 'receivers' of the committed consumer.

> **"Visibility of the brand is the key to successful advertising."**

## 5. How do you evaluate your advertising effectiveness?

How do you evaluate whether your advertising is 'working'? The best way of doing this is to commission a continuous tracking study, measuring the commitment of your brand's users, as well as the availability of non-users on a continuous basis. Using this approach, you can identify the impact of various marketing stimuli on these key measures. However, it must be noted that a lot of successful advertising will not have any impact on commitment. It will hold it in place. But, for a successful brand, this is a significant achievement, as the brand is continually under threat from competitive brands. Hence, the commitment of consumers to your brand always runs the risk of being eroded.

One-off quantitative ad testing should be approached with caution, due to the pitfalls already described. At the very least, if quantitative ad testing is used, a distinction should be made between users and non-users of a brand, in terms of their reaction to the advertising. Even better, reactions of committed and uncommitted brand users should be contrasted, as well as those of available and unavailable non-users.

To use advertising testing that only presents results in aggregate is extremely dangerous, and can yield misguided recommendations. This is particularly the case when norms are used in order to evaluate the comparative effectiveness of the advertising campaign. Small brands will be severely prejudiced, while larger brands run the risk of being unfairly flattered, in terms of their advertising efforts.

> **"To use advertising testing that only presents results in aggregate is extremely dangerous, and can yield misguided recommendations."**

## Marketer's summary: advertising in relation to commitment

In summary, then, this chapter has attempted to describe a new conceptualization of advertising. We have pointed out that many of the advertising testing techniques used internationally are flawed, and can result in incorrect recommendations.

The fertile soil for advertising is usage. Within the commitment segments of brand users, the committed user is the one most likely to 'receive' and like the advertising. Advertising plays an invaluable role, but it is a rifle in the armoury of communication techniques, not a shotgun. Addressing the needs of the committed consumer leaves the marketer pondering on how best to communicate with the uncommitted users, and non-users, both available and unavailable. Inevitably, these decisions need to be based on the value of these segments. It is highly unlikely that any marketing campaign will address the needs of all these segments, as the funds are simply not big enough to cover them.

The task of conceptualizing communication to commitment and availability segments in terms of setting communication and marketing objectives, as well as measuring your success, is radically different to traditional approaches used in the past. But not to change will mean that the marketer is dealing with meaningless aggregates of information, with the risk of incorrect decisions being unacceptably high, and a resultant erosion of the bottom line.

The key points for marketers contained in this chapter are:

- Despite the popularity of hierarchical models of advertising, few, if any, researchers have been able to provide convincing evidence that these hierarchical models exist.

- Advertising *nudges* consumers towards their next purchase, providing a measure of reinforcement for brand choice, rather than *persuading* consumers to buy the brand. Do not rely on advertising alone to sell the brand.

- Usage is the fertile ground of advertising. The more users a brand has, the more effective its advertising will be.

- Brand users are approximately 50% more likely to recall the brand's advertising than are non-users.

- Because of this, small brands typically underperform advertising norms for the product category. They simply do not have enough users to produce high scores.

- Usage does not only impact on the propensity to 'see' advertising. Users of a brand are also more likely to 'like' the advertising for the brand, as well as receive the advertising message in a positive way.

- Advertising tends to be more effective among *committed* users than among uncommitted users.

- For this reason, it is often worth while formulating advertising campaigns with the single-minded objective of *maintaining* consumers' commitment.

- If you do not know what the prior relationship is that the consumer has with the brand, you are unable to evaluate the effectiveness of your advertising. Do not make the mistake of condemning advertising unnecessarily because of a lack of understanding of the prior relationships that exist between consumers and the brand.

- Advertising is particularly inappropriate when a significant segment of consumers are uncommitted because of dissatisfaction with the brand. Even though they may 'see' the advertising, they are unlikely to receive the message in a positive way.

- Quantify the wastage in an advertising campaign prior to flighting, by examining the size of the non-user segment unavailable to the brand. This can help decide the weight that advertising should have in the overall execution of the marketing strategy.

- Treat unavailable non-users of the brand as a very distinct category. The brand will have to force itself into their field of vision to get noticed. Advertising, on its own is unlikely to be successful in achieving this.

- In terms of achieving trial of your brand, it will often be the case that advertising, without product sampling, will be one of the least effective and most expensive ways of getting a consumer to buy your brand for the first time.

- To use advertising testing that only presents results in aggregate can yield misguided recommendations. The reaction of consumers to a campaign will depend on their level of commitment to the brands they use, as well as their availability to brand switching.

# References

1.  Vakratsas, D. and Ambler, T. (1999) How advertising works: what do we really know? *Journal of Marketing Research*, January.
2.  Schultz, D. (1994) Attitudinal segmentation is dead! Attitude and Behavioral Research Conference, San Diego, CA, January.
3.  Deighton, J., Henderson, C.M. and Neslin, S.A. (1994) The effects of advertising on brand switching and repeat purchasing. *Journal of Marketing Research*, **31**.
4.  Barnard, N. and Ehrenberg, A. (1997) Advertising: strongly persuasive or nudging? *Journal of Advertising Research*, January/February.
5.  Rice, J. (1992) In the mind, out of sight, 14th Southern Africa Market Research Association, Wild Coast, Transkei.
6.  Stewart, D.W. (1994) Advertising in a slow-growth economy. *American Demographics*, **16**(9).
7.  Ehrenberg, A. (1998) How advertising works – an opposing view. Admap Conference, London, January.
8.  Du Plessis, E. (1998) The advertised mind. A Commissioned Telmar Awards Paper, New York City, April.
9.  Lacayo, R. (1995) An ugly end to it all. *Time Magazine*, **146**(15).
10. Bruner, J.S. (1983) *In Search of Mind*. Harper & Row, New York.
11. Rice, J. and Bennett, R. (1998) The relationship between brand usage and advertising tracking measurements. *Journal of Advertising Research*, May/June.
12. Jones, J.P. and Blair, M.H. (1996) Examining 'conventional wisdom' about advertising effects with evidence from independent sources. *Journal of Advertising Research*, **36**(6).
13. Lodish, L.M. (1997) Point of view: J.P. Jones and M.H. Blair on measuring advertising effects – another point of view. *Journal of Advertising Research*, October.
14. Ehrenberg, A. (1997) Differentiation or salience. *Journal of Advertising Research*, November/December.
15. Campbell, J. (1998) Creating salience vs. creating differentiation: implications for marketers and advertisers. Southern Africa Market Research Association Annual Convention, September.

# 7

## Fine-tuning your Customer Relationship Management

### *Profiling your customers in terms of their commitment*

It is every marketer's dream to eradicate the wastage in all communication programmes to consumers. Every marketer would like to be able to identify exactly with which consumers it is worth attempting to have a relationship, as well as the tone, content and frequency of the conversation that should take place, continually being adapted to the responses from the consumer.

Commitment is the key to the appropriate management of the relationship with the consumer. The degree of commitment and involvement of the individual consumer will dictate the appropriate conversation that should be taking place with the consumer, and, indeed, whether the conversation should be taking place at all.

In mass communication strategies, wastage is inevitable but it can sometimes be horrendously large. Direct marketing campaigns suffer from the same problem, with the possibility that the bulk of direct marketing effort is discarded without even being read. Ideally, a marketer would like to be able to identify every consumer of the brand at an individual level, with the amount of money being invested in a communication programme being directly related to the potential value that that consumer has for the brand. This approach will result in complete accountability for communication programmes, as well as adhere to the investment criteria applied by the rest of the organization – something to which advertising, in particular, has tended to be an exception in the past.

The marketer's dream has now become a reality. It is no longer a pipe dream to be able to invest funds in a communication programme with the same precision as investing funds in a new factory, in terms of calculating rates of return. Marketers are now able to merge everything they know about an individual's behaviour with all the relevant measures of what is in that consumer's mind, continually updating these measures so as to fine-tune the tone and weight of the communication programme.

These principles are now being applied in the field of database marketing, with data mining becoming increasingly popular, particularly for databases in which attitudinal and behavioural variables have been merged. For telemarketing, the principles are already well entrenched, while Internet-based marketing is ideally placed to take advantage of these principles and implement them in communication strategies.

The issue of privacy is continually being debated in many countries, with marketers increasingly under fire for what is seen to be unethical use of customer data. However, if customers are aware that data is being gathered and that this will be to their benefit, there is the potential for a positive response from them. In this chapter we describe case studies in which customers have been told that their anonymity will not be preserved, but that the data will be used to provide better service. This has resulted in better responses from customers than when promises of anonymity were made. Customers want better service. They want to be recognized as individuals. If it is explained to them that the amount of information to be supplied in the future will be exactly what they want – no more and no less – a very different type of relationship is formed with the customer, with benefits to both marketer and customer.

In terms of communicating with customers, the aim is not to unfairly exploit the relationship, but to tailor a relationship that is optimal in terms of satisfying consumer needs. For some people, the product category is important enough in their lives to warrant enthusiasm and energy in acquiring as much knowledge as they can about the brands that are available. They will want as much information as they can get. On the other hand, there are always consumers of the product category who are relatively uninvolved. They couldn't be bothered with learning more about the brands and have no interest in a relationship. The less information they receive, the happier they are. It is necessary to understand the relationship between the person and the product category in order to effectively tailor communication programmes for them, with the result being a more profitable relationship for the marketer, and a less irritating or frustrating one for the consumer.

In this chapter we provide case studies which describe the experiences of marketers who are already well advanced in implementing customized customer communication programmes based on the commitment and involvement of their customers. These initiatives are happening across the globe, with exciting results. The formulation of communication strategies offers one of the most fertile areas for increasing the profit potential for the brand. The marketer's objective should be to communicate just the right amount to consumers – not too little and not too much. The content of the communication should be finely balanced in line with the individual consumer's needs, ranging from no communication at all to detailed communication about the brand and what it stands for.

> **"The marketer's objective should be to communicate just the right amount to consumers – not too little and not too much."**

Some of the earliest pioneers in applying the principles of commitment-led marketing to the management of individual customer relationships were in the banking industry. Banks are ideally placed to use these principles, as they have databases which summarize the behaviour of their customers. However, no two databases are alike in their complexity and in their ability to satisfy marketing needs. All too often, the needs of marketers enjoy a far lower priority than they should when a database is designed. But this is changing rapidly, as the impact of efficient utilization of databases on marketing profitability becomes apparent.

# The problem with databases

Most marketers nowadays have either successfully constructed customer databases, are in the process of building them, or are wondering how they should go about it. This applies across all categories, including packaged goods. Having said this, however, most databases suffer from a serious defect – they only record the activity of the customer with regard to the marketer's own brand. Some marketers attempt to get rid of customers who have a low value to the brand or under-market to them. This could be a serious mistake. Low value to the brand often correlates with low commitment. Among uncommitted customers we often find those who are the heaviest users of the product category, with the highest growth potential for the brand. Typically, although uncommitted, they are involved. Brand choice *does* matter, but they spread their purchases over a range of brands. These are the consumers we would like to be able to identify in a database, so that specially tailored marketing programmes for them can be launched.

> **"Most databases suffer from a serious defect – they only record the activity of the customer with regard to the marketer's own brand."**

Figure 7.1 shows an example from the retail clothing sector in the UK, which illustrates a typical scenario. The example was first described in a paper by Trevor Richards of RSGB.[1] The analysis focused on the importance of involvement. Committed customers, although only representing 25% of the customer base, account for 53% of sales. This is because the higher the commitment, the larger the share of repertoire devoted to the store to which the customer is committed.

The importance of understanding commitment and involvement is underscored in Table 7.1. For committed customers, 81% of their spend in the category is devoted to the retail chain. However, it is clear that the major loss in terms of share of wallet, in *absolute* terms, is among those customers who are uncommitted but for whom store choice matters. However, in the absence of complete purchasing knowledge, their potential is difficult to identify in a customer database.

The measurement of commitment provides the marketer with a perfect link to identifying customers in the database who are low value to the brand but high value to the category. The modelling process is a fairly

**Figure 7.1**  *Clothing retailer*

Source: Richards (1997).

**Table 7.1** *Value to category and to brand*

|  | Committed | Uncommitted involved | Uncommitted uninvolved |
| --- | --- | --- | --- |
| Value to category (£) | 5137 | 10 269 | 4656 |
| Value to brand (£) | 4146 | 3767 | 1910 |
| Share of 'wallet' (%) | 81 | 37 | 41 |
| Lost value (£) | 991 | 6502 | 2746 |

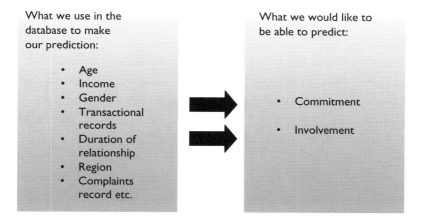

**Figure 7.2** *Building a model*

simple one, with the dependent variables – that is, the variables we would like to predict – being commitment and involvement (Figure 7.2). A model can be constructed which uses other variables in the database to predict commitment and involvement, usually with a high degree of accuracy. So, for the first time, we are able to make deductions about the value to the *category* of all the customers in our database.

> **"The measurement of commitment provides the marketer with a perfect link to identifying customers in the database who are low value to the brand but high value to the category."**

The bulk of the lost value to the marketer in the retail example is among those customers who are uncommitted but to whom store choice matters – the *involved*. They are heavy category spenders and are promiscuous in their behaviour. Those customers who are uncommitted, to whom store choice does not matter, deserve different management of the customer relationship. For these customers, the marketer has to decide whether buying loyalty is a worthwhile strategy. It might well be that for these kinds of customers, loyalty or retention programmes could do the trick, building loyalty without commitment.

## Business-to-business banking example

In the UK, several banks have implemented a system to measure the commitment of their customers, in order to identify those most likely to defect and those least likely, as well as to understand the reason for the imminent defection. The approach taken is straightforward, and mathematical modelling is not necessary. The key objective of these programmes is to empower front-line staff to be able to take actions which will enhance the profitability of the bank.

Questionnaires are mailed to a different set of customers every month, inviting them to express their feelings about the bank and competitive banks. An accompanying letter explains that their identity will be revealed to the bank, so that action can be taken if necessary. It is interesting to note that the research supplier (Taylor Nelson Sofres Finance) reports that removing anonymity has resulted in the response rate almost doubling, compared to other surveys of a similar kind in which the respondent does not disclose their identity.

When the results of the survey are received, they are analysed so as to classify customers by commitment. This information is then merged with other information from the customer database, and used to produce a one-page summary (see Figure 7.3).

In this example we see that the commitment of this customer is extremely low, as he has been classified as convertible. However, profitability is very high. Hence, the contact priority for this customer is the highest possible.

It can be seen that database information has been combined with data gleaned from responses to the questionnaire. Not only is the customer's attitude to the client bank measured, but their usage of other banks is recorded, as well as their attitude to those banks – information willingly given by the customer.

| | |
|---|---|
| 1. Customer name | Dave Hannay Enterprises |
| 2. Customer ID no. and branch code | 10001/123456 |
| 3. Length of time customer has been financial decision maker for the business | 6 years or more |
| 4. Main business account is with | Retail Bank but has secondary a/c at Bank B |
| 5. Overall satisfaction score out of 10 | 7 |
| 6. Does Bank B perform better than us? | Yes, 9 out of 10 and Bank B shows that it values his custom |
| 7. Desired frequency of contact by business manager | About once every 6 months |
| 8. Preferred method of contact by business manager | By telephone |
| 9. Best time of day for business manager to make contact | Morning before 11 a.m. |
| 10. Mistakes handling, last 12 months | Mistakes made and not dealt with satisfactorily |
| 11. Complaint handling, last 12 months | Felt like complaining but did not |
| 12. Key aspects of importance to customer (rating out of 7) | (7) A business manager who knows and understands my business<br>(7) A business manager who stays in place for a reasonable length of time<br>(7) A business manager who has the authority to lend whatever my business requires<br>(7) A business manager with whom I feel at ease<br>(7) A bank that makes me feel valued as a customer |
| 13. In what areas are we giving poor service (score out of 7) | (1) Business manager does not stay in place for reasonable length of time<br>(1) Business manager does not know and understand my business<br>(1) A bank that doesn't make me feel valued as a customer |
| 14. Commitment level | Convertible |
| 15. Profitability (1–10) | 10 |
| 16. Contact priority (1–10) | 10 |

**Figure 7.3**  *UK bank summary output for managers*

Source: Taylor Nelson Sofres Finance, 1999.

The calibration of profitability levels is defined by the bank's marketing team. The research team and the marketers then discuss the matrix of all possible combinations of profitability with the different levels of commitment, setting contact priorities for each cell in the matrix.

The process of producing these summary sheets is completely automated, resulting in an extremely fast and efficient delivery of information to branch managers. These one-page summaries of the client relationship with the bank are sent to the relevant branch managers on a monthly basis. This enables the branch manager to prioritize customer contacts, providing areas of focus for the appropriate management of the relationship between the bank and its customers. To ensure that the branch manager is not swamped by information, the sample of customers being interviewed is rotated every month, to break the customer base into manageable chunks.

A report is produced for divisional management which contrasts the commitment of customers of each branch with previous time periods, as well as comparing its performance with branches regarded as similar.

Most importantly, customer commitment can be tracked over time, as shown in Figure 7.4.

Implementation of the system has several implications. Branch managers of the bank are given an actionable tool to enable them to identify those customers most likely to defect, establishing a priority in terms of personal contact and relationship management. The feedback form provides an insight into what is in the customer's mind. Knowing what is in the customer's mind is essential for understanding how best to manage the relationship. Perceptions of service delivery need to be understood, as well as the strength of the relationship. In the event of an erosion of the relationship, it is important to be able to identify the competitor who is wooing the customer, as well as which attributes of the competitor appeal to the customer.

> **"Knowing what is in the customer's mind is essential for understanding how best to manage the relationship."**

Profitability is key to prioritizing management time. By combining customer perceptions, commitment and profitability in one simple form,

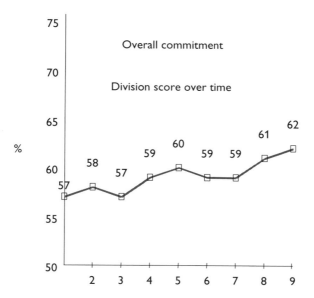

**Figure 7.4** *Commitment tracking*

*Source*: Taylor Nelson Sofres Finance, 1999.

the branch manager is effectively empowered to enhance the profitability of the branch.

> **"Profitability is key to prioritizing management time."**

# Nissan Ireland

The motor car market is notorious for high levels of satisfaction but low levels of commitment. In an effort to increase commitment, and gain additional insight into the minds of customers, Nissan Ireland has embarked on an ambitious marketing programme, in which the database is being enriched with measures of commitment at regular intervals. This programme was initiated as a result of a research study which revealed that:

- 34% of customers were not contacted after their purchase;
- 61% were not contacted after their first service to ascertain their satisfaction;
- 66% had not been informed of the accessories range;
- 31% had not had the warranty explained to them;

- 42% of customers have two or more cars in a household, yet no offer had been made on a special deal if they bought a second car.

Having discovered this, Nissan was certain that a programme needed to be instituted to alleviate these problems. A two-year mailing programme was designed, and an intelligence centre established to coordinate it. Key aspects of the new programme included:

- A welcome pack one month after purchase;
- A service telephone call after four months;
- A telephone interview six months after purchase;
- A relationship-builder pack eight months later;
- A second car offer eighteen months into the relationship;
- A follow-up telephone interview on the second anniversary of the sale.

A key component of the customer interviews conducted six months and twenty-four months after purchase is the measurement of commitment to the car purchased, as well as availability to competitive makes. Respondents are asked whether they are prepared to have their survey details attached to their names in the database. To date, over 90% of those who have taken part in the interviews have been happy for this to happen. Generally, customers do not mind revealing relevant information if they know that this will lead to better service and recognition of their specific needs as individuals.

This programme enables Nissan to fulfil its key objectives of:

- Building a database of customers, including the profiling of customers in terms of standard demographics and commitment levels;
- Assessing the perception of the brand versus major competitors.

Figure 7.5 shows the sorts of analyses that Nissan is able to undertake. The company is now able to identify, on an ongoing basis, which competitors are the major threats.

This database has also enabled the marketing team to confirm the instability of satisfaction as a predictive mechanism. Figure 7.6 shows the sort of example that the survey has yielded. It can be seen that 55% of

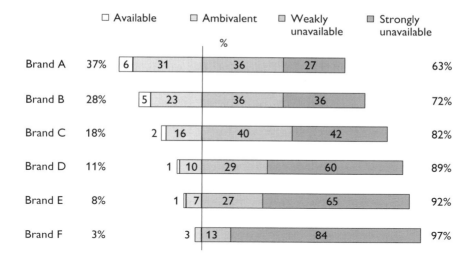

**Figure 7.5** *Nissan owners' disposition towards major competitors*

*Source*: MRBI, 1999.

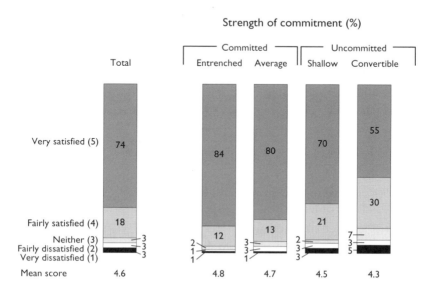

**Figure 7.6** *Level of satisfaction with dealer's handling of purchase*

*Source*: MRBI, 1999.

*convertible* customers were *very satisfied* with the way in which dealers had handled their purchase. Hence, satisfaction would be a relatively poor predictor of the likelihood of customer defection. Not only are customer perceptions monitored, but media usage is recorded, enabling the marketing team to target the media used by uncommitted owners, if necessary.

A summary report is produced for each customer, in which the customer details, the model purchased, and the availability of the customer to all competitive makes are recorded. In addition, the expected time for replacing the car is recorded, providing an actionable summary in terms of prioritizing contact with the customer.

With the passage of time, this database will be expanded, giving Nissan Ireland the ability to monitor the commitment of its customers to its products, and manage the relationship appropriately.

# Lloyds TSB

Lloyds TSB has provided us with one of the finest examples we have encountered of the comprehensive implementation of a commitment-led marketing philosophy. Much of the credit is due to Alan Gilmour, of Lloyds TSB. The example described below draws heavily on the paper presented by Alan Gilmour and Tony Smith of Taylor Nelson Sofres[2] at the Market Research Society Annual Conference in 1998.

We first met Alan when he worked at TSB prior to the merger with Lloyds. At that stage, Alan was not happy with traditional customer satisfaction studies, which had proven disappointing in terms of identifying which customers were most likely to defect. He had heard about commitment models from Tony Smith of Taylor Nelson AGB (now Taylor Nelson Sofres).

Intrigued by the concept of commitment, Alan decided to embark upon research in order to test the practicality of applying the philosophy of commitment-led marketing to the bank. His key objective was to investigate the extent to which profitability could be maximized, using the principles of commitment. Among those customers who were open to do more business with the bank, the objective would be to maximize the level of profit that could be obtained, while those customers who were unprofitable were to be investigated to ascertain what the potential was for increasing their profitability.

As with many markets, the majority of the profits of the bank came from a minority of customers. Relationships were shared with other suppliers, and in many instances the bank was getting a relatively small share of the customer's wallet.

The bank's database was sophisticated. Cheque account customers were segmented according to the amount of profit derived from each customer, which in turn depended on the repertoire of products and services that the customer was using. Cheque account customers range from those who only have a cheque account with the bank and use no other products and services, to those who use a wide range of the products and services available. Clearly, the least profitable customer to the bank will be one who only has a cheque account, maintaining an average balance of such a small magnitude that the account is unprofitable to service.

In contrast, other customers contribute a significant amount of income to the bank year after year. Typically, they will use several of the bank's products, and will often have been customers for many years. In terms of past behaviour, they would be classified as loyal, although not necessarily committed.

## The marketing objective

The marketing objective was to supply the right proposition to the right customer at the right time through the right channel. In order to do this, an accurate profile of the customer was necessary, together with a model that would determine the propensity to the customer to do additional business with the bank. The bank would obviously need a decision engine to determine the most profitable way of managing the relationship with individual customers. Having formulated a strategy in terms of the way the relationship should be managed, the offer would then have to be delivered through the appropriate channel, at the right time.

The problem with most database models is that they only use 'hard data'. This provides only a limited assessment of the strength of the relationship and other softer issues. It is here that commitment offers itself as a promising new variable. By using commitment, Alan hoped to improve the usefulness of the segmentation models that were being used as measures of a customer's potential. This would result in more appropriate management strategies in terms of the relationship between the bank and the customer, with improved communication targeting, both in terms of the media used and the creative approach. The end objective was clearly to improve customer profitability.

> **"The problem with most database models is that they only use 'hard data'."**

## The initial study

As an initial study, it was decided to analyse the most and least profitable customer groups of the bank separately in order to determine what the potential was in terms of future profit. Could an unprofitable customer be changed into a profitable one? Or was there little hope of achieving this, with the result that the bank would be better off without these customers?

Among profitable customers, the concern was a different one. Obviously, the bank would like to retain their custom, but what was the likelihood that they would stay? Their past loyalty did not necessarily mean that they were committed to the bank. Here, a retention strategy was most appropriate.

## Unprofitable customers

The study that was carried out revealed that, perhaps not surprisingly, six out of ten unprofitable customers were uncommitted to the bank. Their low profitability was a result of their low commitment. Only 8% of these unprofitable customers were entrenched (Figure 7.7). Even the committed customers in this segment provided little comfort. They had relatively few products in their repertoire, and, even worse, intended to buy fewer in the future than the convertible customers, who were those most likely to be growing their banking business generally. Thus, the greatest potential for the bank lay among those customers with whom the relationship was weakest, where the customer was most likely to defect.

The unprofitable customers who were committed to the bank were not likely to enhance their profitability in the near term as a result of a combination of age and income levels, as well as their low intention to purchase additional products. It was clear that this segment offered little potential in terms of further investigation.

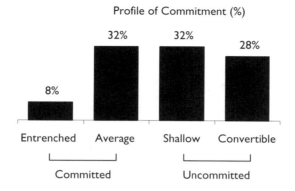

**Figure 7.7**  *Unprofitable customers*

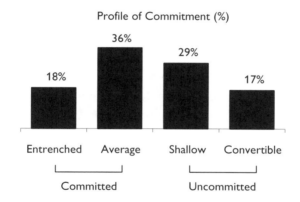

**Figure 7.8**  *Profitable customers*

## Profitable customers

The most profitable customers at the bank were analysed in order to see how they contrasted with those who were least profitable. Their commitment profile was significantly different (Figure 7.8).

Although the commitment of the most profitable customers was higher than that of unprofitable customers, with 54% being committed, some 17% of profitable customers were still at risk and likely to defect. These uncommitted customers were likely to be more affluent and more likely to be a prime target in terms of cross-selling of products and services at the bank, due to their high propensity to do more business generally.

This is a typical finding. The more affluent a consumer and the better educated, the less likely they are to be committed. It is often the case that the customers the marketer would most like to keep are those most likely to leave.

An interesting finding of this initial investigation was that there was no relationship between the length of time that the customer had been with the bank, and their subsequent commitment. Commitment could not be deduced from the duration of the relationship. Hence, commitment was an essential overlay to determine the true nature of the relationship existing between the bank and the customer, so that the appropriate management strategy could be implemented.

## Understanding commitment

Alan needed to understand why some profitable customers were committed and others not. As has been pointed out, there are factors such as education and affluence which influence commitment, but there will also be factors related to the level of service delivery. It was found that there was a strong relationship between the level of commitment and the level of complaints to the bank. Whereas 8% of committed customers had complained to the bank in the last six-month period, an astonishingly high 50% of convertible customers had complained. Of those convertible customers who had not complained, four out of ten had felt like complaining but had not done so. Although complaints to the bank were recorded in the customer database, there was no way of identifying those who had felt like doing so, but had not.

> **"The more affluent a consumer and the better educated, the less likely they are to be committed. It is often the case that the customers the marketer would most like to keep are those most likely to leave."**

An additional analysis of image dimensions shows that there were other relationship issues related to the lack of commitment, some of which are shown in Table 7.2.

Further rubbing salt in the wound was the fact that convertible customers showed greater potential for business, but with other banks (Figure 7.9).

**Table 7.2** *Image association of the bank among profitable customers*

|  | Entrenched (%) | Convertible (%) |
| --- | --- | --- |
| Have customer's best interests at heart | 89 | 21 |
| Have knowledgeable/helpful staff | 95 | 42 |
| Good reputation for customer service | 94 | 32 |
| A bank I would recommend to a friend | 97 | 27 |

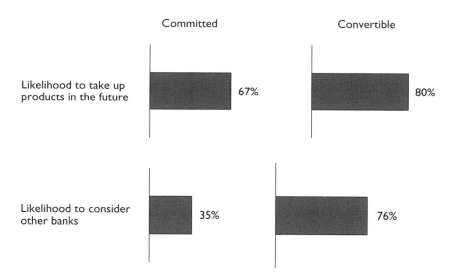

**Figure 7.9** *Convertible customers showed greater potential . . . but for other banks*

As a result of the findings of the initial study, the bank devised marketing strategies to address the issues. However, at this stage the customer segments could only be addressed in aggregate, because individuals could not be identified in the database according to their commitment. Putting it another way, the bank had to decide where to focus its efforts, in terms of retention versus acquisition, as well as what the service issues were, but would still not know whether a specific customer was committed or uncommitted.

It was clear that, in order to fully implement the philosophy of commitment-led marketing, a customer communication strategy would have to be developed that allowed for customized one-on-one customer communication according to the relationship that existed with the bank.

## Enriching the database

In May 1996 TSB began publishing a magazine for its customers called *Money Talk*. The content of the magazine was customized, with 35 variants of each edition being produced. The target audience of *Money Talk* was the 350 000 most profitable customers of the bank. Articles were selected for inclusion in the magazine based on the age of the customer, their product holdings and other variables in the database.

*Money Talk* provided the perfect base for the experiment that Alan wanted to embark on. Questions designed to measure commitment were added to a questionnaire included in a flyer in the magazine, which sought to obtain feedback on the magazine itself. As the covering letter made it clear that the information would be returned to the bank, customers realized that their responses would not be anonymous. This straightforward approach yielded more than 20 000 completed questionnaires. The process which had been embarked upon is summarized in Figure 7.10.

The bank was now able to identify the commitment of 20 000 of its customers and integrate this information with the customer records which existed in the database. The interrelationships between commitment and other variables in the database were then explored, using a variety of statistical analysis tools, including Chaid, a statistical analysis designed to uncover relationships between different variables in a database. A model was successfully developed that was able to predict the commitment of customers with a more than 80% level of accuracy. Some of the variables that were used to build the model included:

- Age
- Terminal education age
- Income
- Products held
- Channel usage
- Transaction patterns
- Complaint record

As commitment could now be predicted from other variables in the database, the bank was in a position to update the measure of commitment for each of its most profitable customers on a monthly basis. This

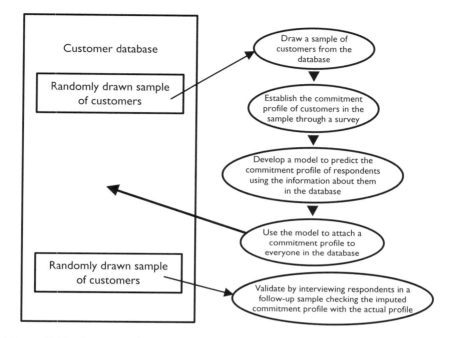

**Figure 7.10**   *Summary of customer communication strategy*

Source: Hofmeyr and Rice, 1999. Reproduced by permission of Henry Stewart Publications.

would allow for not only the commitment of customers to be measured, but changes in commitment, which might require a different relationship management strategy.

Many customers who become uncommitted to their bank do not close their accounts. They simply give the bank less of their business, or give more of their new business to another bank. It is often difficult to identify these customers, as they 'hibernate', rather than terminate the relationship. Hence, attrition rates are not always helpful in identifying poor relationships.

The outcome

For the first year, Alan did nothing but observe. Twelve months after customers were first tagged with levels of commitment, it was found that the profitability of those who had been identified as being least committed had declined by 14%. In the same period, those customers who had been identified by the modelling process as being most committed increased their profitability to the bank by 9%. Thus, the profitability changed by 23%, according to commitment.

A further finding was that those who had been identified as committed were 20% more likely to increase the number of products they held during the 12-month period.

During the 12-month experimental period, Alan found that approximately 5–10% of all customers changed their commitment levels on a quarterly basis. This is broadly in line with the findings we had observed in a Canadian banking validation study, in which about 30% of committed customers declined in commitment in a one-year period.

## Implementing a strategy

It had now been shown that the inclusion of commitment in the database was practical and, more importantly, that it correlated with current and future profitability. By including a commitment tag for each customer in the database, the management of the relationship could be significantly enhanced, as appropriate action could be taken when necessary.

The next step was to implement a management process of the relationship. As an example of this, no attempt would be made to promote products or services to customers who had a low commitment to the bank. Their commitment would have to improve before they would be open to approaches from the bank, in terms of doing more business with them.

### Step 1: Seduce the uncommitted

A programme to seduce high-value uncommitted customers was launched, beginning with a questionnaire to assess channel preference, product preference and service issues relating to the relationship with the bank. A personal review was held with the customer, and special customer product offers were made. The results of this programme have been impressive. Within six months of implementing the programme, the level of consideration of the bank's products increased from 24% to 66%, with a 5% increase in actual product holdings, in contrast to the 9% drop in profitability which was observed in the experimental study.

*Step 2: Reward the committed*

For those high-value customers who were committed, the Personal Choice Programme was launched early in 1998. Key features included the appointment of dedicated Personal Choice managers, the creation of a loyalty scheme for customers, and differentiated product and service offers. These were customers who already enjoyed a good relationship with the bank, and were open to doing more business.

For this segment, profitability has also increased, with a higher level of sales than previously, and improved account balances.

Applying the philosophy of commitment-led marketing by integrating commitment measures into the database for the most profitable customers, has allowed the marketing team to:

- Identify the link between commitment and profitability;
- Isolate the variables which are related to commitment;
- Predict the commitment and risk of defection of the individual customers;
- Develop marketing strategies to manage commitment and enhance profitability.

# The lifetime value of customers

If marketers have a database at their disposal, they will often want to integrate survey data and database data, in order to provide a comprehensive marketing database to assist in making investment decisions. For some of the most critical decisions they need to make, they will need the lifetime value of customers as input. Only by measuring the lifetime value of a customer are we able to decide how much we should be spending on the segment to which they belong, or on that individual, if we have access to the information at that level of detail. At the very least, however, we need to know what the relative weight of our investment spending should be on our customer and non-customer segments according to their commitment and availability. This will then feed into the decision regarding the total investment we make in the execution of our marketing strategies.

Commitment has proven to be a useful concept in helping to calculate the lifetime value of customers. Let us explain how we use the concept to go about calculating the lifetime value of different customers.

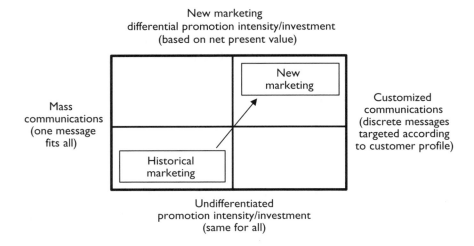

**Figure 7.11**  *The move from historical marketing to new marketing*

*Source*: Schultz (1994).

Different users of your brand will stay with the brand for varying lengths of time. Some will flirt with it and move on. Others, being committed, may stay with the brand for pretty much their entire lives. The anticipated lifetime of a customer is correlated with commitment. The more committed customers are, the longer they stay with the brand.

Non-customers also have a lifetime value for your brand because some of them will switch to your brand at some point. The key question is where to spend your marketing money in order to derive the maximum benefit in targeting your current customers, as well as non-users of your brand or service. Don Schultz[3] of Northwestern University in Chicago has produced a useful summary of how he sees the move from historical marketing to new marketing, shown in Figure 7.11.

In the past, marketers spent the same amount on consumers, regardless of who they were. Communication tended to be in mass media, and differential spending did not occur. This does not make sense, and marketers are now endeavouring to invest more intelligently in customers who are more likely to yield a profitable return, spending less on those who are worth less to the brand.

The principle is simple, but how does one calculate the value of different customers? It is very straightforward. All it takes is an initial consumer survey, followed by the recontacting of respondents. (This example draws heavily on a paper published in the *Journal of Database Marketing*.[4])

> **"The more committed customers are, the longer they stay with the brand."**

Here is a step-by-step guide, followed by a practical example.

1. In order to calculate the net present value (or lifetime value, which is the same thing) of the brand's users as well as non-users, the starting point is to conduct a research study in which the commitment of your customers to the brand is measured, as well as the availability of non-customers to the brand.

2. Measure the current value of your customers to the brand by ascertaining how much of the brand is used relative to their category consumption. For non-customers, all that needs to be ascertained is the level of consumption of the product category. By definition, their consumption of your brand is zero.

3. After waiting for at least six months, recontact the original respondents in order to determine what the defection rate of customers is, as well as the acquisition rates of non-customers. Analyse these acquisition and defection rates by commitment segment.

4. Once you know what the defection rate of customers is, you are able to calculate their expected time with the brand. For example, if the defection rate of the convertible segment is 33%, then the average lifetime of a convertible customer will be three years, and so on.

5. You now have all the components you need to calculate the net present value of customers and non-customers. For your customers, you know how long they are likely to be with the brand, and how much they spend on the brand currently. Hence, all you need to do is discount the future revenue stream, using an appropriately conservative discount rate.

6. For non-customers, you have calculated the probability of acquisition. For these consumers, you take a rather rough and ready approach, and calculate what their average lifetime expectancy would be were they

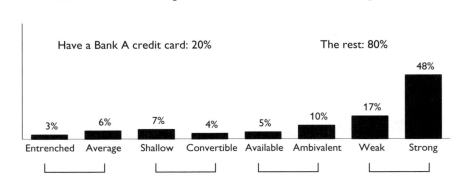

**Figure 7.12**  *The commitment/availability segmentation*

to be acquired, as well as their average value to the brand, and multiply all of this out, using the same discount rate as for brand users. If you want to be more precise with your calculation, you could identify which segments they were most likely to fall into, if acquired, and fine-tune the calculation in that way.

7. You have now calculated the value of each of your customer segments, according to the commitment they have to your brand. This enables you to calculate the total value of your brand, in terms of its net present value, based on the relationship it currently has with users and non-users.

In order to make this all a little bit more real, and easier to understand, we will work through an example. Figure 7.12, a disguised real-world example, shows the commitment segmentation for a credit card – Card A. Every respondent in the study, based on a representative sample of credit card holders, has been assigned to a segment based on the strength of their relationship to Card A. The card has a 20% penetration of the market; 9% of all credit card holders hold Card A and are committed to it (i.e. are entrenched or average in their relationship), and 11% of all card holders hold Card A but are uncommitted to it. They are potentially at risk. The remaining 80% hold other cards, and 5% of all card holders are strongly attracted to Card A, but are using other credit cards.

Information for the segmentation is obtained through conventional survey research methods. The segmentation allows us to answer the following critical questions about the card and its competitors:

- What is its customer equity profile – how committed are the users, and how available for aquisition are the non-users?
- Who are the committed and who are the uncommitted? Who are the available and unavailable? Who should we be targeting?
- To which competitors are the uncommitted users thinking of defecting? From which competitors are the new recruits coming?
- What motivations are driving commitment and convertibility? How can commitment be improved? How can we recruit the availables?

The segmentation enables us to tell how close individual customers are to defecting, to which competitors (if any) they are thinking of defecting, and what may be done to prevent defection from taking place.

We began by drawing a representative sample from the database of current Card A holders. We sent them a questionnaire which included the questions needed to generate commitment segments.

We supplemented the survey with a second survey of a representative sample of non-customers holding other credit cards. The second survey included conventional questions about attitudes and behaviour in the credit card market, as well as the commitment questions.

We then combined the results from the two surveys to produce the customer equity profile of Card A. To establish the value of both customers and non-customers to Card A, we need the following information:

- The average annual value to the credit card industry of the holders of competitive cards as a function of their segment membership.
- Of the total value of a Card A holder to the industry, the proportion of the value which goes to Card A as a function of their commitment to it.
- The likelihood that a Card A holder will drop the card from active usage in the following year, as a function of their commitment to Card A.

- The likelihood that a non-cardholder will subscribe to Card A in the following year, as a function of their availability to Card A.
- The number of people in each commitment segment.

The approach combines database information with survey-based information to produce a valuation of both the current customer and potential future customer base of Card A. Figure 7.13 shows two essential rows of new information: the average value to the industry of card holders in each segment, and the average value to Card A of card holders in each segment. These are empirically based values derived from a combination of database and survey information. Notice that the immediate annual value to Card A of all the non-Card A holder segments is £0 – obviously, because they do not hold Card A.

The next step, calculating the net present value of the current customer base of Card A, is shown in Figure 7.14. Some explanation is in order. The first line of values expresses the average value of a card holder in each segment to Card A. So, for example, the average entrenched customer is worth £1648 per annum to Card A. By contrast, the average convertible customer is only worth £579 per annum. These values are real; that is, they are established by linking the segmentation obtained in the survey to the database information about card holders.

The second line of information shows the likelihood that a customer in a particular segment will switch credit cards in the course of the following year. The respondents' relationship with the card was established through a normal usage and attitude study, including the commitment segmentation. A year later, respondents were recontacted and their current card membership and active usage compared with their card membership the year before (when the original study was conducted). This allowed us to establish real conversion probabilities as a function of commitment – derived as the result of a follow-up study on cardholders.

The third line shows the lifetime value (LTV) of a customer in each segment as a function of their membership of the segment. Following Hughes,[5] we used a conservative discount rate of 20% when working out LTV. It was calculated as follows:

- Take the current value of the customer
- Multiply by the reciprocal of their likelihood of conversion

Total number of card holders in this market: 2.5 million
Total value of the card holders to the industry: £5.42 billion per annum
The penetration of Card A in this market: 20% (500 000 card holders)

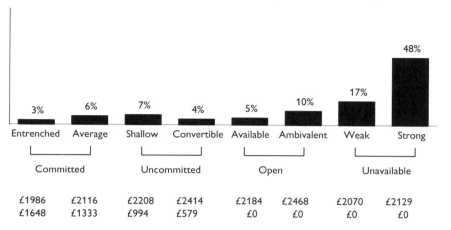

| | | | | | | | |
|---|---|---|---|---|---|---|---|
| £1986 | £2116 | £2208 | £2414 | £2184 | £2468 | £2070 | £2129 |
| £1648 | £1333 | £994 | £579 | £0 | £0 | £0 | £0 |

The first row of values indicates the annual value to the industry of the average person in each segment. The second row of values indicates the current annual value of the average person in each segment to Card A

**Figure 7.13** *Valuation of current and potential future customer base for Card A*

Total number of card holders in this market: 2.5 million
Total value of the card holders to the industry: £5.42 billion per annum
The penetration of Card A in this market: 20% (500 000 card holders)

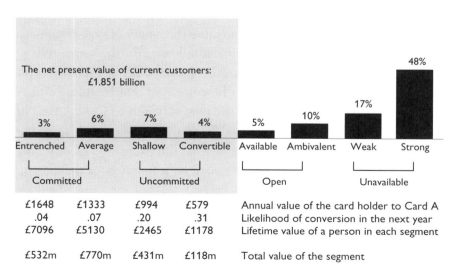

| £1648 | £1333 | £994 | £579 | Annual value of the card holder to Card A |
|---|---|---|---|---|
| .04 | .07 | .20 | .31 | Likelihood of conversion in the next year |
| £7096 | £5130 | £2465 | £1178 | Lifetime value of a person in each segment |
| £532m | £770m | £431m | £118m | Total value of the segment |

**Figure 7.14** *Calculating the net present value of Card A customers*

- Work out the net present value on a discount rate of 20%
- For the customer's expected life-span (from the conversion rate).

The value of each segment to the company was then simply the average lifetime value multiplied by the number of people in the segment.

When measured in this way, we get a finer description of where the value of the card lies than we would normally get in a gross valuation of a customer database. It gives us a powerful insight into the value of commitment. A convertible holder of Card A is worth only about one fifth of what an entrenched holder is worth to the company, partly because they tend already to be spending less with the card, and partly because they have a significantly shorter expected life-span.

The fact that we can be precise about the value differences for different levels of commitment means that we can model the way in which customer equity changes, given changes in the commitment profile of a customer base. In this case, we can tell precisely what the bottom-line gain or loss will be when someone changes their relationship with the card.

## Establishing the customer equity of non-customers

Most customer equity valuation methods stop with the measurement of the value of existing customers. Clearly, however, high-equity products or services achieve their equity in part by building equity among non-customers. Figure 7.15 shows how we measure the equity of non-customers. The key points about how this is done are as follows: first, the survey tells us what the average value to the industry is of customers in each segment. Second, our customer database tells us how much of that business Card A can expect to get, on average, should the person switch to Card A (in our real-world example, the amount was 70% of the total). Third, from our longitudinal study of this market we know what the likely rates of switching to Card A are for each person in a segment as a function of their membership of that segment. Fourth, we know from our customer database records how long the average customer stays with Card A once they have joined.

All of this information is put together to give an average value for non-customers using a 20% discount rate once again. Quite simply: the average lifetime value of a non-customer for Card A is:

Total number of card holders in this market: 2.5 million
Total value of the card holders to the industry: £5.42 billion per annum
The penetration of Card A in this market: 20% (500 000 card holders)

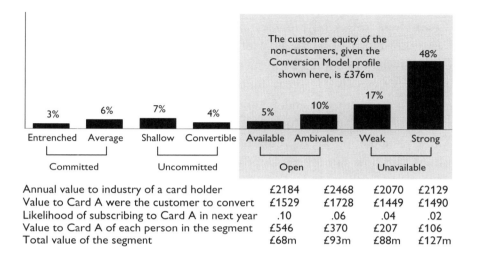

| | | | | Annual value to industry of a card holder | £2184 | £2468 | £2070 | £2129 |

Annual value to industry of a card holder | £2184 | £2468 | £2070 | £2129
Value to Card A were the customer to convert | £1529 | £1728 | £1449 | £1490
Likelihood of subscribing to Card A in next year | .10 | .06 | .04 | .02
Value to Card A of each person in the segment | £546 | £370 | £207 | £106
Total value of the segment | £68m | £93m | £88m | £127m

**Figure 7.15** *Measuring the equity of non-customers*

- Their likely value once they have switched
- Multiplied by their likelihood of switching
- With the net present value worked out on a discount rate of 20%
- For the expected lifespan of the customer once they have switched.

As can be seen, the lifetime value of non-customers increases significantly as they move closer to switching, i.e. as they gravitate from the strongly unavailable segment to the available segment. The customer equity of the segment is then simply the average lifetime value of each person in the segment multiplied by the number of people in the segment.

The total customer equity of Card A, that is to say, the real value of all the people in the market to Card A's issuing company, turns out to be:

£1.851 billion + £0.376 billion = £2.227 billion

This illustration, which is based on real data, is not atypical. It illustrates the extreme imbalance in the allocation of many marketing budgets. It is clear from the above example that the majority of the value of the brand lies with current customers, rather than non-customers. Yet many marketers stubbornly pursue the acquisition of customers who are not using the brand, despite the futility of doing so in many cases.

Research of this kind provides us with a baseline against which to measure the return on investment of our marketing actions. It allows us to establish whether our marketing activity is building real customer equity or not. Are the sales we see a function of a real improvement in our relationship with current and potential future customers, or are they a function of factors which achieve sales without building a relationship?

Clearly, marketing for the long term is about building profitable relationships. But how can the marketer tell whether or not that is what they are doing, unless they integrate information about both their current and their future potential customers in the above sort of way?

## Marketer's summary: commitment and customer profiling

The concept of commitment has many uses, but its primary use when allied to databases is to dig below behaviour in a way which links a customer's or potential customer's attitudes to their bottom-line value to a brand. It provides a way to value both customers and non-customers. It provides a means to identify customers who are at risk of leaving and understand why and what, if anything, should be done about them.

> **"Clearly, marketing for the long term is about building profitable relationships."**

With respect to non-customers, it provides a means of identifying the source of new potential customers to replace those who inevitably defect. All of this is is achieved in the context of an empirical evaluation of the bottom-line impact of gains or losses. Combining attitudinal information with database information in this way seems the obvious route to the future.

Using this approach to valuing a customer base, as well as potential non-customers, provides the marketer with a clear focus as to where the marketing spend should be concentrated. All too often, we find that marketers spend far too little on retaining the commitment of those who are happy with the brand, and far too much time trying to acquire customers who are out of reach. By calculating the lifetime value of customer segments, the marketer can allocate marketing funds based on the normal rules of investment used by the company.

The key learning points for marketers contained in this chapter are:


- The problem with most database models is that they only use hard data. The addition of commitment to databases significantly enhances their marketing value.
- The vision of all marketers should be to integrate behavioural data with commitment measures and the lifetime value of all customers. This will enable marketing resources to be optimally allocated.
- The technology is now available to integrate attitudinal, behavioural and profit information in the same database, making it available to marketers in a user-friendly format which can easily be analysed.
- The elimination of wastage in direct marketing programmes is, if anything, easier to achieve than with advertising. If brand choice does not matter to a consumer, they are unlikely to be interested in receiving additional information about the brands or the product category. It is relatively easy to identify these individuals in any database, providing the necessary marketing research studies are undertaken.
- It is not necessary to interview every single customer on a database. Sophisticated modelling techniques now exist which allow the marketer to infer what the commitment of customers is, based on a sample of customers, rather than the entire universe.
- If a customer has a low value to the brand it does not mean they have a low value to the category. Often the customer with the highest value to the category will have the lowest value to your brand. Do not make the mistake of automatically attempting to discard all low-value customers.
- The integration of commitment into databases allows for the marketer to formulate customized communication strategies, with the tone, content and weight of the communication being varied according to the commitment and profitability of each customer. This impacts significantly on profitability.

# References

1. Richards, T. (1997) Buying loyalty vs. building commitment: developing the optimum retention strategy. Esomar, Spain, November.
2. Smith, T. and Gilmour, A. (1998) Using research and database marketing in managing customer profitability. Market Research Society Annual Conference, Birmingham, March.
3. Schultz, D. (1994) Attitudinal segmentation is dead! Attitude and Behavioral Research Conference, San Diego, CA, January.
4. Hofmeyr, J. and Rice, J. (1995) Integrating the psychological conversion model with database information to measure and manage customer equity. *Journal of Database Marketing*, **3**(1).
5. Hughes A. (1995) Evaluating database strategy by lifetime value. *Journal of Database Management*, **6**(4), 343–354.

# 8

# Case Studies: Marketing Fast-moving Consumer Goods

*Beer, carbonated beverages, household cleaning products*

In previous chapters we laid a foundation for understanding commitment and what drives it. We looked at the theory of commitment, the impact of our way of thinking on some classical marketing problems like the definition of brand loyalty and equity, examples of how consumer commitment to brands impacts on consumer behaviour, and the implications of our thinking for understanding how advertising works and for customer relationship management.

In this chapter we illustrate what can be done with a commitment-led approach by looking at case studies from the world of fast-moving consumer goods:

- First, we look at an early project from the beer market to show how *commitment* and *availability*, when properly measured, can act as leading indicators of market share changes.
- Then we go to the USA for a look at the 'cola' wars. Our main purpose in this case is to show how what we call the *traffic pattern* can be used to identify the real source from which competition is coming.
- Our third case takes us to the laundry detergents market in France. We look at the market leader, Ariel, and show you how to analyse uncommitted consumers and what to do with them.
- Finally, we look at the launch of a new brand of household cleaner in a developing country. The purpose of this case study is to aid in the development of effective new product launch strategies.

# Case 1: Commitment as a leading indicator of brand health

This case disguised for the purposes of client confidentiality comes from a project done for Green Hop Breweries, a large international brewer. It has two main purposes:

- It illustrates the value of the commitment–availability profile as a measure of brand health. Changes in a brand's commitment–availability profile can act as leading indicators of changes in its market share.
- It illustrates the importance of understanding committed, rather than just loyal, consumers. Committed consumers are the heart of your brand – they like it just the way it is. Changing their perceptions can have deadly consequences.

In the mid-eighties, Green Hop Breweries had an overwhelming share of the market in a country, in which their leading brand was Bear Beer. Although Bear Beer's market share had fluctuated significantly over the years, by the mid-eighties it was the undisputed market leader. It had achieved its position of dominance on the back of a very consistent message: 'the best beer from the best hops . . . for over a hundred years'. In addition, it was marketed as 'popular and sociable' – the brand you drink with your friends. These perceptions lay at the heart of what made it a very powerful brand and defined the way committed drinkers of Bear Beer saw the brand (Figure 8.1).

The main challenge to Bear Beer at the time came from a brand called Lakes, with about a 20% market share. Lakes had a more substantial and slightly sweeter taste. This difference in taste was reinforced by its dark, golden colour. Other smaller brands were Hogshead and Oaken, both of them lighter in colour and seen by consumers to be milder or weak. Then there was Star, manufactured under licence from the Star Brewery, priced at a premium and sold in an up-market blue pack, and Mountain Beer, positioned as the 'strong and alcoholic' beer, a positioning which was reinforced by the fact that it had a high alcohol content.

Late in 1985, the Bear Beer brand management team decided that Bear Beer needed new packaging. Bear Beer in the new pack was launched in

| Too alcoholic **Mountain** | **Star** | For special occasions |
|---|---|---|
| Substantial | | |
| **Lakes** | **Hogshead** | Too watery |
| A sociable drink **Bear** | | **Oaken** |
| The ideal beer | | |

**Figure 8.1**  *How committed Bear Beer drinkers saw the different brands, February 1985*

April 1986. Green Hop Breweries ran a well-publicized campaign about the coming new packaging to ensure a smooth transition. Consumers were invited to design new packs themselves and submit them in a competition. Adverts featured a light-hearted look at committed Bear Beer drinkers trying their hand at pack designs. But no one knew then what the pack would look like.

When Bear Beer in the new pack was launched it met with mixed reactions. Although not noticeably different in style, the designers had taken some of the darker colouring out of the packaging. Unfortunately for Bear Beer, this coincided with a strike among workers at Green Hop Breweries. The workers had started a rumour that the company couldn't sell all the Oaken Beer it was producing. According to the rumour, Oaken Beer was being added to Bear Beer. The rumour and the lighter pack created a situation in which beer drinkers believed that Bear Beer's quality had been compromised and that it was now a weaker beer.

The effect on the consumer equity of Bear Beer was dramatic: although about 66% of all beer drinkers continued to say that they were regular drinkers of Bear Beer, a significant number of them became uncommitted. Among non-drinkers of Bear Beer the brand's consumer equity also worsened significantly as many beer drinkers who had previously been available for conversion to Bear Beer became unavailable. Our analysis showed that the brands most likely to benefit were Lakes and Hogshead (Figure 8.2).

We told Green Hop Breweries that Bear Beer's position had deteriorated and that Lakes and Hogshead looked as though they would be the main benefactors. Formerly committed Bear Beer drinkers had become

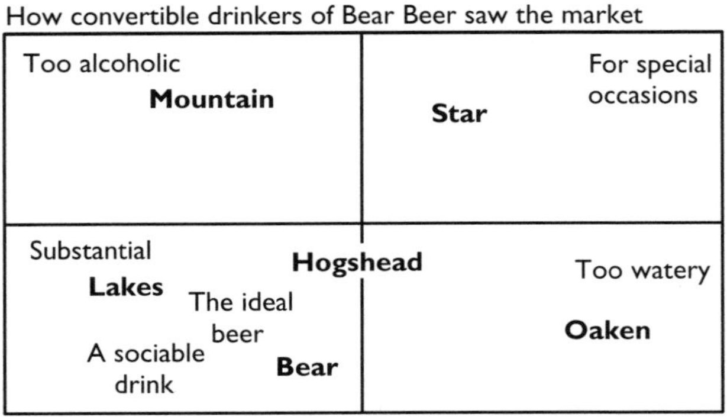

How convertible drinkers of Bear Beer saw the market

| Too alcoholic<br>**Mountain** | **Star** | For special<br>occasions |
|---|---|---|
| Substantial<br>**Lakes** **Hogshead**<br>The ideal<br>beer<br>A sociable **Bear**<br>drink | | Too watery<br><br>**Oaken** |

**Figure 8.2**  *Why the equity of Bear Beer declined – and how it became clear which brands would win*

uncommitted because they believed that Bear Beer had become 'weak and watery'. We hypothesized that the lighter colours in the pack had helped to reinforce this impression. Bear Beer, we suggested, could be on the verge of a 'flight from perceived weakness'.

Bear Beer's market share held relatively steady for about two months. Then it began a dramatic decline (Figure 8.3). Over a four-month period, Bear Beer fell from a market share of more than 50% to about 35%. In the eight months after that it continued to slide, steadying eventually at just below 30%. Lakes became the market leader with a market share in excess of 35%. Hogshead also gained significant share – moving up to about 15%. While Lakes picked up defecting Bear Beer drinkers who wanted to stay with 'strength', Hogshead picked up those who wanted to stay with something 'milder'.

It took Green Hop Breweries almost two years to turn the situation around and set Bear Beer on a path to recovery. The company did so by reaffirming the core positioning of Bear Beer. And it ran a series of adverts called 'roots' which linked a return to drinking Bear Beer with getting back to one's culture and history.

Meanwhile brand management at both Lakes and Hogshead were patting themselves on the back for a job well done. But they failed to appreciate that their success was due more to Bear Beer's failure than to their own marketing genius. As Bear Beer clawed back its market share, so the market shares of both Lakes and Hogshead suffered. It was to be the start of a long-term decline in the market share of Lakes which has still

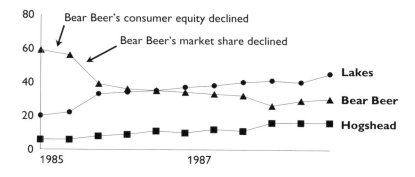

**Figure 8.3**  *Changes in the market shares of Bear Beer, Lakes and Hogshead*

not been reversed. Hogshead went back to being a smaller brand for a year or two, then began a long-term and solidly based increase in its market share which continues to this day.

Four important lessons come from this case.

1.  With a proper measure of commitment and availability, you can use changes in the underlying consumer equity of your brand as a leading indicator of future potential market share changes. Obviously, as a marketer you do not want to be at the mercy of these kinds of changes. So the purpose of these measures is to help you recognize what is happening with your brand and take preventative action. In this case, however, the changes that occurred were almost inevitable once the process was under way. The best Green Hop Breweries could do was to understand why it was happening and develop a recovery strategy.

> **"You can use changes in the underlying consumer equity of your brand as a leading indicator of future potential market share changes."**

2.  Committed consumers – not merely loyal consumers – are the key to understanding the health of your brand. For two months after commitment deteriorated, Bear Beer's consumers remained loyal. They continued to drink Bear Beer heavily, as a result of which Bear Beer's market share remained relatively steady. Quite simply, conventional measures of loyalty completely failed to pick up the fact that Bear

Beer's equity had weakened. It was the deterioration in commitment that flagged the impending problem.

> **"Committed consumers – not merely loyal consumers – are the key to understanding the health of your brand."**

3. When you are managing a big brand, it's the way your committed consumers see the brand that matters most:

   - Committed consumers drive your brand's volume – they pull it through the trade and encourage their less committed friends to drink it.
   - It is therefore critical that you understand who your committed consumers are and why they are committed.
   - If you embark on a marketing exercise which has the potential to interfere with their perceptions, then you are taking a huge risk.

> **"Committed consumers drive your brand's volume."**

4. The case reinforced a lesson that all marketers know but apparently often forget: never underestimate the importance of packaging. Marketers often measure consumer brand perceptions and ignore the pack. Yet we know from the way that consumers react to unbranded products that packaging plays a huge role in reinforcing consumer perceptions. Anyone who has participated in a wine tasting will know how divergent judgements about a wine can be, depending on whether or not the label and price are known. Packaging helps to drive the way consumers experience a product. Yet we spend little time researching the connections between packaging and the direct experience of the product.

> **"Never underestimate the importance of packaging."**

We have already mentioned the Marlboro incident. After our experience with Bear Beer, we picked up a weakening in the commitment–availability profile of Marlboro in the USA. Our client at the time did not believe us. Yet within a year Marlboro was in trouble. On 2 April 1993 the price cut announced by Marlboro management to try to stem the tide knocked $13 billion off the market value of Marlboro's parent company, Phillip Morris.[1]

# Case 2: Using the traffic pattern to identify threats to a brand

One of the measures that a commitment-led approach to marketing involves is a measure of the availability of non-users of a brand to become users. Sometimes, these are people who merely 'flip-flop' from one brand to another – the 'brand switchers' of classical marketing. But sometimes they are more than that: they are people who are giving up one brand in favour of another – 'pilgrims' (if you will) in search of a new favourite brand. One of the ways in which we use this information is to identify, before any brand switching takes place, what the main threats to or opportunities for a brand are.

The purpose of this case, taken from one of marketing's great battles, the 'cola' wars in the USA, is to show how this can be done. Specifically, we show how it was possible to:

- Identify to which brands Coke and Pepsi drinkers were going to switch;
- Quantify how many consumers were involved in each case;
- Understand the reasons for the emerging switching patterns.

In the summer of 1991, our business partners in the USA did some non-proprietary work on Coke and Pepsi.[2] At the time, 36% of all consumers in the four regions studied drank Coke regularly; 24% had Coke as their main brand. Pepsi had a lower penetration, with 31% of regular drinkers, 21% of whom had Pepsi as their main brand. Dr Pepper, Diet Coke, Diet Pepsi, 7-Up and Sprite were the other important brands in the market. They ranged in size from Dr Pepper with 19% penetration to Sprite with 13% (Figure 8.4).

Pepsi had a significantly stronger 'commitment-availability' profile than Coke. But the brands with the strongest profiles of all were Dr Pepper, Mountain Dew, Orange Crush and 7-Up. The strength of the latter brands could be seen from the fact that, although fewer consumers were drinking them regularly, those who were tended to be committed, and many non-

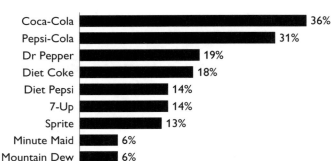

**Figure 8.4**  *Soft drinks market*

drinkers were open to conversion to them. The three weakest brands at that time were Coke itself, Diet Coke and Diet Pepsi (Figure 8.5).

It is easy to identify the uncommitted users of a brand and quantify to which competitor brands they may switch in the future. This is because the attraction that competitors have for consumers is one of the key measures that must be made when measuring commitment. Once the measure is made, we establish what we call the *traffic pattern*. We simply look at how many of a brand's uncommitted consumers are attracted to, but not yet consuming, each of the competitor brands.

We show the results of such an analysis for Coke and Pepsi in Figure 8.6. What was clear was that, while Pepsi was pulling consumers from Coke, many of the other brands were pulling consumers from both. In particular, although Pepsi might win some consumers from Coke, both were likely to lose consumers to Dr Pepper, Sprite, 7-Up, Mountain Dew and fruit-flavoured drinks like Orange Crush. Further analysis showed that the main reasons for this were that convertible drinkers of Coke and Pepsi saw the challenger brands as more 'thirst-quenching' and 'refreshing'.

> **"The attraction that competitors have for consumers is one of the key measures that must be made when measuring commitment."**

In the months that followed, here is what happened. On 27 April 1992 *Business Week* reported that 7-Up had gained 8% in terms of volume in

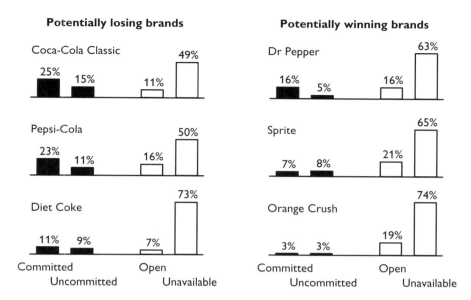

**Figure 8.5** *Commitment–availability profiles for key brands*

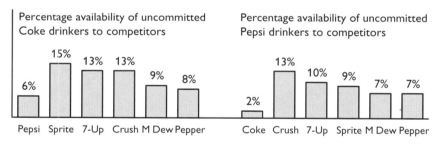

**Figure 8.6** *Availability of Coke and Pepsi drinkers to competitor brands*

the first quarter of 1992. And the *Beverage Industry Soft Drink Report* of March 1992 noted that 'Pepper-type drinks are making gains . . . Colas are seeing some slippage . . . Lemon limes are growing'. These trends were further confirmed by a report in *Advertising Age* (25 May 1992) which stated that the cola market share was in a downward trend while orange flavoured and lemon-lime drinks were growing.

Now, the purpose of commitment-led marketing is not to predict the future, but to change it. This approach would therefore be useless if all that it did was to foretell impending doom for your brands. Instead, you should be put in a position to get a clear idea of what the future will look like *unless* you take appropriate action. And in this case, the major finding was that non-colas were a bigger threat to both Coke and Pepsi than either of them were to each other.

What action should have been taken to respond to this threat?

> **"The purpose of commitment-led marketing is not to predict the future, but to change it."**

Let's begin by considering the sort of advice marketers are usually given in a situation like this. Imagine that you are the brand manager of Coke. In our experience, you would almost certainly be told that 'Coke has two weaknesses – refreshment and thirst-quenching'. You would probably be advised that Coke had the potential to lose market share unless you addressed these weaknesses. You would probably then be told that you should develop marketing communications which boost consumer perceptions about Coke's thirst-quenching and refreshing characteristics.

We do not underestimate the importance of advertising's role in reinforcing consumers' perceptions of brands. But we have seen enough over the years to believe that this sort of advice is overly simplistic. There are two reasons for this:

- First, the dimensions of image which need reinforcing may not be appropriate, given the way consumers think of your brand.
- Second, the switching patterns indicated may involve fundamental shifts in consumer tastes.

Consider Coke: 'thirst-quenching' is what advertisers tell us a brand like Sprite is. Coke's core attributes, by contrast, are captured in one of its classic marketing slogans 'the pause that refreshes' – Coke is refreshment in the sense that it 'recharges' you. Strengthening the brand should therefore involve reinforcing its core attributes (i.e. those that drive its committed consumers) rather than trying to make the brand seem something that it isn't. So, the way to address its weakness – 'thirst' – is to leverage its strength – 'the pause that refreshes'. Put simply, the problem should be addressed by reinforcing the things about the brand that make it more salient to consumers rather than by trying to change the way the brand is seen. It is not a matter of 'make people believe that Coke is more thirst-quenching than other brands', but rather 'make the revitalization that Coke offers more relevant to people'.

This still leaves the problem of changing tastes. No matter what Coke brand management does, there are going to be people for whom 'thirst-quenching refreshment' is more important than 'revitalization'. In addition, it is likely that many of these people will identify other brands, and not Coke, as being 'thirst-quenching'. What should brand management do?

> **"Strengthening the brand should involve reinforcing its core attributes rather than trying to make the brand seem something that it isn't."**

In our view, the only problem here tends to be a lack of courage. No matter what market you are in, there will always be people who are motivated in a way that just doesn't suit your brand. Trying to get them all to want the same things is futile. Over time, the numbers of people looking for one thing, say 'the quenching of thirst', rather than another, say 'revitalization', may change. Once this is recognized the answer to the marketing problem is simple: address the diversity of motivations and the reality of changing tastes in a market by offering consumers a range of brands from which to choose. Brand portfolio management is the key.

> **"Address the diversity of motivations and the reality of changing tastes in a market by offering consumers a range of brands from which to choose."**

# Case 3: What to do about uncommitted consumers

In the two cases that we have looked at so far, we have seen how our commitment–availability profiles anticipated what would happen in markets. Both cases involved leading brands whose shares declined as a result of the defection by uncommitted consumers to competitor brands. But we have made the point in both cases that information of this kind is useless unless it serves as a guide as to what to do. Let's look at a case, therefore, in which we show you how to handle uncommitted consumers.

Our case is based on data collected in 1998 on the laundry detergents market in France. To make it more real, let's suppose that you are the marketing director for Procter & Gamble. Ariel is your leading brand of laundry detergent. In the past number of years, it has established a commanding lead over the Unilever brand, Skip. But you are not sure how secure Ariel's position is:

- Does it have the potential to grow even more, or is it under threat?
- Either way, what must be done to increase your domination of the market?

We begin our analysis with an overview of the market. Ariel dominates with a market share of around 26%. Skip comes second with about 16%. Then there are three brands – Omo, Le Chat and Xtra – of which each has about 7% market share. Super Croix and Dash 2-in-1 (another one of your brands) are two more brands with about 5%. Then there are a range of brands with 3% or 4%. In all, the top 13 brands account for about 94% of the market (Figure 8.7).

Functionally the market divides into brands which emphasize cleaning power and fragrance – Ariel, Vizir (also one of your brands, but available only in liquid form), and Axion; mainly just cleaning power – Skip, Omo, Persil and Super Croix; value for money – Bonux, Gama, Xtra; environmental friendliness coupled to being good for baby clothes – Le Chat; and your brand which combines cleaning with a fabric softener – Dash 2-in-1. Both the 'fragrance' and the 'cleaning power' brands are used by everybody. But the value brands are more likely to be used in bigger households, especially those in which there are teenage children.

To answer the question: 'how secure is Ariel?', we have to look at a table of the commitment–availability profiles of all the main brands (Table 8.1). We see that Ariel is in a strong position: 27% of all consumers are committed users of it. This means that about one in four buyers of laundry detergent walking into any general store in France will

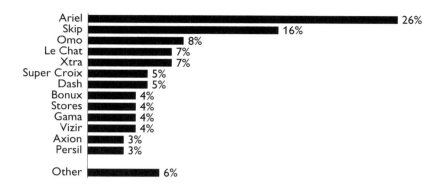

**Figure 8.7** *Percentage market share of laundry detergents in France (claimed purchase)*

**Table 8.1** *The commitment–availability profiles of laundry detergents in France*

| Brand | Committed (%) | Uncommitted (%) | Open (%) | Unavailable (%) | CR* | PR† | CE‡ |
|---|---|---|---|---|---|---|---|
| Ariel | 27 | 18 | 24 | 32 | **.60** | .57 | 1.14 |
| Skip | 16 | 14 | 26 | 44 | **.53** | .65 | 1.13 |
| Omo | 5 | 12 | 23 | 61 | .29 | .66 | 0.94 |
| Le Chat | 7 | 9 | 23 | 61 | .44 | .72 | 1.09 |
| Xtra | 4 | 11 | 14 | 71 | .27 | .56 | 0.77 |
| Super Croix | 4 | 9 | 24 | 63 | .31 | .73 | 0.98 |
| Dash | 5 | 5 | 25 | 65 | **.50** | **.83** | 1.24 |
| Bonux | 3 | 8 | 23 | 67 | .27 | .74 | 0.95 |
| Stores | 1 | 6 | 5 | 88 | .14 | .45 | 0.65 |
| Gama | 3 | 7 | 17 | 74 | .30 | .71 | 0.99 |
| Vizir | 3 | 6 | 24 | 68 | .33 | **.80** | 1.09 |
| Axion | 3 | 5 | 20 | 71 | .38 | **.80** | 1.03 |
| Persil | 1 | 6 | 25 | 67 | .14 | **.81** | 0.99 |

\* CR (ratio of commitment): committed divided by total users.
† PR (ratio of potential): open non-users divided by open non-users plus uncommitted users.
‡ CE (index of customer equity): based on a weighted average of the percentage committed and the PR.

want to buy Ariel. It is the one brand in France that has enough committed buyers that the trade actually has to take notice. Retailers cannot afford not to stock it. But there is a bewildering amount of information in this table.

**[?]** *Is there any way to simplify it so that we can get a true comparative picture of the brand health of Ariel?*

The way we simplify the picture is to turn the commitment–
availability profiles of each brand into a set of ratios, which are also shown
in Table 8.1.

- The *ratio of commitment*: divide the percentage of committed brand
  users (i.e. entrenched plus average) by the total percentage of users.
- The *ratio of potential*: divide the percentage of non-users who are open
  to the brand (available plus ambivalent) by the total of those who are
  uncommitted (shallow plus convertible) added to those who are open.
- The *customer equity index*: create an index of commitment and an
  index of potential. The index of commitment should be based on the
  percentage of committed users each brand has. The customer equity
  index is a weighted average of the two.

## What a high commitment ratio tells us

Ariel, Skip, Dash and Le Chat have high *commitment* ratios. This tells you
that significant numbers of the regular buyers of these brands think that
brand choice is important and identify their brand as having what they
look for in a laundry detergent. Each of these brands is a market leader in
some way: Ariel for cleaning power and fragrance, Skip for sheer cleaning
power, Dash for combining a laundry detergent with a fabric softener, and
Le Chat for baby clothes and environmental friendliness.

In our cola wars case we talked about the fact that there are a variety
of motivations in every market. What these results are telling us is that
there are four sets of motivation in the market for laundry detergents in
France, and that each set is dominated by a strong leading brand among
consumers motivated in that way – Ariel for those looking for cleaning
power and fragrance, Skip for those looking for sheer cleaning power, and
so on.

Most of the remaining brands have a low ratio of commitment. This
means either that they are a distant second to a leading brand, or that
they are price- or distribution-driven. Vizir, for example, has a low commitment ratio because it competes in the 'cleaning power plus fragrance'
sector of the market and runs a distant second to Ariel. By contrast, Xtra,
Bonux and Gama all have low commitment ratios because they are

marketed as 'value' brands and therefore compete on price rather than brand features.

At this point the numbers are telling you that Ariel is in a strong position – it scores above average in terms of commitment among regular users. And it has lots of committed users – nearly 70% more than Skip.

## What the ratio of potential tells us

One of the big problems that faces the brand management of market-leading brands like Ariel is to establish at what point the brand has reached market saturation.

 *Is Ariel so big that it cannot get any bigger?*

To answer this question we look at the ratio of potential.

The *ratio of potential* is a measure of a brand's relative momentum. In other words, it is a measure of the percentage who could start using it against uncommitted users who could stop. And the point about Ariel is that, in comparison to many of the other brands in France, it has a relatively low ratio of potential. Compare it with Dash, for example – 0.57 as against 0.83. Axion, Persil and Vizir also have high potential ratios.

What these results are telling us is that although most of Ariel's users are committed, it has become so big that it cannot but help having many regular users who are uncommitted. And the uncommitted users act as a counter-force to open non-users who could still become users. Ariel has reached a point where the recruitment of new users will become increasingly more difficult. It can be done – but it is a situation in which the brand is facing diminishing returns in its attempts to increase its market share.

## How strong is Ariel? What is its consumer equity?

On the one hand Ariel is in a very strong position because of all the laundry detergents users in France who are committed to it, but on the other, we have just seen that because of its sheer size it is the weakest of all brands in terms of momentum.

**?** *How do we put these results together to get an overall feel for Ariel's strength? And, more importantly, what are the implications for marketing strategy of these results in relation to Ariel?*

We answer these questions by looking at the *index of consumer equity* – a measure of the overall strength of Ariel in the minds of laundry detergents users in France. Table 8.1 tells us that despite the fact that Ariel has weak momentum, it still has considerable consumer power. Its power derives from the impact that its very large core of committed users has on the market.

Skip also has significant consumer power and largely for the same reason. By contrast, the other brands that have above average consumer power – Le Chat, Vizir, Axion and Dash – all have it because they have momentum. Dash, although one of yours, is a brand that looks dangerous from Ariel's point of view: it has significantly more non-users who are open to it than users who are uncommitted, and its users are relatively strongly committed to it.

## Going from consumer equity to brand equity

Now that we have established the consumer equity of Ariel and its competitors, it is relatively easy to produce a picture of the brand equity for all the brands. In Chapter 4 we argued that brand equity is a function of factory equity, market equity and consumer equity. If we suppose that market share is a good surrogate for market equity, then we can combine our index of customer equity with an index of market share to present a brand equity matrix. We show this in Figure 8.8. Clear marketing implications follow from where your brand falls (Figure 8.9):

- *Rising stars*: a brand with high customer equity but low market equity usually gets that way because it has momentum – although small, so many people are open to it that it has above-average potential to grow.

**?** *The question for a marketer is then: how do I find those who are open to start using my brand? And what are the market obstacles preventing my brand from reaching its true potential?*

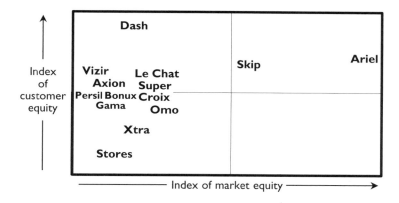

**Figure 8.8**  *The brand equity of laundry detergents in France*

**Figure 8.9**  *The brand equity matrix for brands in a market*

In our experience, the most common obstacles are poor distribution, low visibility and price.

- *Fading stars*: diagonally opposite the small brand with potential are big brands with low customer equity. These are the 'fading stars' of the marketing world – big brands whose users are no longer enthusiastic and whose momentum is below average. Brands in this position are extremely vulnerable. If you are not prepared to relaunch a brand like this, then it should be milked or allowed to become an aggressive commodity brand.

- *Commodity-like brands*: to the left of the 'fading stars' are 'commodity-like brands': they have neither customer nor market equity. In strongly branded markets this quadrant will usually be occupied by distribution-driven or price-fighter brands, bought by the relatively small proportion of consumers in the market who need the product – laundry detergent – but who don't really care about which brand they buy. Brands like this stay small as long as most consumers in the market stay brand oriented. This is a bad quadrant to be in if you are trying to create a brand that consumers will take seriously.

- *Strong market leaders*: the last quadrant in Figure 8.9 is that of the strong market leaders. This is where we find brands that have high customer and market equities. They are the 'current stars'. The most common difficulty that brands in this position have is that of finding new users because they may be approaching market saturation. This is why one of the most common strategies for strong market leaders is not to aim to convert still more consumers from the other brands, but to increase the size of the category. Hence the strategic imperative: maintain the brand, grow the category.

## Given these results, what should you do with Ariel?

We see from Figure 8.8 that Ariel has high brand equity. As the marketing director for Procter & Gamble, you note with satisfaction that Omo is in the worst possible position that a brand can be in: they occupy the 'commodity-like' quadrant.

> **[?]** *Dash and Vizir, two of your brands, have potential to grow, but so do Le Chat and Axion. What should you do?*

The problem Ariel has in France is that there is nowhere else for it to go other than to attack existing brands. Because the French population is static, the market will not grow as a function of population growth. And because most French people are wealthy enough to buy branded laundry

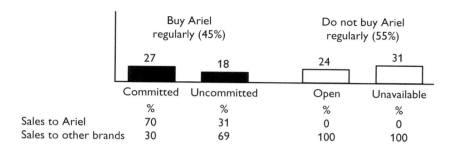

**Figure 8.10** *How commitment to Ariel influences sales*

detergents, the category has reached market saturation. Ariel can only grow by creating new, committed users. Let's see how we can do this.

Figure 8.10 shows how commitment to Ariel impacts on the sales that you get from regular buyers of Ariel. The impact is significant: whereas committed users of Ariel give you 70% of their business, uncommitted users of Ariel give you only 31% of theirs. By targeting uncommitted users successfully you should be able to achieve a significant increase in sales.

To find out how best to attack other brands we have to know two things:

- First, what is it that consumers are looking for in a brand?
- Second, how does Ariel perform in terms of what consumers are looking for?

The starting point must be Ariel's existing committed consumers. The mind of the committed Ariel user is shown in Figure 8.11. It is very clear that these people are looking for cleaning power and fragrance and that they believe they have found it in Ariel. This, then, is the heart of your brand. It should not be violated. Communication for Ariel must continue to support these two premises.

Now we look at Ariel's uncommitted users. Figure 8.12 quantifies them in terms of the different reasons why they are uncommitted. There are three main groups:

- The biggest group are the 52% who are uncommitted to Ariel because they are committed to a competitor brand.

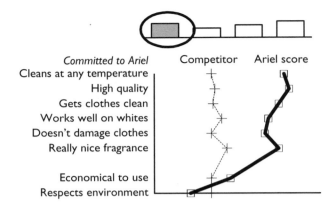

These consumers look for cleaning power and fragrance. They are not interested in economical or environmentally friendly laundry detergents. They believe Ariel is far superior to any other brand in terms of the things they look for in a laundry detergent.

**Figure 8.11**    *Understanding what is in the mind of consumers who are committed to Ariel*

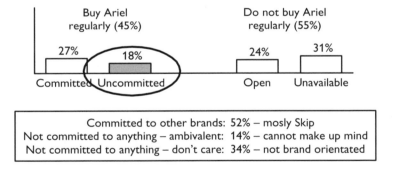

**Figure 8.12**    *Reasons for low commitment to Ariel*

- The smallest group are the 14% who are uncommitted because they care about the brand choice, but are ambivalent about which brand is best.
- Finally, there are the 34% who are uncommitted because they don't care about the brand choice.

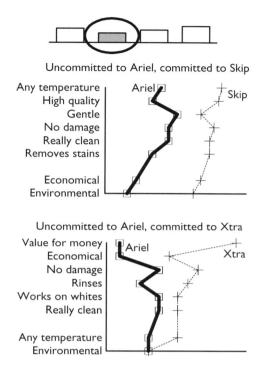

Uncommitted to Ariel, committed to Skip

Uncommitted to Ariel, committed to Xtra

Consumers who are uncommitted to Ariel and committed to Skip are not interested in 'fragrance'. Cleaning power matters more to them. Skip is seen to be far better than Ariel. It will be difficult to win these consumers for Ariel. By comparison, uncommitted Ariel consumers who are committed to Xtra are very clearly 'value' orientated. Again, it would be very difficult for Ariel to win more business from these people.

**Figure 8.13** *Understanding what is in the mind of uncommitted consumers of Ariel who are committed to some other brand*

## The mindset of uncommitted Ariel users who are committed to something else

Let's begin by looking into the minds of consumers who are uncommitted to Ariel because they are committed users of some other brand. We show two such groups in Figure 8.13 – those who are uncommitted to Ariel because they are committed to Skip, and those who are uncommitted to Ariel because they are committed to Xtra.

The two 'mental' pictures make it clear that you would have difficulty achieving dominance for Ariel in the minds of these consumers. The subgroup of committed Skip users are looking for a gentle cleaner with knock-out cleaning power. In their minds, Skip is it. Ariel's main source of competitive advantage in this market – fragrance – is not relevant to these people. The best you can do is continue to communicate 'fragrance' in as salient a way as possible, but it is clear that you will have an uphill battle with these consumers.

The second group, the committed users of Xtra, are clearly a 'value for money' group. Ariel is a premium brand. It cannot fight this battle. Again, the mental map of these people makes it clear that you cannot hope to convince them that Ariel is a good substitute for Xtra. As in Skip's case, the best you can hope for is that advertising will somehow make 'fragrance' more relevant to these people. But as in Skip's case, it is clear that this will be difficult.

### The mindset of uncommitted Ariel users who are ambivalent

Our look into the minds of uncommitted Ariel users who are committed to Skip and Xtra may be depressing. Ariel has a long way to go before it challenges for a spot in their minds. However, when we look into the minds of uncommitted Ariel users who are not committed to any other brand (Figure 8.14), we see a much more encouraging picture.

Among consumers who care about brand choice, Ariel scores exactly as well as the best competitor brand. This is not a 'value for money' group. It is a 'fragrance plus cleaning power' group. Any marketing spending which increases the visibility (i.e. share of voice, market presence) of Ariel will increase Ariel sales in this group, as long as it gets noticed. Notice that discounting is not needed for this group – they are prepared to pay for a premium brand. They are just ambivalent about which of the premium brands is best. In total they make up a small group, 2.5%, which should get added to the 27% who are already committed to Ariel, because they are like committed Ariel users in that the same things are important to them.

### The mindset of uncommitted Ariel users who do not care about the brand choice

The very large group of uninvolved uncommitted Ariel users are a real problem. They are clearly not motivated by brands. 'Value for money' does

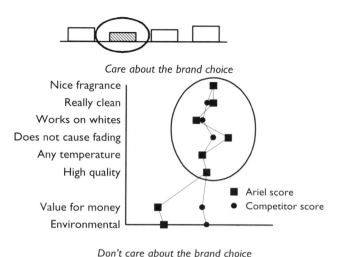

**Care about the brand choice**

Nice fragrance
Really clean
Works on whites
Does not cause fading
Any temperature
High quality

■ Ariel score
● Competitor score

Value for money
Environmental

**Don't care about the brand choice**

Any temperature
Nice fragrance
High quality
Value for money
Fresh clothes
No damage

The winning brand is 'don't know'!

■ Ariel score
+ Competitor
● Consumers who 'don't know'

Economical
Environmental

The first chart shows us a great picture of the ambivalent mind. These consumers do care about which brand they use – but they are undecided. A small improvement in the salience of Ariel when they actually come to buy a brand will ensure that Ariel gets chosen. This is a mindset that we can do something about.

The second chart shows us a great picture of the uninvolved mind. These consumers don't care about the brand choice – and don't have very strong images of any of the brands. Because they are not brand driven they will tend to be market driven, i.e. they will buy whatever is easiest, most convenient, best value on the day etc.

**Figure 8.14** *Understanding what is in the mind of uncommitted consumers of Ariel who are committed to nothing*

matter to them. But they are not paying much attention to your marketing – or to the marketing of any other brand, for that matter. When we ask them about the image of different brands, their most common response is 'I don't know'. Consumers in this state of mind are market rather than brand driven. They buy brands without always knowing which brands they have bought. Often it will be Ariel, simply because Ariel, being the biggest brand, will tend to have the highest in-store visibility. But it just as well might be something else. Any brand will do.

## Marketing recommendations for Procter & Gamble in France

Now that we have seen what is in the minds of the different groups of uncommitted Ariel users, what should we do? Here are our recommendations:

- Maintain significant visibility for the brand both above and below the line, emphasizing 'cleaning power' and 'fragrance'. This will lock in committed users and win uncommitted and involved users. They are the heart of the brand, and there are a lot of them. Keep them happy.
- Do not discount the brand. The willingness of both committed and uncommitted but involved users to pay for the brand should be leveraged. Ariel has enough committed users who are willing to pay the price for the brand to make discounting and price-orientated promotions unnecessary.
- You need to evaluate Vizir critically: while it has potential to grow, the motivational platform on which it appeals to consumers is exactly the same as that of Ariel – cleaning power and fragrance. You have to ask yourself: is there a need to give a brand like this a different name just because it comes in a different form – liquid? It runs a poor second to Ariel in terms of image.
- There is clearly room in this market for a well-marketed 'value' brand. Ariel should not be used to fight a brand like Xtra. You may therefore give some thought to doing more with Bonux in the 'value' arena. You may have to give up some Ariel sales for the incremental sales you would gain in a brand portfolio which included a strategy 'value' brand.
- Leave the 'cleaning power plus gentleness' arena to Skip. Unilever has over-populated the 'cleaning power' arena already, with apparently harmful consequences to its brand portfolio. Continue to fight the Unilever brands by striving to make 'fragrance' more salient than sheer 'cleaning power'.

- Although the current market potential of Dash has an upper limit, this brand has the highest customer equity of all the brands in the market at the moment. You may want to put more money behind the brand. Your reason for doing so would be to hit Skip – although you recognize that it will cannibalize volume from Ariel.

Ariel is in a fascinating position in France – it is the position of a strong market-leading brand with nowhere to go. An aggressive portfolio approach may be the only route to scooping up more of the market, even if you launch new brands which cannibalize Ariel. The trouble is that market leaders, having defined the most important attributes in the market, simply cannot be stretched to cover any more of the market. It is therefore a matter of continuing to maintain the integrity of your main brand's positioning, while managing other brands to fight in the other attribute territories.

## Case 4: Launching new products successfully

The fact that new products often fail is well known. Some 60% of the new products launched in the USA every year fail. In Chapters 2 and 4 we pointed out that consumers who are committed to the brands they are already using spend most of their money on those brands and stay with them for years. We also showed that such consumers ignore competitive discounts; and in Chapter 6 we showed that they ignore competitive advertising. The purpose of this case study is to answer two questions:

- What are the implications of existing commitment levels in a market in terms of the likely success or failure of new products?
- How can an understanding of commitment in a market help with the development of strategy for a new product launch?

In late 1994, we were working with a marketer who decided to launch a new brand of household cleaner called Brand B. At the time Brand A, with a market share of some 56%, dominated the market. Store brands accounted for 18% of the market and other smaller brands for 26%. None of the smaller brands had more than 10% of the market.

**Table 8.2**  *Commitment and market share changes, 1995–1999*

| Brand | 1995 | | 1999 | |
|---|---|---|---|---|
| | Market share (%) | Commitment to brand (%) | Market share (%) | Commitment to brand (%) |
| Brand A | 56 | 85 | 56 | 84 |
| Brand B | 0 | 0 | 22 | 82 |
| Store | 18 | 46 | 10 | 44 |
| Others | 26 | 48 | 12 | 41 |
| Average (weighted) | | 68 | | 74 |

By 1994 it was already clear to us that committed consumers simply are not available to competitor brands. Their defection rates are low, they give little business to competitors, they resist competitive discounts and so on. We therefore believed that commitment could be an important variable in determining the success or failure of a new brand. So marketing research was commissioned to establish the commitment of consumers to Brand A and other brands in the market. In addition, the research established who in the market were committed and who were uncommitted. And, finally, the research established why.

The results were clear: Brand A was a very powerful brand – it combined a 56% market share with a highly committed consumer franchise. Of the people regularly using Brand A, 85% were committed to it. Commitment to the other brands was significantly lower: about 46% of the regular buyers of store brands were committed to their brands while commitment to the remaining brands was about 48% (Table 8.2).

Brand A was a premium brand that had positioned itself in terms of cleaning power and versatility. However, although it dominated the market, there remained a significant number of consumers who were not committed to any brand and who treated the market as a commodity market – buying the cheaper store and value brands instead.

Against this background, the marketers of Brand B decided to attack Brand A, but with a new message: a decent household cleaner shouldn't just offer 'cleaning power' and 'versatility'. It should also promise 'not to damage' surfaces.

Our view was that any attempt to attack Brand A would be futile. As we have already shown (see Chapter 6), the problem is not just that committed users of a brand are unlikely to convert. The problem is that

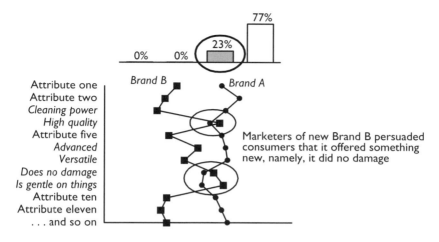

**Figure 8.15** *The image of Brand B among consumers who were available for conversion to it*

committed users of existing brands are unlikely to hear the marketing messages for new brands. We therefore argued that the fact that Brand B had something new to offer would pass by the committed users of Brand A.

When Brand B was launched it was a success, but not in the way anticipated by Brand B's marketing team. As predicted, Brand B failed to take market share from Brand A – the market share of Brand A stayed rock solid at about 56%. What Brand B did instead was to capture significant market share from the weaker brands. In the four years from 1995 to 1999, Brand B grew from 0% to 22% of the market. The market shares of the smaller brands were decimated. Store brands went from 18% to 10% while the others went from 26% to 12%.

The reason for Brand B's success was that the message its marketers were putting out got through to the uncommitted consumers of the smaller brands. The analysis showed that they were responding to the fact that Brand B was offering something new and important, namely a 'gentler cleaning power' (Figure 8.15).

> **"Committed users of existing brands are unlikely to hear the marketing messages for new brands."**

Brand B was launched with a campaign which targeted Brand A's consumers with a new message – but it succeeded because it captured the uncommitted consumers of the weaker brands. Because this message – 'does no damage' – was relevant to these people, it managed to turn them into newly committed consumers in the product category. Not only did Brand B end up with 22% of the market, it ended up with committed users in that market. This led to aggregate commitment in the market going up! Whereas before there had been only one strong brand with lots of committed consumers, now there were two.

Figure 8.16 shows how committed consumers are to Brands A and B these days: 85% of Brand A's users are committed to it while 82% of Brand B's users are committed to it. Figure 8.16 also shows what is in the mind of committed users of each of the brands. Brand A is seen to offer cleaning power and versatility. Brand B is seen to offer a 'gentler' cleaning power.

What lessons can we learn from this case?

With respect to the potential success or failure of new product launches:

- The greater the number of committed consumers in a market, the harder it will be to launch a new product successfully.
- It is the uncommitted consumers of existing brands who are most likely to try new products than committed consumers.
- It is one thing to get uncommitted consumers to try a new product; it's quite another to keep them.
- You will only keep uncommitted trialists if you can turn them into newly committed consumers of your new brand.

With respect to refining new product launch strategies:

- Target the uncommitted consumers of existing brands. Committed consumers are less likely to 'hear' your message, and even if they do, they are less likely to convert.
- Give uncommitted consumers a reason to become committed. To create a stable market share, your product must offer something new that matters to consumers

It's one thing to create trial of a new product, particularly among uncommitted users of existing products; it's quite another to turn them

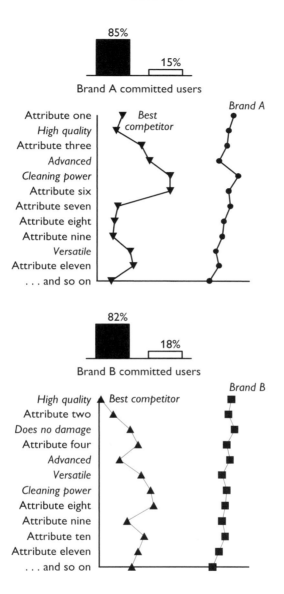

**Figure 8.16** *Understanding what is in the mind of committed buyers of Brands A and B*

into committed users of the new product so that you create a stable market share. In order to do the latter, it is essential that you give formerly uncommitted consumers a reason to be committed to your new brand. Usually this is achieved by identifying an unmet need in the market and then making sure that consumers get to know that your brand can satisfy that need. In Brand B's case it was 'does no damage'.

> **"It is essential that you give formerly uncommitted consumers a reason to be committed to your new brand."**

One last point: if you do want to launch a new product or brand at people who are committed to their existing brands, then conventional marketing methods will probably not work. Committed consumers do not see competitive advertising and are not interested in competitive offers and discounts. You will probably have to force your brand into their hands to get them to try it at all. This means that sampling is the main tool available to marketers to get really committed consumers to look at a new brand.

## Marketer's summary: what we have shown in the case studies for packaged goods

What you can do with a proper measure of commitment

Understanding the psychological commitment of people to your brand (and not merely their loyalty) is critical to brand management because:

- It can act as a leading indicator of potential market share shifts.
- It can identify which brands are truly the most serious competitive threats.
- And in both cases, it can help you formulate defensive strategies.

Unless you are managing a commodity brand, you need to analyse the motivation of people who are committed to your brand to understand what drives your sales. There are two steps to this: first, analyse what they are really looking for in your market; and second, understand why they believe your brand fulfils their needs. Maintaining the salience of the things that they believe about your brand is critical to maintaining ongoing sales to these people.

## What you should do about uncommitted consumers

To manage people who are uncommitted to your brand, you must establish what the reasons for low commitment are:

- They are uncommitted because they are committed to something else: often these people aren't looking for what your brand offers. Do not try to make it look as though your brand can do what they want. Rather:
    - Change what they want by promoting the salience of your brand's strengths;
    - Or fight the battle with a different brand which does offer what they want.
- They are ambivalent because they believe another brand is just as good as yours: in this case it is appropriate to strengthen perceptions about your brand, i.e. to make more people believe that it's your brand which offers what they're looking for.
- They are *ambivalent* in that they like another brand, but for reasons which are different from the reasons they like your brand: make your brand's attributes more salient, and develop a new brand to fight the 'other reasons'.
- They are uncommitted because the category doesn't matter to them: you win sales from these people by reinforcing your brand's market power. If you cannot do that, then you have to find a way to make them care about the brand choice.

The problem is seldom outright dissatisfaction with your brand. Often therefore, it's a matter of improving the *salience* of your brand rather than fixing perceptions about it. Either way, there is always a point beyond which your brand cannot be stretched so that a portfolio approach will be needed.

## Developing new product launch strategies

In any market, people who are already committed to the brands they are using will be difficult to convert. Therefore, when launching new products:

- Establish who are committed and uncommitted, and how many of them there are.
- Target the uncommitted first, they will be easiest to win.
- Make sure that you have given uncommitted trialists a reason to become committed.

If you must go for committed consumers, then you will probably need to use some form of 'demonstration marketing' to convert them, for example sampling.

# References

1. Kluger, R. (1997) *Ashes to Ashes: America's Hundred-Year Cigarette War, Public Health and the Unabashed Triumph of Phillip Morris*. Vintage Books.
2. This is a much shortened version of our paper 'The impact of consumers' commitment to existing brands on new product launch strategies', Hofmeyr, J. and Rice, J. (1999) Esomar Congress: The Race for Innovation, Paris.

# 9

# Working with the African National Congress

*Applying a commitment-led approach to political marketing*

The first time that we tried out some of the ideas in this book was in the penultimate, mostly white election in South Africa in 1987. At the time we were working with a mainly white South African political party, the Progressive Federal Party (PFP), whose stated purpose was to bring democracy to South Africa through the existing electoral process. The most well-known spokesperson for the PFP was Helen Suzman.

Going into the elections, we had identified significant voter ambivalence. On the one hand voters wanted to 'reform apartheid'; on the other they were afraid of the African National Congress (the party to which Nelson Mandela belongs). The ruling National Party (NP) tried to mobilize around 'fear' while the PFP offered 'change'. Neither was able to respond credibly to both needs.

In situations like this we would usually predict the potential for dramatic fragmentation – and that, in fact, is what happened. A small new political organization calling themselves the 'Independents' achieved stunning successes at the polls. Within two years there had been a significant realignment in the white politics of South Africa. By 1989, the Democratic Party (DP), an amalgam of the PFP and the 'Independents', was in a position to convert many voters from the NP. And just a year later, the final negotiations for a democratic South Africa began.

We moved from the DP to the ANC in about 1991. Among the most enjoyable and interesting marketing challenges on which we have worked have been the ANC's election campaigns. That is what this chapter is about.

In this chapter we look at a number of questions. We look at how research helped us to:

- Understand the nature of political polarization in South Africa and define realistic electoral goals.
- Develop a message which remained true to the long-term goals of the ANC while at the same time maximizing support for it.
- Understand the 'swing' voters and what made them ambivalent about voting for or against the ANC.
- Position the ANC in a way which made it possible to convert significant numbers of voters in later elections.

# The African National Congress in South Africa's first general election: 1994

On 2 February 1990, F.W. de Klerk, then the president of South Africa, lifted the ban on the ANC and other previously banned political organizations. Some months later he announced the release of Nelson Mandela, probably the world's most famous political prisoner at the time. So began the irrevocable process which led to South Africa's first general election on 27 April 1994.

We were social democrats in South Africa when the ANC was unbanned. We had worked for largely white political organizations dedicated to establishing non-racial democracy in our country. When the ANC was unbanned we thought that it would surely lead to peace and a lessening of social tension. How wrong we were. The reforms announced by de Klerk unleashed a storm of political violence, mostly from forces resisting change. In 1989 alone, 1403 people were killed as a result of political violence. By 1993, over 300 people were being killed in political violence every month. Killing due to political violence peaked in March 1994, the month before the election, at 537 people.

As the elections drew near it seemed impossible that they would be peaceful. A series of bomb blasts ripped through the country at taxi ranks, sites designated as polling stations and in the central business district of Johannesburg, headquarters of South Africa's gold industry. Bombs in the election month of April killed 21 people and injured more than 200. These deaths came on top of the continuing death toll from political violence. The world's news media descended on the country expecting –

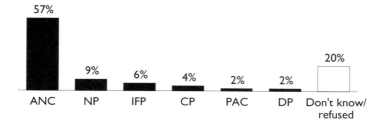

**Figure 9.1**  *Support for political parties in South Africa, August 1993*

we don't know what – but we suppose they were expecting a violent drama to the end.

In the event, the media got drama – but it was the drama of more than 19 million people standing peacefully in non-racial queues for days, waiting to vote. South Africa's first democratic general election *was* a miracle. Having gone through the process we cannot but wonder at what an elegant solution to the problems of war and conflict democratic elections are: you stand in a queue, put a cross on a piece of paper and go home. Citizens count the crosses and tell you who won. You let the winners govern while you get on with your life. If the winners mess things up, or even if you just decide you want a change, you go back after about five years and throw them out.

We were asked to join the ANC's strategy team in early 1993. Apart from ANC insiders, our team included Mark Orkin, now president of the Human Sciences Research Council, and Stan Greenberg, at that time a pollster for former president Bill Clinton of the USA. Apart from Stan Greenberg and Jannie, none of our team had been involved in modern, conventional election campaigning.

Let's have a look at what was in the public mind when we got involved. Figure 9.1 shows the levels of declared party political support in about mid-1993. The ANC had 57% of the vote. De Klerk's NP with just 9% were second. There was clearly no real opposition to the ANC on a national basis. But the overwhelming support for the ANC masked some significant social differences in political support patterns.

The single factor most strongly associated with voting intention was race and ethnicity. This we show in Table 9.1. The ANC was getting 76% of the black vote, but only 3% of the white vote. Within the black vote,

**Table 9.1**  *Sharp ethnic differences in voter support patterns*

| Party | Black (%) | White (%) | Coloured (%) | Indian (%) | Xhosa (%) | Zulu (%) | Afrikaans (%) | English (%) |
|---|---|---|---|---|---|---|---|---|
| ANC | 76 | 3 | 16 | 21 | 88 | 57 | 7 | 11 |
| NP | 1 | 34 | 30 | 33 | 0 | 1 | 33 | 32 |
| IFP | 5 | 12 | 1 | 2 | 0 | 17 | 5 | 11 |
| CP | 0 | 24 | 1 | 0 | 0 | 0 | 21 | 4 |
| PAC | 2 | 0 | 0 | 0 | 4 | 1 | 0 | 0 |
| DP | 0 | 6 | 4 | 4 | 0 | 0 | 2 | 11 |
| Don't know | 16 | 21 | 47 | 40 | 8 | 23 | 33 | 30 |

the ANC was getting over 80% of the vote of most ethnic groups, but only 57% of the Zulu vote. De Klerk's NP, by contrast, was getting 30% or more of the white, coloured and Indian vote, but only 1% of the black vote.

Figure 9.2 explains these patterns. Most South Africans wanted peace and justice. But while the voting intentions of most black South Africans were driven by hope, the voting intentions of most white, coloured and Indian South Africans were driven by a mixture of concern and outright fear.

ANC's national priorities:    Equality – equal say, economic and social justice, jobs
Reconciliation – peace, racial and ethnic harmony

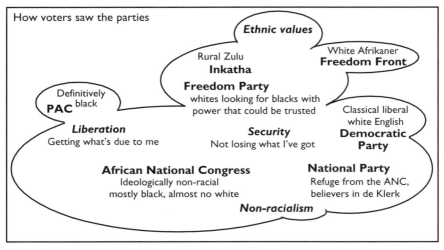

**Figure 9.2**  *How South African voters saw the parties*

Coloured and Indian communities had played a pivotal role in the anti-apartheid struggle, yet when it came to voting they indicated support for de Klerk's NP – the very party that had been responsible for apartheid – or for no one. They described themselves as 'the meat in the sandwich' and as 'caught between the devil you know (de Klerk) and the devil you don't (the ANC)'. They indicated that while white and black South Africans each had parties that would represent their interests – the NP and the ANC respectively – coloureds and Indians had no one. In the event, they decided to support 'the devil you know' and came out in favour of the NP.

Liberal whites in the meantime were also looking for a meaningful political home. Traditionally they would have supported the DP – historically the party of anti-apartheid campaigner Helen Suzman. But the DP was seen to be ineffectual, so they deserted it in droves for the NP or for Mangosuthu Buthelezi's Inkatha Freedom Party (IFP). As a result, the NP ended up being a party mostly for non-black ethnic minorities who were looking for a party that could protect their relatively privileged position against the ANC, but within a declared framework of non-racialism.

The trouble with the NP was that, while its declared ideology was non-racial, it could not attract much black support. Many white South Africans thought that Buthelezi's IFP would be a credible non-racial alternative to the NP. As a result, the IFP ended up being a curious mixture of mostly ethnically orientated rural Zulus, and whites who recognized that the NP wasn't credibly non-racial and who were looking for a black leader 'with power' who they thought could be 'trusted' – Buthelezi.

On what was called 'the white right' a political party called the Freedom Front emerged to fight for the preservation of the cultural values of Afrikaans-speaking white South Africans. Like the IFP, they represented mostly ethnic interests – only white Afrikaner interests rather than mostly rural Zulu interests.

Apart from Buthelezi's IFP, black opposition to the ANC appeared to be minimal. Only 2% declared their intention to vote for the Pan Africanist Congress (PAC) during 1993. This was very low considering that this had been one of the top two liberation movements, along with the ANC, for many years.

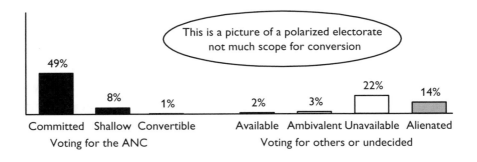

**Figure 9.3**  *Commitment and availability to the ANC, 1993*

The ANC set itself the target of winning handsomely and capturing all nine provinces of South Africa. From the start, our research showed that while winning handsomely would not be a problem, winning all nine provinces would. Because of the ethnic balance in a province called the Western Cape – mostly coloured and white – we were certain that the ANC would lose the Western Cape. Other provinces that were marginal because of the ethnic make-up of the voting public were the Northern Cape (mostly coloured), Gauteng (centre of South Africa's gold industry with a very large white vote) and Kwa-Zulu Natal (rural Zulu).

Against the background of these realities, we planned the election campaign themes. As Figure 9.3 shows, we were dealing with a polarized electorate in 1994. Most ANC support was committed – and most of those not voting for the ANC were strongly unavailable. Only a small proportion of the ANC vote was at risk and an even smaller proportion of those who had not indicated support for the ANC were open to conversion. The election would therefore not be primarily about conversion this time round – there were very few people available for conversion one way or the other. It would mostly be about consolidation and mobilization. Consolidate both the existing 58% and the 5% available and ambivalent, and then run a campaign which maximizes the turn-out.

When we turned to an analysis of who was in these different target groups the results were striking (Figure 9.4). Of the ANC's committed supporters, 97% were black and 2% coloured. Committed white and Indian support was negligible. Even the marginal groups (uncommitted and open) were mostly black with some coloured. Whites were almost

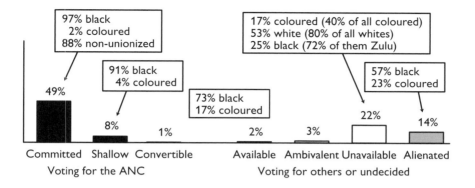

**Figure 9.4** *Commitment and availability to the ANC – where South Africans positioned themselves in 1993*

uniformly opposed to the ANC, as were many rural Zulus. Coloureds and Indians were divided, but with most support going to de Klerk's NP. A brutally pragmatic analysis would have suggested that the campaign should be aimed at black South Africans.

Running a campaign which mobilized black support around an anti-apartheid, liberation theme would have been easy. But that would have been to mobilize the vote around past injustices, and that would surely have been bad for the country. While 'injustice' had been an important tool of mass mobilization in the days of revolutionary struggle, there was a question as to whether it would be appropriate as South Africa attempted to rebuild.

Discussions within the ANC were lively around this issue: should the elections be about liberation from the past, or should they focus on hope for the future? Some critical factors intruded on the strategic direction that the ANC decided to take. First, the ANC is deeply committed to non-racialism. But the research showed that racial polarization was a deeply embedded political reality in South Africa. Given its commitment to non-racialism, the ANC did not want to run a campaign which exacerbated that polarization.

Second, while conversion may not have been a realistic prospect in the short run, it was essential that the ANC did not run an election which made conversion in the long run more difficult. The campaign would therefore have to lay a foundation for the eventual conversion of voters in, for example, the Western Cape. Since the Western Cape was mostly coloured and white, such a campaign would have to embody non-racial themes, despite the fact that coloured and white voters were mostly unavailable to the ANC.

Third, research showed that black South Africans wanted to look forward, not back. They wanted to approach the election with hope for the future rather than anger at the past. It was as if they were saying 'at last, now the history of our country can really begin – we trust you, the ANC to have a vision that will take us forward. Now show us that vision in your campaign'. Black South Africans wanted a reason to vote which had to do with South Africa becoming, at last, a normal, prosperous and just democracy.

Finally, the ANC was deeply conscious that the election campaign should not make South Africa even more difficult to govern than it already was. The ANC was therefore committed to running a campaign which would create a positive mood in the country that could be carried over into the days after the election. The research was telling us that ethnic minorities would probably not believe this message of hope. For the time being that was irrelevant. The ANC was determined to run a positive, forward-looking campaign rather than one that dwelt on the past.

The campaign theme was simplicity itself: a better life for all. A better life for black South Africans, certainly. But a better life for all because the social tensions which currently divided the country would be eliminated. Coupled to that went a relentless focus on policies and plans – plans to build houses, to provide communities with basic services like clean water and electricity, to provide affordable education, and to provide jobs. About a month before the election, in speeches around the country to mark the Sharpeville massacre of 1961, the ANC spelled out its campaign: 'to build a better life for all we plan to: create 2.5 million new jobs, build 1 million houses, provide 10 years of free schooling, bring electricity to 2.5 million houses in five years'. The plan became known as the reconstruction and development plan. Apart from pointing to the future, it was intentionally drafted to give people a sense that the ANC, although a revolutionary party, was thinking about normal government.

The campaign was simple, positive, almost mundane. It was saying to people 'we're going to be a normal government – there will be no vendetta – we aim to be inclusive so that South Africa will succeed – we do have priorities and our plans include jobs, housing, schooling and basic

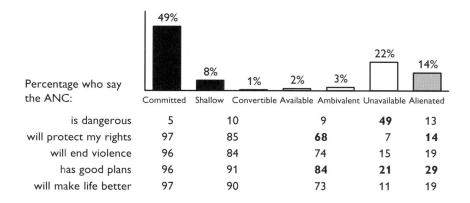

| Percentage who say the ANC: | Committed | Shallow | Convertible | Available | Ambivalent | Unavailable | Alienated |
|---|---|---|---|---|---|---|---|
| is dangerous | 5 | 10 | | 9 | | **49** | 13 |
| will protect my rights | 97 | 85 | | **68** | | 7 | **14** |
| will end violence | 96 | 84 | | 74 | | 15 | 19 |
| has good plans | 96 | 91 | | **84** | | **21** | **29** |
| will make life better | 97 | 90 | | 73 | | 11 | 19 |

**Figure 9.5**  *The impact of issues on commitment and availability to the ANC early 1994*

services – and it is true that our priority is poor, mostly black South Africans – but by attending to these priorities we will ensure that the future for everybody in this country involves a better life for all'.

By early 1994 the campaign had begun to 'bite'. Figure 9.5 shows the state of the public mind. Even voters who were strongly unavailable to the ANC were beginning to believe that it was serious about normal government. As the research continued to show, however, conversion would not take place in this election. Unavailability to the ANC was too deeply rooted in fear and in the belief that the ANC would ignore the rights and needs of communities who were not its traditional supporters. A startlingly high percentage of voters who were unavailable to the ANC – 49% – still believed it was outright dangerous.

The ANC ended up getting 62.7% of the vote. De Klerk's NP came second with 20.4%. Most of the undecided vote among non-black minorities went to his party. It came from liberal whites who had voted for the DP in the last all-white elections of 1989, and from coloureds and Indians who had decided to support 'the devil they knew' even though the NP had been responsible for apartheid. Buthelezi's IFP sewed up the rural Zulu vote in Kwa-Zulu Natal and won that province as a result. Country-wide the IFP got 10.5%. No other parties featured.

The ANC did better than most pollsters were expecting. Most pollsters thought the Northern Cape would go to the NP. Our strategy team didn't – and we were right. The ANC won the Northern Cape, albeit by a very narrow margin. Most pollsters thought that Gauteng, the 'gold centre' of the country, would be won by the ANC, but by a narrow margin. Again, we didn't – and we were right. The ANC won Gauteng with a comfortable 56% majority. Although the ANC didn't want to believe that they would lose the Western Cape, they did, as we and other pollsters thought they would. Both the Western Cape and Kwa-Zulu Natal were lost decisively as a result of ethnic voting patterns. Few pollsters picked up how poorly the ANC would do in Kwa-Zulu Natal, but its successes elsewhere more than compensated.

The positive campaigning had paid off. And it would become clear, within two years, that the campaign had created a foundation for the future conversion of disillusioned opposition voters, particularly in the Western Cape.

## A picture of ambivalence: local government elections in 1996

There have been two elections in South Africa since 1994. In 1996, South Africa held its first nationwide, democratic election for local government. In many countries, participation in local elections is poor. These elections, however, were treated as something of a referendum on the ANC's performance to date. For the ANC, doing well was seen to be central to the implementation of policy at a local level.

The aftermath of the 1994 elections had seen an immediate drop in political violence. And by 1996 there had also been notable gains in some basic areas, especially water, roads and electricity. On many big issues, however – housing, education, jobs – the ANC had little to show. Levels of crime were high and a new problem had emerged in perceptions of government corruption. The majority understood that achieving change would take time. And they believed that the country was going in the right direction. But they still felt that more should have been done.

If there was disappointment in the ranks of ANC supporters, there was disarray when it came to de Klerk's opposition NP. By 1996 it had become clear that the NP's role in government had been completely ineffectual. In addition, the NP was apparently learning a harsh lesson: you cannot take a group of white South Africans who have been trained for more than

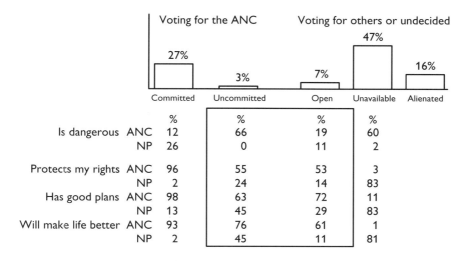

| | Committed | Uncommitted | Open | Unavailable | Alienated |
|---|---|---|---|---|---|
| | % | % | % | % | |
| Is dangerous ANC | 12 | 66 | 19 | 60 | |
| NP | 26 | 0 | 11 | 2 | |
| Protects my rights ANC | 96 | 55 | 53 | 3 | |
| NP | 2 | 24 | 14 | 83 | |
| Has good plans ANC | 98 | 63 | 72 | 11 | |
| NP | 13 | 45 | 29 | 83 | |
| Will make life better ANC | 93 | 76 | 61 | 1 | |
| NP | 2 | 45 | 11 | 81 | |

**Figure 9.6**  *The impact of issues on commitment and availability to the ANC in 1995: coloured voters in the run-up to the local elections*

40 years to think of apartheid as 'God's natural order' and get them to behave in non-racial ways.

Apart from the nationwide focus on mobilizing voters who already supported the ANC, the strategic focus for the local elections in 1996 was very much on 'swing' areas in which the ANC had a chance of winning new support. According to the research, the most promising of those areas was the rural Western Cape and the Northern Cape. In 1994, rural communities in the Western Cape had voted against the ANC by a ratio of close to five to one. But the failures of de Klerk's NP had resulted in a significant shift of rural coloured support towards the ANC.

Figure 9.6 is almost a copy-book picture of the ambivalent mind. Take a look at the swing voters – those who were either uncommitted to the ANC or open to conversion to the ANC. In 1994, many of them had voted for the NP. But by 1996, large percentages of these groups had come to believe that the ANC really was committed to creating a 'better life for all' and that it had the plans to do so. There was still a hangover from 1994 in terms of whether or not the ANC really would 'protect the rights' of 'people like me'. By contrast, the NP was not seen to be offering a better life for all. But many voters still believed that the NP would 'look after' their rights.

In 1994 the ANC's campaign theme had been 'we have the plans to make a better life for all'. The research in 1996 showed that the ANC had achieved credibility in terms of that promise. The party's challenge was to overcome the remaining ambivalence. So the campaign theme was built around a simple extension of the 'better life' theme: 'a better life for all, make it happen where you live'. 'We have the policies', the ANC was saying, 'if you haven't seen the fruits of those policies yet, support our people and they will make sure that it happens where you live'. The campaign invited people to take control in their local areas by voting for the ANC.

The campaign was a stunning success. In the ANC's election offices the mood was electrifying as the results came in. One after another, districts in the Western Cape in which the ANC had got as little as 10% of the vote in 1994, were won. In short, in 1996 the ANC swept the rural and mostly coloured areas of the Western Cape. At the same time, there was no noticeable opposition to the ANC emerging in the areas in the rest of the country which it had won in 1994.

## The second general election: 1999

By 1999, the mood in South Africa was definitely sombre. The country had been through a painful economic adjustment as the government brought down inflation and paid back the huge debts it had inherited from de Klerk's NP. When the ANC took over in 1994, the government deficit before borrowing stood at close to 10% of gross national product – more than three times the limit allowed for joining the EU. By 1999, the ANC had brought this down to less than 3%. Formal jobs were being destroyed as South Africa's previously sanctions-based economy was opened up to the world and South African businesses were forced to become competitive.

In other areas delivery had stuttered. Basic services continued to be a success story and a massive housing programme was at last under way. But organized crime had escalated alarmingly and joblessness was rampant. An overlay to all of this was a sense that people in government had stopped caring about poor people now that they were in office and getting good salaries. Stories of government corruption and incompetence were a daily occurrence.

In developing election themes for the 1999 election we concluded that voter disappointment should be recognized. While the ANC had scored many successes in its short five years – politically motivated killing had all but stopped and basic delivery had begun – there was a cloud of doubt about the ANC in the minds of many people. We concluded that it would be difficult to break through this cloud to focus on the successes. The campaign theme would therefore have to acknowledge the 'cloud of doubt'.

Again, the theme was simple: 'fighting for change – and a better life for all'. The ANC admitted that governing South Africa had proven to be much more difficult than it expected. It acknowledged that the difficulty of government was not made easier by people in its own ranks who simply took advantage of the fact that they were in power to enrich themselves. In campaign speeches, Thabo Mbeki, the president elect, drew attention to his disappointment at the corruption and incompetence in government. He vowed to do something about it. The campaign itself was designed to start with these acknowledgements and then gradually became increasingly positive as the election date grew closer.

Opposition to the ANC was in complete disarray by 1999. All the evidence pointed to the collapse of support for De Klerk's former party, now called the New NP. In addition, once it had become clear that the heart of Buthelezi's support was mainly rural Zulu, white support for the IFP melted away. As a result, the DP managed to consolidate white support against the ANC, becoming the biggest opposition party with 9.6% of the vote. Support for the New NP fell catastrophically from 20.4% to 6.9%. But while the DP celebrated its massive gains, not many commentators pointed out that the combined vote of the DP and the New NP had fallen from 22.1% in 1994 to 16.4% in 1999.

Black opposition to the ANC did emerge at local levels. In one of its strongholds, a region called the Eastern Cape, the ANC lost a fair amount of support to a new party called the United Democratic Movement led by a former member of the ANC, Bantu Holomisa. Holomisa's UDM got 14% of the Eastern Cape vote, knocking the ANC back from 84% in 1994 to 74% in 1999. In the North West Province a former homelands leader, Chief Mangope, took a few percentage points off the ANC.

But ANC losses among traditional supporters were more than made up by its continuing massive gains among non-white ethnic minorities who had opposed it in 1994. Against all expectations, the ANC easily won the Northern Cape, previously a marginal province. It achieved a crushing victory in Gauteng. And in the Western Cape, the ANC increased its support by 33%, becoming the biggest party in the province and forcing opposition parties to form a coalition to keep the ANC out of provincial government. In Kwa-Zulu Natal the ANC got as many votes as Buthelezi's IFP and went into a government of provincial unity. Countrywide, support for the ANC increased from 62.7% in 1994 to 66.4% in 1999.

## Concluding remarks

To date, the three ANC campaigns have been a text-book case of developing a long-term strategy and then sticking to it. 'A better life for all' is still what the ANC is about. Fear, as the main motivator of opposition, has been replaced by a sense that the ANC is incompetent – but among a smaller group of people than before. And ironically, incompetence is a healthier reason for opposition than fear. In fact, it's normal.

In 1994, the ANC laid down three guidelines to campaigning that have continued to inform the development of election campaign themes. It is worth repeating them here. The first is: the election campaign must help to create a national mood which facilitates the task of government afterwards. In other words, the ANC is committed to running elections in such a way that a positive mood is created in the country.

The second guiding principle has always been: no matter what our election research shows, the campaign must be true to the non-racial values of the ANC. The ANC is a party for all people. Its campaigns must reflect that, whether or not it succeeds in attracting a broad band of all people.

The third guiding principle is: the national goals of the ANC must drive strategy, not what's in the public mind. In other words, election strategy will not simply play back what the public wants as seems to happen in so much Western political campaigning these days. Instead, while the campaign will take into account what is in the public mind, it will also aim to present the public with the ANC's vision for government and for the future.

# Marketer's summary: political campaigning

More than any other marketing research, political research involves testing campaign messages. We do not use our approach to commitment to make predictions. Rather, it has four very specific uses:

- To identify very precisely a party's uncommitted supporters on the one hand, and non-supporters who are open to being recruited on the other.
- To classify 'refusals' or 'don't know' voters more precisely in terms of the way they are leaning than conventional techniques make possible.
- To identify voters who are alienated from the political process in a seamless way and with greater reliability than is conventionally possible.
- To provide a simple and powerful framework for communicating what is in the mind of voters to party campaigners.

Modern political campaigning runs the risk of submitting party ideology to public opinion. Politics has lost some of its credibility because the public believe that politicians allow themselves to be driven by public opinion rather than by what they the politicians believe in. In our campaigning we have attempted to avoid this:

- What drives the formulation of campaign messages is the party's vision, not mainstream public opinion.
- Campaigns have therefore had a long-term focus – the party has been aware that it will have to wait for public opinion to catch up with aspects of the vision.
- Because the country is ideologically and ethnically divided, there has been a strong bias towards positive rather than negative campaigning.

In contrast to the more commercial markets in which we have worked, we do not see our commitment-based approach to politics as supplanting conventional political campaign work. In our view, political campaigning is one of the most sophisticated forms of marketing there is. There are no marketers with whom we have worked who focus as intently on persuasion as the politicians.

We therefore see our commitment-based approach as enhancing the way in which political campaigning happens. We can improve what is done by making it more precise and by creating a theoretical framework for understanding the results of political research.

# 10

## Some Practical Tips

### *Some dos and don'ts*

This chapter describes some common errors encountered in marketing. In addition, we provide a brand manager's checklist to be used when drawing up a marketing plan.

All marketers make mistakes, no matter how experienced they are, and regardless of the size of their organization. The Coca-Cola Company made a mistake with New Coke, and the Levi Strauss Company has been castigated for strategic marketing errors by missing opportunities in the youth market in the USA in recent years. More recently, Richard Branson announced the withdrawal of Virgin Cola from the USA, where the brand achieved less than 0.1% of the market. Usually, when the mistakes are big enough heads roll. But a lot of these mistakes are avoidable. Whereas in the past there were areas in the marketing world which were pretty murky, and we had to feel our way around by fumbling in the dark, we now have efficient radar detection systems that can identify the problems and challenges well in advance, mapping out the territory to be conquered or protected, as need be.

Although we make mistakes and learn from our experiences, there are some mistakes which are made more frequently than others. Not only are they made more frequently, but their impact on the bottom line is significant. Some of these mistakes are made with the best of intentions, after having gleaned all available knowledge of the marketing environment, and of the latest analytical methodologies to analyse the data, so as to arrive at an optimal solution. But the methodologies which were used and the thinking employed are reliant on a view of the world that has changed. 'Flat-earth marketing' is now moving to the realization that the marketing world is round. By adjusting to the new reality, which at times is difficult to assimilate into the organization, we are able to avoid costly mistakes from the outset.

This chapter contains a list of the areas in which change is most likely to occur in the near term by applying the philosophy of commitment-led marketing. Typically, they are 'quick hits', resulting in an immediate boosting of the bottom line. If you have committed some of these mistakes in the past, you have not been alone. As an example, armies of marketing researchers have been incorrectly evaluating the effectiveness of ad campaigns, relegating perfectly sound campaigns to the rubbish dump. But we are now in a position to correct some of the misperceptions of the past, for the benefit of the brand and its profitability.

> **" 'Flat-earth marketing' is now moving to the realization that the marketing world is round."**

Let's have a look at the areas in which marketers are most likely to make mistakes, by not utilizing the philosophy of commitment-led marketing.

# 1. Unnecessary price-cutting

Procter & Gamble are marketers for whom we have a lot of admiration. We are surprised that more marketers do not emulate their intelligent stand on price-cutting. Some years ago Procter & Gamble adopted a policy of everyday low prices (EDLP) in the USA. They do not price promote their products, and rely on the strength of the brand for profitable sales.

In most markets, there are too many price promotions, to the detriment of the profits of the brand, as well as those of the retail trade. The larger the segment of consumers committed to the brand, the less appropriate price promotion becomes. Yet it still happens with alarming frequency, often at the insistence of the retail trade.

Unnecessary price-cutting erodes the *total* brand equity in the market, and seldom results in a long-term increase in brand share. By continually indulging in price promotions, all that is achieved is that consumers are trained to wait patiently for the next price promotion, at which time they will stock up their trolleys for the next few months.

Having said this, however, the retail trade often poses a very real problem, particularly when they are used to getting significant discounts at certain times of the year. The challenge in many parts of the world is to educate the retail trade on the dangers of price promotion, and the value in resisting discounting wherever possible.

> **"Unnecessary price-cutting erodes the *total* brand equity in the market, and seldom results in a long-term increase in brand share."**

When price promotions take place, the committed customer will stock up, and the promiscuous price shopper will take advantage of the price promotion. Commitment will not be improved by selling the brand at a lower price unless, of course, it was being sold at a disproportionately higher price previously.

We have found that, in line with marketers underestimating the commitment of consumers in the markets in which they operate, price sensitivity is often overestimated. Typically, when we debate this point with marketers, they will point to share changes which have occurred as a result of price promotions. It is rare for these fluctuations to exceed more than a couple of percentage points. In most markets, a small group of promiscuous price shoppers can give the market a misleading impression of the way in which the market operates, as they flit from price promotion to price promotion.

> **"When price promotions take place, the committed customer will stock up, and the promiscuous price shopper will take advantage of the price promotion."**

One of the best guides to the stability of the market, and the desirability of price promotions is the underlying commitment to brands in that market. By using this approach, the marketer can avoid giving money away unnecessarily, as the committed consumer will buy the brand regardless of price promotions. The more committed consumers a brand has, the less appropriate price promotions become.

> **"We have found that, in line with marketers underestimating the commitment of consumers in the markets in which they operate, price sensitivity is often overestimated."**

It will often be the case that marketers manage more than one brand in the same product category. When this is the case, the brand with the smaller segment of committed consumers should be the one offered to the retail trade when they demand price promotions. The equity of the stronger brand should be protected at all costs.

# 2. Unnecessary new product development

Most new product launches fail because marketers fail to take commitment to existing brands into account.[1] They do not measure the commitment that consumers have to the brands they are already using, and as a result overestimate their chances of success. It is difficult to formulate an effective new product development strategy without the knowledge of the commitment of consumers to competitive products.

Some marketers attempt to boost a languishing brand share by launching new variants of the product. Consider, however, the reasons for not doing so. With each additional variant that is launched, shelf facings of the parent brand are further squeezed and the problems of visibility become more acute. Consumers become confused and the overall brand health suffers.

> **"Markets should be examined by category and geography, in order to identify which markets will be easier to penetrate than others."**

Too often, we see marketers trying to fight their way out of declining sales situations by launching new variants. Bearing in mind that the more alternatives a consumer is offered, the lower their commitment will be to any single alternative, we would recommend that, before embarking on this course of action, the marketer is convinced that launching new variants will result in a significant increase in share. Of course, it may be that the marketer is forced into doing this as a defensive strategy, in order to ensure that the committed users of the brand are not wooed by competitive variants which pose a threat.

The process of new product development should be embedded in an understanding of commitment in the markets in which the marketer is interested. Markets should be examined by category and geography, in order to identify which markets will be easier to penetrate than others. A strongly committed market does not mean that new product development is inappropriate. Rather, it has the implication that the strategy used for entering the market will differ. When markets are highly committed, forced trial is almost essential, in the form of sampling, but when markets are characterized by low commitment, product sampling is seldom necessary.

New product concepts, as well as the products themselves, should be tested on those consumers who are open to the appeal of the brand. Testing the concept of a new product on a consumer who is already committed to another brand can produce negatively biased reactions to a product which may well have strong appeal for the rest of the market. Commitment is an essential overlay to the results of research studies designed to measure the reaction of consumers to the concepts of new products, as well as the products themselves.

> **"New product concepts, as well as the products themselves, should be tested on those consumers who are open to the appeal of the brand."**

# 3. Too much advertising

Advertising plays a nudging role, rather than a persuasive one, and needs the fertile soil of usage, particularly by committed users, to be most effective. If the brand is a small one, in terms of market share, it has few committed users in relative terms. Hence, its advertising is not as effective as that of a brand with many committed users.

The objective of advertising for small brands should primarily be one of creating awareness for the brand, rather than persuading consumers to buy the product. It is the brand *itself* that attracts consumers. Although it could be argued that advertising plays a part in creating this image, the campaigns that are able to achieve this are in the minority. Certainly they exist, but the odds are against the average marketer in terms of developing these types of campaigns. For brands that are ranked number four or lower in terms of brand share, the investment of substantial funds into above-the-line advertising, particularly when the brand is already well known, is questionable. In these situations, lateral solutions to marketing problems are needed. The classic approach of spending more on advertising is seldom likely to produce results.

> **"The objective of advertising for small brands should primarily be one of creating awareness for the brand, rather than persuading consumers to buy the product."**

The frustration of many marketers, then, is how to acquire more committed users, when launching new brands. The harsh truth is that it is often difficult, if not impossible. Some leading marketers, including the likes of Procter & Gamble, will only enter markets in which their brands have a strong probability of being in position one or two. We would support this view and suggest that a harsh approach be taken by culling brands which languish with small shares in over-traded markets. These brands are often unprofitable and only cause stress to the marketing team, as well as sour relations with the retail trade.

For small brands, we would strongly recommend the use of guerrilla tactics to improve the visibility of the brand to consumers. Advertising can be a very expensive way of increasing visibility. There are much cheaper ways of achieving this. Bus shelters, billboards and the sponsoring of sports teams are some of the ways that can be used to enhance the visibility of the brand. When consumers are exposed to a brand in a variety of different situations, the implicit cue is that the brand is well established, and secure and strong in its position in the market. Essentially, the marketer needs to think of every innovative cost-effective way of publicizing the existence of the brand.

> **"For small brands, we would strongly recommend the use of guerrilla tactics to improve the visibility of the brand to consumers."**

## 4. Too little advertising

A brand leader should behave like a true leader. When a brand is large, and has built up a significant segment of committed consumers, these consumers need to be reassured on a regular basis, in the same way as a personal relationship is sustained.

Recent debates in the area of media planning show a strong swing to the attractiveness of 'drip' campaigns rather than 'burst' campaigns.[2] Much of the research we have undertaken supports this view. The role of advertising for a strong brand, with a large segment of committed consumers, is to reassure committed consumers and give them a 'feel good' feeling. Too often, we see leading brands underspending on advertising, indulging in burst advertising, where drip schedules would be preferable.

| |
|---|
| **"A brand leader should behave like a true leader."** |

We have seen examples of brands that have neglected their committed consumers for some years, by cutting off all advertising support. The result of this is that commitment slips slowly but surely. When launching a new ad campaign, after having been absent for some time, it is not unusual to see the size of the committed segment leap dramatically, as those consumers who have slipped in commitment renew their ties with the brand. Equivalently, when the advertising tap is turned off, commitment to the brand edges downwards once again.

The relationships between consumers and brands are similar to relationships between people. If relationships are not nurtured and sustained, they will eventually deteriorate. In the same way as friendship needs sustaining by regular contact, in some or other form, as well as a feeling that a friend 'cares', brands need to make contact with their consumers on a regular basis, reassuring them of the wisdom of an ongoing relationship. Advertising is particularly relevant for this task, when it comes to reassuring committed users of the brand. Given their high propensity to receive and like almost any advertising for the brand, the more committed consumers the brand has, the more relevant significant advertising support becomes in the total marketing mix.

| |
|---|
| **"If relationships are not nurtured and sustained, they will eventually deteriorate."** |

# 5. Inadequate management at point of purchase

Great marketers build strong brands *and* make it easy for consumers to purchase their brand. All too often, we encounter brands which consumers love, but which are inadequately managed at the point of sale. Effective marketing management manages not only the relationship with committed consumers, but that with uncommitted consumers as well. Any brand will have a segment of uncommitted consumers, with many of them uncommitted because brand choice does not matter. These consumers do not want to spend a lot of time thinking about the brand, and the purchase decision must be made as painless as possible. The brand should be the first one that comes to mind, stand out on the shelf, be attractively priced and be available at all outlets. The larger the segment of consumers for whom brand choice does *not* matter, the more important this will become in terms of overall management of the brand.

> **"Effective marketing management manages not only the relationship with committed consumers, but that with uncommitted consumers as well."**

A committed consumer will go out of their way to find the brand, delving into the back of shop shelves if necessary. Uncommitted consumers will not go to these lengths, and the relationship needs to be managed appropriately.

## 6. Believing that advertising can change perceptions

In many marketing departments, the brand teams change every couple of years. We often see brand teams setting the objective of changing the perceptions of the brand, using advertising to achieve this. The chance of doing this is very slim. For mature brands, in well-established markets, the odds against advertising changing the perception of the brand intrinsics are high.

However, it is seductive, in terms of cookie-cutter marketing, to give the ad agency the brief of changing the perception of the brand on certain key attributes. This will usually be a waste of money.

> **"For mature brands, in well-established markets, the odds against advertising changing the perception of the brand intrinsics are high."**

Advertising works best at reinforcing current beliefs. In exceptional circumstances it might change the perception of the brand, but these circumstances will be truly exceptional. What an advertisement can more realisitically aim at doing is making the brand more visible. It is easier to make a brand more salient than to change the way it is seen. Achieving a perceptual shift for well-known brands is exceptionally difficult, takes a long time, and cannot be done without unusually creative advertising.

> **"Advertising works best at reinforcing current beliefs."**

As we have described earlier in this book, advertising is very much a rifle shot mechanism and not a shotgun. It works best at reassuring consumers who are already committed to the brand and non-users of the brand who are already available to it. This is obviously a very valuable role. However, the majority of campaigns cannot be expected to do much more for the brand than that.

## 7. Spending according to value instead of commitment

Relationship managers are often told to lavish attention on their high-value customers. But what if some of your high-value customers are already committed? They like you the way that you are and are already spending as much with you as they can. You are not going to get more out of them by spending more on them.

The key is not to spend indiscriminately on your high-value customers, but to be able to distinguish who among them are committed and who are uncommitted. Committed high-value customers need maintenance spending. Uncommitted high-value customers need retention spending. In our experience, maintenance ought to cost less than retention. Here is what's involved.

First, it's what you're already doing that makes them committed. 'Maintenance' has to do with understanding exactly what it is about your brand that makes them committed – and maintaining that. If you're an airline, it's about maintaining the elements of your image that are attractive to your high-value, committed customers. It's about continuing to deliver the unique parts of the service that delight them. They will almost certainly be frequent flyers – and so it's about understanding exactly what it is about your programme that they like.

In our experience, it's not about how much you spend on high-value committed customers, it's more to do with your failure to recognize them in the first place. Just think about airlines. Or hotels. How many of them know how to recognize the customer who is both worth a lot and committed at every point of contact? Very few. A committed customer can be worth anything up to a hundred times more to the brand than an uncommitted customer. Committed customers not only spend more, but have a dramatically longer life expectancy than uncommitted customers. They are worth nurturing in every way.

The challenge to the marketer is not just to create a database of customers, but to be able to identify customers in terms of their lifelong profitability to the company. We still find that the majority of marketers are unable to quantify the profitability of their customers at an individual level. This is a critical component of an optimal marketing strategy for the future.

> **"A committed customer can be worth anything up to a hundred times more to the brand than an uncommitted customer."**

The more successful you are at maintaining the commitment of your high-value committed customers, the more profitable your brand will be. If you have not yet worked out how to identify your really committed customers, now is the time to start. While you are doing that, start thinking about all the things *you* would like as a customer, to show appreciation for the business that you are giving to a brand.

The happier your committed customers are, the longer they will stay with you and the more likely they are to act as advocates for your brand. Highly committed customers are an extension of your sales force. A focus on your committed customers is one of the most important elements of an effective marketing strategy. Remember – it is easy to lose the commitment of a committed consumer. By maintaining commitment, the profits of the brand will be boosted immediately.

> **"Highly committed customers are an extension of your sales force."**

# 8. Spending too much on consumers who are unavailable

This is probably one of the marketing mistakes that we encounter most frequently – aiming advertising and promotional activities at customers who simply are not available to the brand. Advertising is particularly inappropriate for this task.

> **"The best way of breaking into the consciousness of a strongly unavailable consumer is to 'force' trial."**

A consumer who is strongly unavailable to your brand has a long way to go before they actually make a purchase. They have to change from being strongly unavailable to weakly unavailable. From there, they have to become ambivalent, then into the psychological state of availability before making the actual purchase. It's a long road.

The best way of breaking into the consciousness of a strongly unavailable consumer is to 'force' trial. Advertising has to work unusually hard to break into the consciousness of people in a market who are strongly unavailable to your brand. And even if it does break through, it has to work hard to be received favourably.

The most likely reason for unavailability, in nearly all markets, is that the consumer is just not interested. They are happy with the brands they are using, and see no reason to switch. They don't need any information about your brand. They are not interested in your persuasive messages on television. Their minds switch off when your brand swings into their field of vision. They are incredibly difficult to reach. Yet, time and time again, marketers make them a target of their marketing campaigns, often because of the enticingly large size of the unavailable segment.

> **"The most likely reason for unavailability, in nearly all markets, is that the consumer is just not interested."**

Spending significant amounts of money to woo unavailable consumers, using traditional marketing methods, is probably one of the biggest marketing mistakes a marketer can make. There is no excuse for making this mistake any more. We can now actively quantify, with precision, the size of the segment unavailable to the brand, the profile of that segment, and the reasons why they are unavailable. Armed with this information, the marketer is able to assess whether there is any realistic chance of succeeding in wooing them, or whether they should be effectively excluded from the market in which the brand operates.

> **"Spending significant amounts of money to woo unavailable consumers, using traditional marketing methods, is probably one of the biggest marketing mistakes a marketer can make."**

## 9. Trying to have a relationship with a consumer who doesn't want one

We get irritated when people we don't particularly like or care about try to have personal relationships with us. This can range from irritation when somebody strikes up a conversation in a queue and you prefer to keep your thoughts to yourself, to a negative reaction to an invitation to lunch or dinner with somebody with whom you have little in common. Relationships between consumers and brands are no different. A lot of consumers, in any market, don't want a relationship with a brand. They don't want consumer intimacy. They don't want to have a 'marketing conversation'.

Particularly in direct marketing campaigns, attempting to open a dialogue with consumers who are not interested wastes a significant amount of the expenditure. Direct marketing material of any kind, whether it is in the form of direct mail, e-mail messages or telephone approaches, is rejected out of hand by these consumers. Direct mail pieces are often tossed into the bin unopened.

It is a relatively straightforward process to identify customers in a database with whom it would be relatively pointless to attempt to form a relationship, unless you could change the importance of the product category in their lives. These are the people for whom brand choice has little importance. When a consumer is not involved in the category, they are unlikely to devote much energy to learning more about the brands that are available. In the same way that mass media can incur significant wastage, one-on-one marketing can be guilty of exactly the same crime. So, don't try to flirt with a consumer who is not interested.

> **"It is a relatively straightforward process to identify customers in a database with whom it would be relatively pointless to attempt to form a relationship, unless you could change the importance of the product category in their lives."**

## Acquiring the necessary information

How simple is it to acquire the information necessary in order to avoid the mistakes outlined? Very. There is now a global network of research suppliers and marketing consultants who are able to measure the commitment in your market cost-effectively, in a short space of time.

These measurements can be taken in different geographies for any product category you might care to specify, in applications ranging from product and concept tests through to continuous tracking. Obviously, utilizing these methodologies comes at a cost. But the benefit of applying your new learnings to the strategic management of the brand should result in cost savings and improvements in profitability which far outweigh the cost of acquiring this information.

Understanding the lack of availability to your brand can have a dramatic impact on the reduction of wastage. The commitment of consumers drives new product development programmes, communication strategies, pricing strategies and distribution strategies. Understanding the relationship between your brand and its consumers, compared to competitors, is essential for formulating a strategy that will enable you to win the marketing warfare battle. You need to know when brands are vulnerable, and how to exploit that vulnerability. You need to know when it is appropriate to defend, and when it is appropriate to attack. You need to know what is in the consumer's mind so as to manage the relationship appropriately. You need to understand the relationships that exist between your consumer and your brand, and all competitive brands in the marketplace. Without the understanding of commitment, no marketing strategy can be completely effective.

## Some dos – a brand manager's checklist

Most brand managers draw up a marketing plan at least once a year. This plan usually contains an overview of the brand's position in the market, in terms of its brand share, together with a budgeted increase for the year ahead. The brand's target market is fully described, as well as the desired brand positioning. The marketing strategy is outlined, with all tactical activities for the year described and budgeted for.

Traditional marketing plans do not take commitment into account when describing the market structure and the relative position of the brand. This is a significant oversight. By incorporating the philosophy of commitment-led marketing, savings and increased profitability opportunities exist at every turn.

In this section we explore some of the building blocks of a comprehensive marketing plan, giving suggestions for ways in which tactics and strategy can be improved. The essential components of a marketing plan can be summarized as follows:

- Describing the market
- What makes your brand different?
- Setting growth targets
- Marketing objectives
- Formulating a communication strategy
- Feedback mechanisms

## Describing the market

Typically, a key component of the marketing plan is a description of the market in which the brand operates.

- What is the size of the market in revenue terms?
- How many consumers are there?
- Which brands compete in the market, and what are their relative brand shares?
- What have the trends been in these shares?

Undoubtedly, these questions need answers. But there are additional questions which need answers.

- What is the overall commitment in this market, compared to other product categories?

- How does this product category compare to the same product category in other geographies, in terms of commitment?

One of the most important characteristics of a market is the overall commitment that exists in that market. This information defines the basic rules that will apply to the product category. For example, knowing that the tomato sauce market in South Africa is a very high commitment market means that the market will not be particularly price sensitive. It will be difficult to persuade committed consumers to switch. The market will be relatively inert, and brand shares will change little from period to period, regardless of marketing activities. New entrants are unlikely to have much success, unless vigorously supported by the trade, in attempts to break the dominance of the traditional brand leaders.

In a market which is highly committed, marketing incompetence can be tolerated for an amazingly long time. It is difficult to break a strong relationship between consumers and the brands to which they are committed. In the same way as a strong personal relationship survives ups and downs, a strong relationship between consumers and brands can survive marketing incompetence in terms of lack of advertising support, poor advertising executions, erratic pricing strategies and periodic out-of-stock situations. However, a brand can only take so much abuse, and the relationship will eventually deteriorate, but consumers are sometimes surprisingly resilient when it comes to sustaining the relationships they enjoy with their favourite brands.

On the other hand, for marketers attempting to break into highly committed markets, there can be many years of frustration. They seem almost impossible to gain entry to, in terms of getting a small brand to survive and thrive.

> **"In a market which is highly committed, marketing incompetence can be tolerated for an amazingly long time."**

At this stage of the marketing plan, geographical comparisons can also provide insight, in many instances. By examining a commitment norm base, the commitment in your market compared to other product categories in your country can be examined, as well as the commitment in your product category to similar product categories in other geographies. This knowledge helps you avoid the error of unwise comparisons. For example, the South African and Australian markets are extremely different in terms of the commitment of their consumers, despite occupying the same geographic region. The identification of markets which are similar to yours in structure enable you to study them so as to identify winning and losing strategies.

When we are confronted by markets which are unfamiliar, the single most important piece of information is the structure of the market, as measured by commitment. Once we understand the level of commitment that exists, it is relatively easy to know which strategies might work, and what will definitely not work. If the marketer does not have this information, wishful thinking can result in an inordinate waste of money. On the one hand, if the market is a highly inert one, traditional marketing approaches will result in no change at all, with a massive loss of funds, particularly for smaller brands trying to grow their share of the market. Then again, if the market is characterized by low commitment, and hence pricing sensitivity, an excess of funds spent on advertising could be short-sighted. In low commitment markets, the majority of funds should be spent on street-fighting tactics, promoting visibility and convenience, as well as a perception of being competitively priced.

## What makes your brand different?

The next step is to describe the profile of your brand's users, as well as quantifying the potential for your brand to grow.

- What is the profile of your brand's users?
- How does this compare to your competitors?
- What is the commitment to your brand, compared to those of your competitors?
- Which brands are vulnerable to attack?
- From which brands can consumers be acquired?
- If your brand is strategically vulnerable, which competitor is the biggest threat, and why?

Traditionally, brand plans profile the brand's users in terms of demographics, psychographics, geodemographics and so on. However, it is

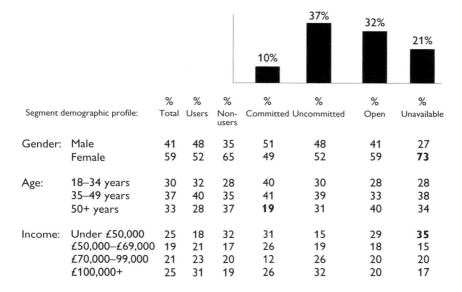

| Segment demographic profile: | % Total | % Users | % Non-users | % Committed | % Uncommitted | % Open | % Unavailable |
|---|---|---|---|---|---|---|---|
| **Gender:** Male | 41 | 48 | 35 | 51 | 48 | 41 | 27 |
| Female | 59 | 52 | 65 | 49 | 52 | 59 | **73** |
| | | | | | | | |
| **Age:** 18–34 years | 30 | 32 | 28 | 40 | 30 | 28 | 28 |
| 35–49 years | 37 | 40 | 35 | 41 | 39 | 33 | 38 |
| 50+ years | 33 | 28 | 37 | **19** | 31 | 40 | 34 |
| | | | | | | | |
| **Income:** Under £50,000 | 25 | 18 | 32 | 31 | 15 | 29 | **35** |
| £50,000–£69,000 | 19 | 21 | 17 | 26 | 19 | 18 | 15 |
| £70,000–99,000 | 21 | 23 | 20 | 12 | 26 | 20 | 20 |
| £100,000+ | 25 | 31 | 19 | 26 | 32 | 20 | 17 |

**Figure 10.1** *Typical brand profile*

more logical to profile your brand's users in terms of their commitment, and non-users in terms of their availability. Figure 10.1 gives a simple example of such an analysis. It can be seen that unavailability to the brand skews to women and those in the lowest income group. Hence, these will be the most difficult demographic targets for the brand. These analyses provide valuable insight in identifying the demographic segment providing most value to the brand, in terms of ongoing commitment, as well as identifying those demographic segments which will be most difficult to acquire.

Ideally, one would always want not only a profile of the brand's users, but the contribution they make to the value of the brand. As has been pointed out earlier, the heavier the user of the category, the less likely they are to be committed to any one brand. What share of requirements is your brand getting from its consumers, and realistically, how much could this grow?

Within any market, there is significant variation in terms of commitment to brands. Figure 10.2 shows the results of commitment to TV channels in South Africa, shortly after the launch of a new TV channel, e.tv, a free to air station, which was launched in October 1998.

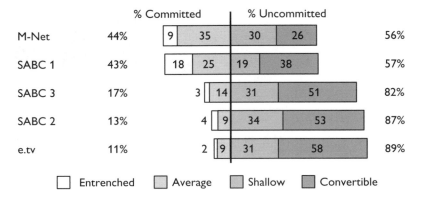

**Figure 10.2** *Strength of commitment to stations watched in past week 28 September–*
*25 October 1998: launch phase*

*Source:* Research Surveys (Pty) Ltd, 1998.

It can be seen that the market is characterized by a high commitment to the leading channels – SABC 1 and M-Net. These are the channels least likely to be affected by e.tv's launch. On the other hand, it can be seen that SABC 2 and SABC 3 are relatively vulnerable. The high commitment to the leading channels means that channel choice, rather than programme choice, drives viewing habits. If a programme's position is switched from one channel to another, it is unlikely to take its audience with it. Although we have measured the commitment in many media markets internationally, the South African television market is one of the few in which we have encountered such high commitment to TV channels.

Having understood the strong commitment to SABC 1 and M-Net, the marketing team at e.tv knew that those audiences would be the most difficult to seduce. In the short term, the objective would be to leap-frog SABC 2 and SABC 3, because of the relatively low commitment of their viewers. SABC 1 and M-Net would be longer-term objectives, in terms of eroding their viewer base.

By identifying the effective competition, e.tv was able to draw up a programme schedule that targeted the most vulnerable viewers of the competitive channels. This strategy proved to be successful, as

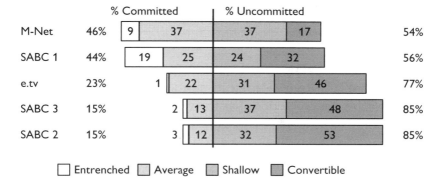

**Figure 10.3** *Strength of commitment to stations watched in past week, 1–28 February 1999*
Source: Research Surveys (Pty) Ltd, 1999.

evidenced by Figure 10.3, which shows commitment to the different channels after e.tv's launch. In a short space of time, e.tv had developed into a stronger brand than SABC 2 and SABC 3, as measured by the allegiance of their viewers.

The predictions of commitment have been fulfilled: e.tv has grown at the expense of SABC 2 and 3, but the tough challenges of SABC 1 and M-Net remain.

Knowing the level of commitment in a market quantifies the size of the marketing challenge. For e.tv, it is clear that the challenge is significant. However, the most vulnerable targets have been accurately identified, the size and profile of the segment available to the new channel has been measured, and the programmes that are most successful in attracting new viewers have been identified. By measuring the total commitment in the market, the ability to predict increases in market share is vastly improved, as the reality of the situation is brought home forcefully.

## Setting growth targets

All too often, we see unrealistic estimates of potential growth of a brand. If you are to grow your brand, where will this growth come from? And how will it be obtained?

> **"Knowing the level of commitment in a market quantifies the size of the marketing challenge."**

The fundamental stance of the brand needs to be clearly identified. Should the brand be consolidating its position or should it be attacking? This is the most basic question that the brand manager needs to address, which can only be answered by looking at the commitment to the brand, compared to that of its competitors. As has been outlined in earlier chapters, it is fairly straightforward to evaluate the size of the segment that can be lost to the competitors, and the size of the segment that can be gained. The next step would be to attach an accurate quantification of growth for the coming year. We need to remind ourselves that not all consumers identified as being uncommitted will leave the brand in the near term, neither will all available non-users be acquired. Estimates need to be made of the proportion of uncommitted consumers likely to be lost, as well as the proportion of consumers likely to be acquired.

The larger the brand, the fewer convertible consumers will be lost, and the more available non-users acquired. However, there are no definitive guidelines in this regard, and one is forced to make estimates. Our advice would be to be as conservative as possible.

The quantification of the acquisition of available non-users can be significantly improved by ascertaining whether non-users of your brand who are available to it are also available to other brands. Most marketing research studies will yield this information, if the appropriate commitment model is being used. For example, if you find that those consumers available to your brand are available to another four brands, on average, it is fairly safe to assume that, at most, you will acquire 20% of them in the near term, unless appropriate marketing strategies are formulated, which are designed to position your brand more attractively than those of your competitors.

Equally important is an understanding of where the product *category* is heading. Far too often, marketers focus only on competitive brands, without ascertaining the potential for growth or decline in the product category in which they operate. Category threats are far more of a potential threat to brand health than other brands. Category threats are one of the most difficult challenges for a marketer to face, particularly when the brand is not a brand leader.

When faced by category threats, the most important thing for the marketer to understand is the reason for another category becoming a threat to the brand. Without this information, it is impossible to formulate an effective brand strategy. Unfortunately, it is often the case that a single brand is unable to stem the tide of an onslaught from another category, particularly when it is a new product category that consumers are finding attractive. In these cases, the decision has to be taken whether the brand is milked for the rest of its sustainable life or sold to the highest bidder. It is not always the case that a solution can be found to combat the threat of a new category. However, the pitfall of wasting funds unnecessarily can be avoided, once the size of the threat has been quantified, using the availability of your brand's users to the new category as the appropriate measure.

## Marketing objectives

Your marketing objective per commitment segment will differ. Broadly speaking, it can be summarized as shown in Figure 10.4.

Of course, you cannot be all things for all segments. Your choice of focus will depend on the value of each segment, as well as your position of comparative strength in the marketplace.

In the past, marketers have set objectives for target market segments, but have not included the important measurement of commitment. For a target market defined only in terms of demographics, psychographics, geodemographics or whatever, the wastage has been significant, because in any geographic market, in any product category, there are consumers who are simply not available to your brand. By including these consumers in your target market, funds are unnecessarily wasted.

The summary of marketing objectives per segment, as outlined above, will result in a far tighter focus of the marketing effort, concentrating on relationships with the consumers which are able to be managed profitably.

## Formulating a communication strategy

Having decided which segments to focus on, the brand manager needs to be as specific as possible in terms of communication strategies for those segments. The questions which need answers are shown in Figure 10.5.

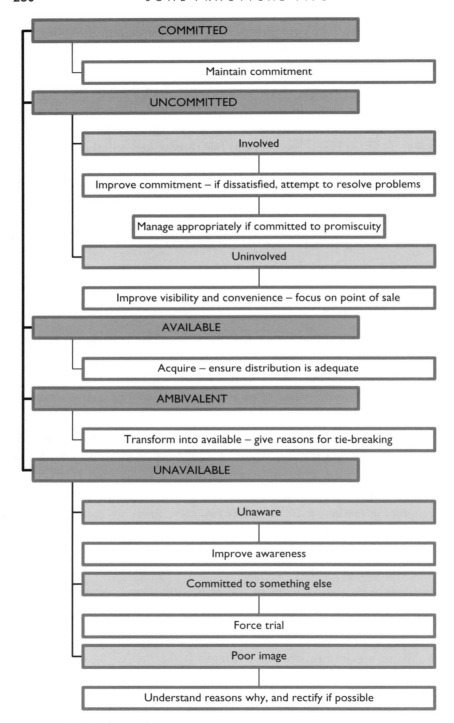

**Figure 10.4** *Marketing objectives*

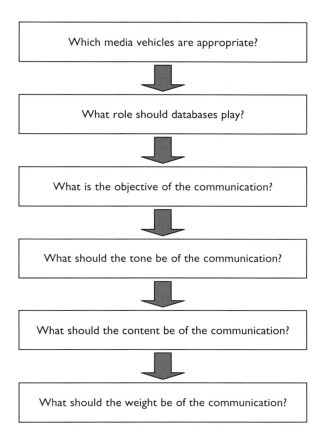

**Figure 10.5** *Communication strategies*

Having decided which commitment segments to focus on, the marketer needs to understand the segments. What is their size? What is their profile? What are their media consumption patterns? What are their lifetime values? All these will feed into the communication strategy, with the amount being spent on communicating with them being commensurate with their value.

Packaging forms an important part of the brand image, and is often ignored, to the detriment of the brand, when evaluating communication strategies. The role of packaging in terms of building the brand image needs to be fully understood, particularly in categories where non-verbal cues are important.

In most cases, our experience has been that pack designs are more likely to influence the consumer perception of the brand than advertising. However, an unnecessary change in pack design can have a seriously negative impact on the relationship between the consumer and the brand, particularly for committed consumers. For this reason, changes in pack design need to be carefully evaluated before final launch, in terms of understanding the impact that they will have on the commitment segments of interest.

The objectives of the communication strategy need to be carefully specified. Is it to reassure already committed consumers, or simply to raise visibility for all consumers? Is it to create a customized one-on-one relationship with consumers, or is the brand simply trying to break into the field of vision of unavailable consumers, making them aware of the brand's existence?

## Feedback mechanisms

It is essential that the effectiveness of the marketing strategy be tracked in a formal way. In particular, the impact of commitment-led marketing on profitability needs to be monitored.

A baseline feedback mechanism is continuous tracking, which has risen significantly in popularity in all markets in the last couple of decades. There are few marketers of successful brands who do not track consumer perceptions and attitudes on a continuous basis. One of the most important features of a tracking programme is the ongoing measurement of commitment to all brands, as well as availability. Figure 10.6 shows an example from the USA, showing the introduction of a new brand in an already cluttered market field.

The first measurement, taken in 1994, shows that the brand had achieved a 29% penetration in the market. However, the striking thing about the brand's position is the extremely high availability to the brand, with 29% of the market being open to the brand. This was a brand operating in the youth market, which was categorized by the ownership of a large repertoire of brands. It can be seen that the brand has a large vulnerable segment, but it is poised to grow given the size of the segment.

Last quarter 1994

|  | % |
|---|---|
| Own | 29 |
| Committed | 9 |
| Uncommitted | 20 |
| Don't own | 71 |
| Open | 29 |
| Unavailable | 42 |

Last quarter 1996

|  | % |
|---|---|
| Own | 45 |
| Committed | 14 |
| Uncommitted | 31 |
| Don't own | 55 |
| Open | 20 |
| Unavailable | 35 |

**Figure 10.6** *Introduction of a new brand in an already cluttered market where penetration changed from 29% at the end of 1994 to 45% at the end of 1996*

In 1996, the predictions of commitment and availability were confirmed. The brand has now grown to a 45% penetration, with its potential to grow even further still remaining.

When the brand was first launched, it had fairly limited distribution. By using the information shown above, the client, who was marketing another brand, was able to identify the size and nature of the competitive threat well in advance. As this product category is one in which purchases are only made every few months, the marketer was in a position to evaluate the size of the threat, and determine what, if anything, could be done to counter it.

We believe that continuous feedback mechanisms improve the wisdom within the brand group, providing that the information gleaned is recorded and stored in a systematic way, and is accessible to the future generations of brand managers who will manage the brand. There are still many unanswered questions in marketing, and continuous tracking provides an ideal way in which to assess the impact of different marketing strategies and tactics. No two markets are exactly the same. It is sometimes only by trial and error that we can discover what is successful and what is a waste of money.

Again, turning to the errors of the past, without examining the commitment of your consumers, as well as the potential of your brand and your competitors to grow, simple behavioural data can be dangerous. It is possible to be lulled into a false sense of security.

For some markets, not only do marketers track the success of their brand and the competition, but also all *categories* deemed to be competitive. If budgets allow for it, we would always strongly recommend this, particularly if new product categories are appearing in the market which could be competitive to your category, or where channels of distribution are changing rapidly, causing consumers to re-evaluate their brand preferences.

Recently, in South Africa, we saw a nice example of this, when petrol companies launched convenience stores on the forecourts of their service stations. This new channel of distribution has proven to be incredibly successful. However, many large packaged goods manufacturers were caught napping by the change. Initially, they paid little attention to this new channel of distribution, enabling smaller brands to take the gap, and gain prominence on the shop shelves in convenience stores. Having lost the opportunity, it is now very difficult for them to reassert the traditional superiority they enjoyed in other channels of distribution.

# In summary

There you have it. Nine frequently encountered don'ts and some dos that can help improve the quality of marketing plans. Managing the relationship between the brand and the customer drives all facets of marketing activities, and understanding the commitment and availability of consumers enhances the profitability of your strategies significantly. The issues which marketers need to focus on are not overwhelmingly numerous. They are relatively few in number and are easy to measure and track.

# References

1. Hofmeyr, J. and Rice, J. (1999) The impact of consumers' commitment to existing brands on new product launch strategies. Esomar Congress, The Race for Innovation, Marketing Research for Pole Position, Paris, September.
2. Ephron, E. (1999) Two views of TV scheduling – how far apart? *Admap*, January.

# 11

## The Road Ahead . . .

### . . . and what it holds for customers and marketers

It is clear that our marketing environment is going through more changes currently than it has for many decades. The impact of e-commerce is still to be fully understood and appreciated. The relative profitability of doing business on the Net remains a subject of fierce debate. But it is clear that the new channels of distribution will have a profound effect on our marketing environment. How will commitment-led marketing impact on this new environment? What will the needs of marketers be, and how can an understanding of commitment enable them to better utilize the opportunities that present themselves?

In this chapter, we look at the road ahead. We highlight three trends in particular in which we believe the ability to measure and service commitment will play a central role. They are:

- The seamless integration of behavioural and attitudinal information for marketing purposes – not just knowing what people are doing, but knowing what they are *thinking* while they are doing it.
- The creation of measurement systems which establish both the short- and long-term returns generated by marketing spending – making marketing truly accountable.
- The inclusion of customers and consumers in the creation of marketing systems with their consent – giving the customer the power to shape the way in which they communicate with marketers.

Let's begin with the integration of information.

# The integration of information

ACNielsen is the largest marketing research organization in the world. One of the things they specialize in is the collection of information on what people buy. With the advent of scanners in retail stores, they formed panels of households which they equipped with laser wands. On returning home from a store, a shopper scans each package purchased, before packing it away. This information is then transmitted to ACNielsen electronically, who market the data as a product called Homescan™.

The Homescan panel enables marketers to profile the use of their brands in the finest detail. People who are recruited to the panel volunteer basic household information, for example, the age and gender make-up of the household. Marketers can combine this information with the information about purchases, and in this way profile pack size use, price sensitivity, responses to promotions in-store and so on. Regional profiles and variations can be examined. Geodemographic patterns of preference can be analysed and understood.

But while the Homescan panel gives marketers a very precise picture of what households are *buying*, it doesn't really tell marketers what they're *thinking*. Nor can the attitudinal gap be filled simply by interviewing members of the panel. Interviewing people on behavioural panels of this kind has the potential to change their behaviour. For this reason, most managers of behavioural panels observe 'from a distance', not wanting to be responsible for any changes in behaviour.

Market Facts, Inc. (MFI) is one of the USA's largest attitudinal marketing research companies. They run a very different kind of panel. Members of some 500 000 households across the USA have agreed to allow themselves to be interviewed regularly about both what they buy and what they think of what they're buying. In contrast to the Homescan panel, which supplies behavioural measures only, the MFI panel is able to supply attitudinal measures. Among the wealth of attitudinal information that MFI collects is information on the commitment and availability of respondents to products and brands.

> **"But while the Homescan panel gives marketers a very precise picture of what households are *buying*, it doesn't really tell marketers what they're *thinking*."**

The difficulty that Market Facts has is that while the panel may provide accurate measures of what people think, many marketers are concerned about it as a measure of what people actually do. The problem lies with the memory of panelists. People are notorious for being imprecise when they report what they're buying. This isn't because panelists wilfully misreport. It's because our memories, as human beings, are not always the best recorders of the things that we have done. Quite simply, *asking* people what they've bought is not as reliable as observing behaviour directly. Marketers therefore often prefer to use something like the Homescan panel for behaviour, but the MFI panel for attitudes.

Recently, Market Facts and Nielsen announced the launch of a new product called 'Segway' which fuses attitudinal and behavioural information using commitment as the link. This product epitomizes the sort of way in which new technologies will make it possible for marketing to be more precise in ways which benefit both the marketer and the customer. Here is an outline of how it works.

The technology has now been developed that has enabled MFI and Nielsen to fuse the data from their two panels. Respondents belonging to MFI's panel are interviewed to obtain their commitment to different brands, whereafter the information is fused with behavioural data obtained from the Homescan panel. Validation studies have indicated that the results are reliable and valid.

The marketer can now be supplied with a CD-ROM, summarizing the purchasing patterns of all households belonging to the Homescan panel. For each panel member, not only is their purchasing behaviour recorded, but the commitment of the household as well, as a result of the data fusion process. Using interactive software, the marketer is now in a position to examine the impact of the relationship between the consumer and all brands in the market on actual shopping patterns. In terms of formulating marketing strategies, the marketer will, for example, be able to identify that it would be best to have a sampling programme in Montana, in order to break down the problem of unavailability, and a strong brand-building campaign in California, to sustain strong commitment, while investigating the potential problem of out-of-stock situations in Florida, as evidenced by high availability but low sales in that region.

> **"Using interactive software, the marketer is now in a position to examine the impact of the relationship between the consumer and all brands in the market on actual shopping patterns."**

This product is sure to be the first of many which will fuse attitudinal and behavioural data into a single-source database. The interface between the data and the marketer will consist of user-friendly interactive software which will permit the marketer to simulate a variety of marketing situations, in order to identify which strategies are most likely to optimize profit.

# Bringing accountability to marketing

Throughout the world, marketers are under pressure to justify the way they are spending their marketing money. Accountability has come to marketing with a vengeance. In some areas of marketing, accountability is easily measured. For example, direct marketers are able to compare the cost of a marketing campaign with the incremental revenues it generates. Similarly for the short-term impact of in-store activity and targeted advertising campaigns. Marketers can compare the sales generated with and without the activity so as to measure exactly what the activity adds to sales. But all of these results are short term and tactical. And we know enough now to know that what works to generate sales in the short term can be harmful in the long run. Take price discounting, for example. While it almost always guarantees increased sales in the short run, in the long run we now know that it harms revenues by depressing what people are willing to pay for brands.

> **"Throughout the world, marketers are under pressure to justify the way they are spending their marketing money."**

So the question arises: can we be more precise about the long-term value of our marketing efforts? The answer is: not yet, exactly – but we are getting there. And it's the new technologies that are helping us to do so. What's getting us there is a three-way combination of abilities, in all of which computing power plays a central role. They are:

- The ability to record and keep track of individual consumer behaviour.
- The ability to predict how behaviour may change under different marketing actions, by understanding commitment.
- The ability to fuse attitudinal and behavioural information about consumer behaviour.

In Chapter 5 we showed how much more business a committed consumer is willing to give a marketer than an uncommitted consumer. We showed that this business accrues to the marketer in three ways. In brief, the more committed someone is to a brand:

- The more the brand will get of that person's spending in the category;
- The longer the brand will get that spending because defection is less likely;
- The higher a price that person will be willing to pay for the brand.

Customer satisfaction researchers have talked for years about the revenue gains that follow if marketers can make their customers more satisfied. Our research shows, however, that the key to increasing the value that a customer has for your brand lies in commitment rather than satisfaction. This is because the ties between commitment and behaviour are much stronger than those between satisfaction and behaviour. Once the gains or losses that follow changes in commitment have been established, it is an easy matter to model how brand revenues will change, either up or down. In addition, it is easy to model how changes in the image that people have of your brands will impact on their commitment. It is therefore easy to go from changes of mind to predictions about changes of revenue.

In terms of simulating the impact on profitability of marketing strategies, the process is a relatively simple one. For many years, companies conducting satisfaction research have modelled the impact of different attributes of service on overall satisfaction. As satisfaction is a key component of commitment, the modelling process can be extended to profitability, as summarized in Figure 11.1.

By modelling the impact of image, service and product attributes on satisfaction, we can derive their impact on commitment. Hence, we can deduce which service attributes or product attributes have the most

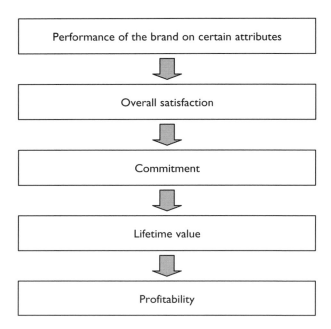

**Figure 11.1**　*Modelling profitability*

impact on shifting the commitment of consumers of our brand or service. Assuming that we know the lifetime value of members of each com‑ mitment segment, we can now calculate the value of changing attributes so as to change commitment. Thus, we are in a position to simulate the impact on overall profitability of changing service attributes, product intrinsics or image dimensions.

The technology to achieve this is already in place, and can be used by marketers to assist them in deciding where to focus their marketing investments.

We said earlier that all these techniques take us closer to accountable marketing. But they do not yet make accountable marketing a reality. The problem lies, as anyone who has had experience of these sorts of models will be aware, in knowing in advance how much it will cost to achieve consumer changes of mind, and in knowing how to achieve those 'changes of mind'. We come across too many marketing consultants who talk glibly about establishing the link between marketing and profits, dazzling their potential clients with models of the above kind, yet failing to point out that the missing link in all of this is the ability to either specify how to achieve these changes of mind, or to predict how much it will cost.

The reason why data fusion has the importance that it does is because it provides us with the empirical tools we need to fill in the missing links. On the one hand, we have been able to measure the direct impact of a marketing activity on behaviour and hence sales, but without knowing what the impact may have been in terms of commitment. On the other hand, we have been able to make strong predictions about the link between commitment and sales which give us the power to model the impact that changes in commitment will have on sales. But we have not been able to put the two together.

With fused data we can close the circle. We can measure the long-term impacts that different marketing activities have on commitment and behaviour. And this will allow us to build up a data bank about what causes change and how much it costs.

## Giving people the tools to shape what marketers offer

Back in the old days in the developed countries of the West, the town library was often the centre of social activity. Many townsfolk would go to the library once or twice a week and the librarian would know everybody by name. Often she (mostly it was a 'she') would know what individual people liked to read, and so she would keep them informed about new arrivals and recommend books to them for reading.

Those days are all but gone. Yet, while we may feel some nostalgia for the small town library, their modern replacements, bookstores and online retailers, do a fantastic job as substitutes. Anyone who has bought anything from Amazon.com will know what we mean. If you have ever bought books from Amazon, then it's highly likely that you will be greeted by name the next time you log on. Amazon will suggest a selection of books for you to look at on the basis of what you have bought before. They may even suggest a range of CDs for you to try, though you've never before bought CDs from Amazon. And so on through all the products that they offer. How do they do it?

They do it in the same way that the small town librarian used to do it – only better. They keep a record of all the things that you've bought. They establish a pattern of interest from that record. They correlate your buying with that of all the other people who have bought similar things. They then simply match these patterns to each other and come up with a likely list of the things you would enjoy. To help prevent mistakes, they solicit customer feedback about all their books and CDs and provide both themselves and you with an immediate, up-to-date record of how their different products have performed. When you are given your list, therefore, you can check what other people have had to say about Amazon's recommendations.

The reason Amazon is better than the small town librarian is that modern computers record, analyse, and collate information better than a small town librarian ever could. Talented librarians continue to be fantastic social resources. But they simply cannot collate all that information. Computers don't forget anything, at least, not as long as the system is properly designed. And they process massive amounts of information at lightning speed. As long, therefore, as people can programme computers to do something like 'thinking', computers can take over some of these tasks – and look after us better than people do.

What Amazon and other marketers like them are doing is to build marketing information systems that allow customers to be in control. With just a little more interactivity, it would be possible for Amazon to allow its customers to tell it when it was making a mistake. Customers could tailor the Amazon offering even more precisely to suit their needs.

What does all of this have to do with commitment? Well, it's clear that by finding ways to put customers in charge of marketing interactions, you should be able to drive up their commitment to your way of satisfying their needs. But it goes beyond that. By offering customers the opportunity to help you measure their patterns of commitment, you can build an even more precise picture of what they want on the basis of very little information.

The Web is just one channel that makes interactive marketing possible. A second and no less important channel is the call centre. The dialogue that takes place between a call centre operator and a customer should depend on the relationship that the customer has with the product or brand. Think, for example, about an airline call centre. If you were managing such a centre, you would agree that calls from high-value but convertible frequent flyers should be handled differently from calls from high-value and committed frequent flyers. And it works both ways. Not only should you be handling the two calls differently in order to preserve your business, the two customers concerned would probably *want* you to handle them differently. A committed frequent flyer would be as irate if they were handled as if they were uncommitted as a convertible frequent flyer would be if they were handled as if they were committed.

> **"By finding ways to put customers in charge of marketing interactions, you should be able to drive up their commitment to your way of satisfying their needs. By offering customers the opportunity to help you measure their patterns of commitment, you can build an even more precise picture of what they want on the basis of very little information."**

One important question that all of this raises is – do people want to be that well understood? In Chapter 7, we talked about what Nissan in Ireland and Lloyds TSB in the UK are doing. In both cases, customers are being asked to communicate to marketers about what they think and what they want. In both cases, the results have been instructive. When people know that the information they are giving will not be abused, but will lead to better products and services, they are only too willing to participate. The key is to recognize that there are two parties who stand to benefit from such information exchanges – the marketer and the customer. Marketing works better for both when appropriate information is exchanged and used properly.

> **"When people know that the information they are giving will not be abused, but will lead to better products and services, they are only too willing to participate."**

Lloyds TSB has shown the way in this new kind of marketing by showing how to tag a customer database with measures of commitment without having to interview the entire customer database. We have pictured the whole process in Figure 11.2.[1] The benefits which follow to customers and marketers alike are significant.

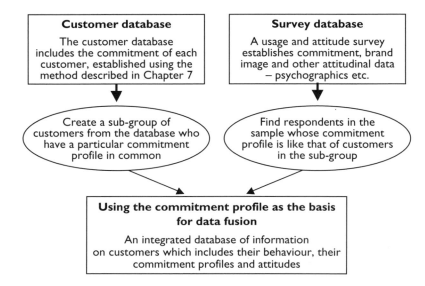

**Figure 11.2**  *Using commitment to link attitudes and behaviour*

*Source*: Adapted from Hofmeyr and Rice (1999). Reproduced by permission of Henry Stewart Publications.

# Individual privacy and the regulatory environment

The power of the new technologies available to marketers has already raised questions about respect for the privacy of the individual. As consumers ourselves, we endorse this questioning unreservedly. Our industry has to take these issues into account. But we also recognize that people do not mind marketers improving what they're doing, as long as it genuinely benefits the consumers.

People need to be given a choice about how deeply they want to be involved in the new kinds of relationships that marketing is making possible. As customers ourselves, we are constantly charmed by the way that better marketers, for example Amazon, appear to be able to read our minds. It takes out the marketing clutter and it improves our experience as consumers. And we are always in a position to switch it off if we want to. We really are in control. But we are also often driven up the wall by clumsy and inappropriate marketing. It is our hope that the tools about which we've talked in this book will help to cause the first to happen more often, and slowly rid the world of the last.

> **"People need to be given a choice about how deeply they want to be involved in the new kinds of relationships that marketing is making possible."**

# Defining commitment

As the popularity of commitment as a marketing measure grows, it is important that the marketers realize that there are different definitions of commitment. Already, there are many companies claiming to measure commitment. But how does a marketer decide which commercially available measure to use?

We would suggest that the following criteria should be used:

- In how many studies has the measure been used? This will be an indication of the experience that the researchers have gained in learning to measure and understand commitment and apply it to marketing situations, as well as the confidence that clients have had in the measure.
- How reliable is the measure? That is, if it is used time and time again, is it stable?
- Is the measure internally valid? That is, does it correlate with other marketing measures in a way that you would expect? For example, you should find that those who are less committed buy the brand less often.
- Is it externally valid? By external validity, we refer to its ability to predict the future.
- Is there an explicit underlying theory supporting the derivation of the measure? It is relatively easy to come up with measures that will satisfy the preceding requirements, but we would suggest that an underlying psychological model is essential for any measure of commitment to be more than just a collection of questions which are shown to correlate with past and future behaviour.

We would hope that, in coming years, the focus on commitment is one of understanding the exact psychological process of what it is, and how to manage it. This is where the debate should lie. Unfortunately, as more and more practitioners become aware of the commercial value of the measure, it is inevitable that some of the measures offered will be less valid than others. We have noticed that many marketers are trusting, and feel that all measures of commitment are more or less the same. Nothing could be further from the truth.

By using the checklist suggested, marketers can avoid the pitfall of using a measure of commitment which is less than fully valid.

# In Summary

So, finally, this is the way we see the path ahead: a marketing environment, in which commitment and the lifetime value of customers are inextricably interlinked, combined with all marketing data, in order to enable marketers to make optimal decisions. A marketing environment in which data is easily available, in a user-friendly format, encouraging the constant use of the database by the marketer, combining both internal and external data sources.

The understanding of commitment and the role it plays in measuring the relationship between consumers and brands impacts on every decision the marketer makes. The next step will be to educate the consumer on the importance of measuring the relationship, explaining how this will lead to the sort of relationship that is 'just right'. Consumers will be communicated with in a way appropriate to the relationship that exists, with the amount of communication between the brand team and the consumer being just right – not too much, and not too little.

With the impressive advances that we are seeing in technological enhancement, particularly in the fields of data fusion and user accessibility, there is no reason why marketing should not be as accountable and as measurable in terms of its financial return to the corporation as every other function within the organization. Those organizations that have been among the first to embrace the philosophy of commitment-led marketing are already reaping the rewards of their efforts. We predict that in the years ahead, the understanding of commitment, the role that it plays and its continuous implementation will be a standard everyday practice for marketers around the globe.

# Reference

1.  Hofmeyr, J. and Rice, J. (1999) A method for using psychological commitment as a window to the motivations that lie behind behaviour in a database. *Journal of Database Marketing*, **7** (1).

# Index